"VALUABLE . . . ACCURATE . . . UNDERSTANDABLE . . . MESMERIZING . . ."

"This book fills a vacuum: it is valuable .  hensive . . . useful . . . understandable . . . n best books on the market on self-hypnosis." –

"If you are willing to learn by trying, *Self-Hy ̣̣̣̣osis* provides an uncomplicated method of changing your thoughts for the better and becoming what you want to be. This is a book to get into, not merely to be read. The outcome will be personal enrichment and self-empowerment." —DANIEL L. ARAOZ, ED.D., A.B.P.P. author of *The New Hypnosis*

". . . a great big happy grab bag of just about every approach to self-hypnosis for just about every problem you'd ever wanted to cope with. Professionals as well as the general public will find it a competent and complete resource." —ERNEST L. ROSSI, PH.D. author of *The Psychobiology of Mind-Body Healing*

"Individuals seeking new strategies for improving their lives will find this book rich in value and easy to use. The chapter on better parenting is a unique application of self-hypnosis training that I highly recommend to all parents. If I had to select only one book on self-hypnosis for my library or to recommend to anyone, it would be this book. A terrific resource." —GEORGE J. PRATT, PH.D.

"This is one of the most comprehensive, easily readable and well thought-out compendiums on the effectiveness of self-hypnosis for achieving individual, specific goals." —BERNICE COHEN SACHS, M.D.

"The book is truly a prescription for wellness for the self-help motivated individual . . ." —ELLIOT V. FELDBAU, DMD

"An excellent resource for both therapists and their patients. The suggestions offered for specific problems provide a great variety of ideas for the novice and the experienced practitioner alike. This is an excellent book." —JOAN MURRAY-JOBSIS, PH.D., P.A.

"Drs. Lambrou and Alman have written an excellent text on self-hypnosis. Their book covers all phases of the subject with remarkably fine presentation of the theoretical and empirical data involved in this field. I recommend it without reservation." —HAROLD B. CRASILNECK, PH.D.

"The current strong interest in mind-body interaction emphasizes the hypnotic process as a powerful intervening factor. Now, psychologists Alman and Lambrou have provided a set of scenarios for enhancing by means of self-hypnosis the role of the individual in the facilitation of his/her own mental and physical well-being." —MELVIN A. GRAVITZ, PH.D., A.B.P.P.

"Has a multitude of suggestions and examples to help the reader acquire and use the necessary skills. It should be read and read again." —SELIG FINKLESTEIN, A.B., D.D.S.

"Alman and Lambrou have done a splendid job of clearly and succinctly describing self-hypnosis. More than that, it is a remarkably useful compendium of hypnotic techniques for a complete variety of conditions. All of it in clear, specific prose." —HAROLD GREENWALD, PH.D.

SELF-HYPNOSIS

The Complete Manual for Health and Self-Change

SECOND EDITION

BRIAN M. ALMAN, Ph.D.
and
PETER T. LAMBROU, Ph.D.

Routledge
Taylor & Francis Group

LONDON AND NEW YORK

First published by Brunner-Routledge

This edition published 2012 by Routledge

2 Park Square, Milton Park, Abingdon, Oxon, OX14 4RN

711 Third Avenue, New York, NY 10017, USA

Routledge is an imprint of the Taylor & Francis Group, an informa business

Library of Congress Cataloging-in-Publication Data
Alman, Brian M. (Brian Mogul)
    Self-hypnosis : the complete manual for health self-change / by
Brian M. Alman and Peter T. Lambrou.— 2nd ed.
        p. cm.
    Includes bibliographical references and index.
    ISBN 0-87630-650-4
    1. Autogenic training.   I. Lambrou, Peter T.
II. Title.
RC499.A8A45   1992   91-29007
                                                         CIP

Contents

• Headache, stomach ache, and other acute pain

Foreword to the Second Edition

Most people have their first—maybe only—exposure to hypnosis through stage show hypnotists and Hollywood productions. From this, they form the impression that hypnosis is something mystical and dangerous. Hypnosis is portrayed as a scary form of mind control, where the helpless victim gives up control of himself or herself.

If this were an accurate portrayal of hypnosis, then hypnosis wouldn't interest me much. As a clinical psychologist who treats people with a wide variety of problems, I've never had anyone ask me to help him lose control of himself. On the contrary, people come in wanting help to establish *more* control over their lives. Hypnosis is the most powerful means for doing so that I am aware of.

What Brian Alman and Peter Lambrou have done admirably in this book is to provide you a means for having more control over your experience. They, too, are clinicians, and their many years of helping people discover skills and resources within themselves for improving the quality of their lives are evident throughout this volume. Alman and Lambrou have done a wonderful job of taking the "hocus-pocus" mystery out of hypnosis, thereby helping the reader discover that "quality of life" is a frame of mind. They have done a good job of acquainting the reader with innovations in the field that usually only other clinicians have access to learning. Furthermore, they integrate abstract and professional literature with common sense applications. And it's the applications that are the strength of this book.

Alman and Lambrou have made it possible for anyone interested in taking care of himself or herself to learn simple and effective ways of doing so. They repeatedly emphasize that the uniqueness of each person is an ally when we learn how to recognize and make positive use of that uniqueness. They teach us that our views of our selves and our individual worlds are changeable, not set in concrete. Best of all, they teach us that we can change our views when we change our ways of talking to ourselves. In their gentle, permissive way, the authors give us lots of guidance, while simultaneously encouraging us to explore and discover what works best for us as individuals.

The authors address so many dimensions of life and provide so many ideas for ways to enhance your experience of life that it would be to your advantage to use this book as both a guidebook and reference manual, reading and rereading sections of greatest personal interest. The practical nature of the material easily lends itself to continuous adjustments and refinements in your self-hypnosis skills as your abilities evolve. For the clinician and layperson alike, the many case examples and sample procedures will undoubtedly stimulate greater mastery on a variety of levels.

Most of all, I think the message in this book that I find the most encouraging and respectful is one of personal empowerment. The authors exude confidence that the reader can learn and benefit from the methods described here. Learning from your own experience that you can gain control over symptoms or experiences that used to seem uncontrollable can provide you with a wonderful sense of pride and accomplishment. I expect you'll discover that in your own way with the skilled help of Alman and Lambrou.

—MICHAEL D. YAPKO, PH.D.
Director, Milton H. Erickson Institute of San Diego, CA

Foreword to the First Edition

Once in a while, progress in the sciences is made through a unique combination of principles which previously were considered to be incompatible. Dr. Alman has succeeded in making such a leap with this brilliant book on self-hypnosis. Most books on this and related subjects require the readers to follow a rigid program for self-development. Due to their standardized format, they allow for little or no variety in individual responses.

This book is different. It offers a very well written, step-by-step program for self-hypnosis, which may be applied to a wide variety of goals. At the same time, it describes an individualized approach. Dr. Alman shows his readers time and again how they can fit this excellent program to their own individual needs, interest, resources, and specific life situations. No one else had done this before.

Moreover, the reader's success with self-hypnosis is not dependent upon a single intervention only. Instead, Dr. Alman suggests many different pathways to achieving results.

While this book is primarily intended for the lay reader, doctors, psychologists, and other qualified professionals wishing to use hypnosis in their work will benefit from this thorough and pragmatic explanation of clinical hypnosis. Indeed, there is no other book where they can find basic hypnotic procedures written in the language in which their procedures ought to be applied—in an imaginative and permissive kind of language, which helps people to realize their own inner resources in their own unique ways.

I suspect that this book will create an uproar among some of Dr. Alman's professional colleagues. They will think that he has given away the very best of their professional work to the general public—that he has made potential clients more self-supporting. Nevertheless, he realizes that hypnosis belongs to the individuals experiencing it and he teaches them to utilize their focused state of consciousness in a very safe and rewarding manner.

Dr. Alman is a very experienced psychologist and hypnotherapist, who has had two of the best teachers. The first was the late Dr. Milton H. Erickson, the man who revolutionized both hypnosis and psychotherapy. The second was Dr. Alman's own extremely painful physical condition for which self-hypnosis proved to be the only remedy available.

There should be no doubt that Dr. Alman's program in self-hypnosis is rooted in both the best clinical approaches to hypnosis and his own personal experiences, as-well-as in his therapeutic work with hundreds of clients. Moreover, his teaching abilities are internationally recognized. Dutch colleagues, for instance, of which I am one, who have been trained by many internationally well-known hypnotherapists, rate Dr. Alman at the top.

—ONNO VAN DER HART, PH.D.
Dutch Society of Clinical Hypnosis
Professor, University of Leiden, The Netherlands
Clinical Instructor, Dercksen Center, Amsterdam
Author, Rituals In Psychotherapy

Preface

The pain was horrible. It disrupted my work, my home, my whole experience within me for many months. I was told by the doctors that I would need a body cast for six months, surgery, then a body cast for another six months. That *possibly* would get rid of some of the pain in my lower back. Still, no guarantees that I wouldn't be worse off than before the lengthy and costly procedures.

A friend suggested that I try hypnosis for the pain.

After waiting, hurting, and remaining undecided about the surgery, I went for help to a psychologist trained in hypnosis. I had no noticeable success the first couple of visits, but I was learning to understand more about my pain. In a few more weeks, I began to get some relief. After about three months, nearly half the pain in my back was gone. I thought this was a miracle.

I went back to the orthopedic surgeons who had recommended surgery. They thought hypnosis was ridiculous and that very quickly the pain would come back—that I would be on the operating table soon. This only fueled me to work and learn more about what was happening to me.

These surgeons had my respect in the beginning, but I was disappointed by their closed-minded attitude about my success in controlling the crippling pain I had been suffering. I began to read everything that was available on hypnosis at the time.

The journey that began with solving my own chronic pain condition developed into a career choice to better understand hypnosis. In the mid-seventies, I studied with Milton H. Erickson, M.D., a well-known physician and innovator in hypnotherapy, at his home in Arizona. His tutelage and his sensitivity with his patients and students were an inspiration for that group of us who studied and even brought our own patients to work together with him at his office.

Nearly twenty years now, since my first back pain—I am running and am free of 99 percent of my discomfort and pain and have been for most of those years.

Still I practice self-hypnosis every day.

I have been traveling to medical schools and other learning institutions in this country and abroad, teaching clinicians and the public how to include the natural abilities of self-hypnosis in their practices and their lives. I had been working on this book for many years and at each seminar and class I was asked when it would be completed. Finally, with the help of my co-author, I described the most complete methods for learning and using self-hypnosis that are available. And now the second edition of this book incorporates the further experience and learning I have accumulated since the first edition appeared almost 10 years ago.

In writing this book, I hope I can share the benefits and personal enrichment of self-hypnosis with many more individuals than I ever could in several lifetimes of classroom teaching. This book is not intended to replace conventional therapies or medical treatments and you are advised to seek professional help should you have concerns.

The methods and techniques in this book represent the most recent developments and applications in the use of hypnosis for a variety of problems, as well as for understanding and enhancement. Often, these methods are a departure from "old line" hypnotic practices that were limited in their scope and effectiveness.

Most recent studies and my own experiences in my private practice show that the combination of techniques that we have assembled here can be used by virtually anyone. This includes people who have been found to be unhypnotizable by rigid and specific testing.

Arranged in a convenient, easy-to-read, self-teaching fashion, this book can be used by both individuals and therapists to learn self-hypnosis on their own or as part of an overall therapy program. It is written in plain language, with full explanations and many examples.

Modern self-hypnosis operates under a variety of labels—visualization, guided imagery, goal-directed relaxation, autogenics, self-suggestion, and others. Call it what you will, the principles and the goals are the same.

All of us look for ways to be more effective in our lives. The intention of this book is to open some new doors, perhaps reopen some old ones, and to keep all present doors open for positive changes.

The techniques described here are not static or unchangeable. You are encouraged to put yourself into the techniques and adapt them for your own adventure into understanding and changing yourself. Read this book and enjoy your new skills for self-change and good health.

—BRIAN M. ALMAN, PH.D.

Acknowledgments

I am grateful to the relationships that inspired me to write this book and pursue more of life's natural resources, both conscious and unconscious.

To my mother, Phyllis, for her unconditional love, and to my father, Mel, for his kindness.

To my three children, Rebecca, Shishana, and Michael, thank you for your loving playfulness and closeness.

To my brother, Prem, and my sisters, Margie and Risa, thank you for your deep friendship and trust.

To Shelley, thank you for the love and encouragement; and her children Willie and Karen for their support, too.

To Peter Lambrou, I am grateful for your creativity and devotion to this book and our friendship.

To my clients, I appreciate your openness in sharing so many of your life lessons with me.

To the publisher and staff at Brunner/Mazel for their motivation and top quality approach to this book project.

And, to Dr. Milton H. Erickson, who encouraged my skills of observing and listening to the unconscious potential of the human mind.

BRIAN M. ALMAN, PH.D.

I wish to thank my wife, Dottie, for her patient understanding and loving support and encouragement during the writing of this book.

I thank Natalie Gilman and Mark Tracten at Brunner/Mazel for their help and confidence in this project. And a grateful thanks to the staff at the University of California at San Diego Central and Bio-med libraries for their kind help in the literature research.

I want to thank Brian Alman for his wisdom and inspiration. You are a very good friend.

PETER T. LAMBROU, PH.D.

Section 1
LEARNING SELF-HYPNOSIS

Welcome to Self-Hypnosis . . . a tool for making changes in your life. Everyone knows that problems are a part of living that we all face. However, perhaps not everyone realizes that all of us carry around, within ourselves, the resources for survival . . . personal evolution . . . and success.

This section of the book is devoted to helping you develop your ability to enter self-hypnosis and provide yourself with meaningful and effective suggestions for self-change. Read this part of the book through completely and then proceed to the chapters that interest you in Section II.

1
What You Can Expect from This Book

Doctor Albert Schweitzer once said: "Patients carry their own doctor inside. They come to us not knowing that truth. We are at our best when we give the physician who resides within each patient a chance to go to work."

Are you investigating self-hypnosis for the first time? You may be interested to know that nearly everyone can learn how to use self-hypnosis to make specific changes in himself or herself. To stop unwanted habits. To prevent headaches. To reduce stress. To control pain.

Perhaps you want to enhance your decision-making and to increase your concentration? To improve your athletic ability? To cultivate better communication in personal relationships? To be more effective in your own personal goals? Even to improve your business achievements?

This book will help you achieve or enhance success in all these areas and more.

It will provide you with detailed explanations of how to develop your capacity for self-hypnosis to reach your goals.

WHO CAN USE SELF-HYPNOSIS?

Clinical use of hypnosis has been linked with susceptibility test scores for a long time. Doctors who used hypnosis in their practice might first have given patients one of several tests to determine the likelihood of success.

In the last several years, studies have shown that even people who score low on these tests *are* hypnotizable. There are innumerable variations of hypnotic techniques. A poor score on a particular test shows only that a person is not responsive to the specific method used in *that test*.

Self-hypnosis that takes into account people's perceptions of their own experiences has been found to be successful with nearly everyone. The idea of using the personal experiences and perceptions of the individual was pioneered by Dr. Milton H. Erickson, a noted physician, teacher, and author.

Erickson's view was that hypnosis was most likely to be successful if the suggestions were meshed with words, symbols, and images to which the individual could best relate. He was adept at picking up these impressions from a patient in just a few moments.

Often, patients who had been given up as hopeless after all other treatments had been exhausted were referred to Erickson. These were frequently people who had tested as unsusceptible to hypnosis. His method not only blended the patient's own experiences into the suggestions, but also used a more indirect, permissive, and flexible language.

Most people think hypnosis uses commanding language such as: "You will feel . . ." or "Now you are going to . . ." But Erickson's suggestions would contain many phrases such as: "You may feel . . ." or "Perhaps you will notice that . . ." These suggestions do not command or direct the person. They imply and leave open the possibility of some different experience. And many people who have difficulty accepting "commands" find it much easier to respond to the more flexible suggestions.

Dr. Milton H. Erickson, a leader and innovator in developing the indirect, flexible, and personalized clinical applications for hypnotic techniques. (*Photo courtesy of Milton H. Erickson Foundation, Inc.*)

Many others have now come to believe, as Erickson did, that with the right approach practically everyone is able to enjoy the benefits of the hypnotic phenomenon. It is only a matter of finding the *right technique for the individual.* Erickson, as a therapist and a teacher, pioneered the use of individualized techniques and variations to accommodate the unique experiences and needs of each person. We also follow that approach.

You will find many places in this book where you are asked to look for something in your own life experiences with which to blend the suggestions. If you take the few moments necessary to personalize the techniques for yourself, you will reach your goals more quickly.

We describe many methods for developing a self-hypnosis trance and for accomplishing goals. You can find the method or methods that you are most comfortable with and that work best for you. We will show you how to modify and adapt them to the uniquenesses of your own personality, situations, and experiences. Many readers will be successful using several or all of the methods described; however, if one or another does not seem right or comfortable to you, encourage yourself to be patient and try one of the other methods for developing your trance.

HOW YOU CAN GET THE MOST OUT OF THIS BOOK

There is an old story about a young man rushing down the street with a violin case under his arm. He frantically stops an old gentleman and asks, "How do I get to Carnegie Hall?" The old man looks at the impatient young man and somberly replies, "Practice, practice, practice."

Self-hypnosis is a skill. Like throwing a ball, it is a skill that nearly all of us can do naturally. With practice and instruction, you can not merely pitch the ball aimlessly; you can pitch to the target.

You may have one or more goals in mind to work on with self-hypnosis. First become experienced with the techniques for entering trance. It is while in a self-hypnotic trance that the drawbridge is down for suggestions to your unconscious mind.

Some people learn self-hypnosis quickly and others take more time. How quickly or slowly you learn has little to do with how effective it will be for you once you have mastered it.

If you are in pain or have some other immediate use for self-hypnosis, you will be tempted to jump right into work on that goal. However, wait until you understand the techniques of self-hypnosis; then feel free to start blending suggestions for the specific change you seek into your practice.

SELF-HYPNOSIS TO REMOVE LIMITATIONS

The hypnotic phenomenon is not magic, not occult. It is a natural, normal state of mind that you can use to instruct and direct your unconscious mind and body. We all carry around the abilities to reduce stress, control pain, conquer fears, overcome allergies, and alter unwanted habits.

George, a 48-year-old salesman and client, suffered from low back pain for over seven years. He had disk surgery and had been on various pain medications for most of those years.

The pain had interfered with practically every aspect of George's life—sleep, sex, exercise, social functions, dancing, and even his job enthusiasm. He sought help through hypnosis after he developed an allergic response to the most recent pain medication.

Within eight weeks, he learned self-hypnosis well enough to get as much pain relief as the medication gave him. After six months, he had more comfort and a greater freedom from pain than anytime since his injury.

After one year, he reported a definite improvement in all those areas of his life that had suffered as a result of his pain. And he was taking practically no medication.

Julie, a 35-year-old waitress, had been struggling with her weight problem for nearly a decade, ever since her first pregnancy. She seemed to have been on a continual diet.

She didn't like the way she looked. Her physician had urged her to lose weight for the sake of her health. The final straw came when she overheard two customers in the restaurant where she worked, commenting about her size.

She began instruction in self-hypnosis with the motivation to change her eating and exercising habits—specifically, to decrease the former and increase the latter.

She altered her perception and desire for food. She used posthypnotic suggestions to resist excessive eating and encourage herself to exercise. Julie lost 65 pounds in nine months. More important, two years later, the excess weight was still off. She was still exercising regularly and she loved the way she looked and felt.

What you will learn from this book is a way to redirect your internal resources to achieve your goals. You can make yourself more capable with self-hypnosis. Most of us use only a thimbleful of our potential; even the brightest people may use only a tenth of their natural capacity. The natural mental potential you were born with is waiting to be tapped.

REFERENCES

Alman, B.M. & Carney, R.E. Consequences of direct and indirect suggestions on success of posthypnotic behavior. *American Journal of Clinical Hypnosis*, Vol. 23. (Oct), 1980.

Barber, J. Hypnosis and the unhypnotizable. *American Journal of Clinical Hypnosis*, Vol 23. (July), 1980.

Pratt, G.J., Wood, D., & Alman, B.M. *Clinical Hypnosis Primer, Expanded and Updated.* New York: John Wiley and Company, 1989.

2

What Are Hypnosis and Self-Hypnosis

Nearly everyone has experienced a trance-like state many times—though they might not have called it hypnosis. Have you ever caught yourself daydreaming and not noticed routine things happening around you? Have you ever been absorbed reading a book or engrossed in an intricate project and not heard someone speak to you or not noticed how much time passed?

Perhaps you have had the experience of being so engrossed in a movie that you realized that it was almost over and yet it did not seem like over an hour and a half had passed. Or, you may have been driving on the freeway, absorbed in your thoughts, and then noticed that you had missed your exit.

These are hypnotic-like trances. The main differences between these sorts of trance and self-hypnosis are specific motivation and suggestions toward a goal. Hypnosis channels the trance to achieve some desired result, like relaxation or relief of pain.

It is common for people to disbelieve that they have been hypnotized the first time or two it occurs. The reason is that the hypnotic trance is not a completely unique feeling. The absorption you may feel is familiar.

Hypnosis is not a form of sleep, though a person in a trance often appears to be asleep. Actually, the opposite is true. The brain-wave patterns of people in hypnosis show alert wakefulness.

Hypnosis has been given various definitions. Since no one has discovered exactly how it works, we can only describe its effects. And like the seven blind men describing the elephant, our descriptions differ depending on our unique perspectives and perceptions. Each person experiences the hypnotic phenomenon in his or her own way.

Here is a definition that seems to explain the effects of the phenomenon: Hypnosis is a state of mind in which suggestions are acted upon much more powerfully than is possible under normal conditions. While in hypnosis, one suppresses the power of *conscious* criticism. One's focus of attention is narrower and one's level of awareness on a focal point is much higher than if one were awake. During this heightened focus and awareness, suggestions appear to go directly into the unconscious mind.

Nearly all scientists and researchers in this topic recognize that the trance-state we call hypnosis has special qualities. In it, you can control areas of yourself that are normally out of reach of your conscious mind.

If you doubt this, sit down and passively but consciously try to slow your heart rate by 10 percent or try to raise the temperature of your hand a degree or two. Those are examples of internal changes that are normally out of your conscious control. Yet, in hypnosis *you can make changes in chemical, physical, psychological, and emotional parts of yourself.*

ALL HYPNOSIS IS REALLY SELF-HYPNOSIS

Many people think there is a difference between hypnosis guided by someone else and self-hypnosis. Many experts agree, however, that all hypnosis is really self-hypnosis. A hypnotherapist may help you guide or develop the trance, but you are always in control. It is your hypnosis.

That may seem contrary to what you've heard or read. Novels, movies, and stage shows are poor teachers of what hypnosis is really about. They've given hypnosis a mysterious aura that is not deserved. This mystique has clouded the true value of hypnosis as a tool for making important positive changes in ourselves.

STAGE HYPNOTISM VERSUS CLINICAL HYPNOSIS

There is a big difference between clinical hypnosis and the stage hypnotism many people are familiar with. The stage variety is a performance, a show purely for entertainment.

When you examine the process of the stage hypnotists, you recognize some of the techniques they utilize. First, the performer asks for volunteers from the audience. These are people who might well have had a drink or three, and their inhibitions are reduced. Many subjects are repeat visitors who are easily hypnotized and are nearly always selected when recognized by the hypnotist. Clearly, those who venture on stage have self-selected themselves to be part of the show.

Onstage, the performer will try to select those volunteers he or she feels will most readily comply with commands. Those who are judged to be "fighting" or "resisting" will be dismissed. The showman is often very adept at reading body language and other subtle signs that indicate that the subjects want to do as they are told and put on a good show.

After the performer has carefully culled the group to a handful of willing participants, the show begins. Whether the entire group is really hypnotized or not doesn't matter. The participants may be in a trance, they may believe they are, or they may simply act as if they are hypnotized. Once they are on stage, there is a powerful pressure to go along and not "spoil the show."

By this time, all the participants have been given tacit permission to let their inhibitions remain offstage. They have the perfect excuse for whatever they do—"they were hypnotized." Let the show begin.

It's not necessary to hypnotize people to get them to quack like a duck, croon like Frank Sinatra, or laugh uncontrollably. People will do both foolish and fantastic things without being hypnotized. A visit to a singles' bar on a Friday night can attest to that fact.

THE SVENGALI EFFECT?

A question often asked in regard to hypnosis is whether someone can be made to do something against his or her will. This has been called the Svengali effect. Many people who have seen stage hypnotism, read novels, or seen movies that include hypnosis ask this question.

In the old John Barrymore film, *Svengali*, a bearded madman, hypnotized women to do his bidding and commit crimes for him. Even very recent films and television shows inaccurately depict hypnosis. Because of these, many people balk at the notion of being hypnotized in fear of allowing someone to make them act foolishly or do something they would regret.

We recommend that you NEVER ALLOW AN UNQUALIFIED PERSON TO USE HYPNOSIS WITH YOU. However, research has shown that people will follow only those hypnotic suggestions that are within their fundamental interests.

Of course, in a clinical or scientific setting a researcher would not ask a subject to actually commit murder or robbery. But, many examples exist demonstrating that subjects in deep hypnosis who are asked to do something against their "fundamental interests" will either ignore the command or, if pressed to comply, come out of the trance.

Certainly, people do not need to be in hypnosis to break the law or do harm. Only in movies, television, and novels is hypnosis linked to such actions. It makes for interesting plots, but is just not based on facts.

There is no relinquishing of your "willpower" with hypnosis, despite fiction to the contrary. You still understand what is right for you and what is not.

Of course, in self-hypnosis—where you are giving yourself suggestions—such considerations are not even an issue. You will always be giving yourself positive, constructive suggestions.

ARE THERE LIMITATIONS WITH SELF-HYPNOSIS?

When doing hypnosis for yourself, you are both the operator/guide and the subject. This is like being both the director of a movie and the lead actor. This poses some limitations, however, since some techniques, such as age regression, may take more practice.

There are remarkable hypnotic effects you can achieve on your own. In areas such as pain control, for instance, major surgeries have been performed with self-hypnosis as the only anesthesia.

Take the documented case of Victor Rausch (1980). A dental surgeon, Doctor Rausch had used hypnosis and self-hypnosis in his practice and was very experienced and confident with hypnotic procedures. When he had to undergo gall bladder surgery, he used self-hypnosis as the only anesthesia. The surgery was performed without complications and without pain. You'll learn more about this case in the chapter on pain control.

Another physical change possible with self-hypnosis is ridding yourself of warts. In fact, you can get relief from many skin conditions by using self-hypnosis.

Still other effects you can create are control over fears, increased self-confidence, and relief from allergies. All of these subjects are discussed in detail in later chapters.

The hypnotic phenomenon is a naturally occurring state that virtually everyone, with practice, can learn to use for achieving goals that might otherwise be too difficult or even impossible to achieve.

It is important to know that hypnosis allows you more control rather than less. In hypnosis, you are conscious of the outside world and you can react to it if you choose. How you can use hypnosis on your own is limited only by your desire to change.

REFERENCES

Erickson, M.H. *Healing in Hypnosis, Vol. 1*, (Eds. Rossi, Ryan, & Sharp). New York: Irvington Publisher, 1983.

Fromm, E., Brown, D.P., Hurt, S.W., Oberlander, J.Z., Boxer, A.M., & Pfeifer, G. The phenomena and characteristics of self-hypnosis. *International Journal of Clinical and Experimental Hypnosis*, Vol. 29(3), 1981.

Rausch, V. Cholecystectomy with self-hypnosis. *American Journal of Clinical Hypnosis*, Vol.22 (Jan), 1980.

3

Practical Matters of Self-Hypnosis

As you develop a desire to practice self-hypnosis you may have some questions about the practical matters of where, when, or how long. This chapter will answer those questions and others.

SELECTING A PLACE TO PRACTICE

Some people can read a book practically anywhere—in a crowded airport terminal, a busy doctor's office, or a restaurant. Are you able to concentrate on your reading and "tune out" everything else? If you can, you will likely find you can practice self-hypnosis anywhere. Most people, however, will want to find a quiet, private place for their first sessions. In today's world, it may be difficult to find a place free of all sounds.

Nevertheless, select a place that is personal and as quiet as possible. Do your best to get as comfortable and relaxed as you can.

After you are comfortable entering a trance easily and quickly, you will be able to use outside sounds and "distractions" to relax even more. You will be able to do your self-hypnosis while sitting in a theater waiting for a movie to start, relaxed in your airline seat, or sitting in a crowded bus depot. You will be able to enjoy a trance anywhere. For now, though, try to find a place that is as free of outside sounds as possible in order to best develop a trance that will soon become familiar.

If you choose an outside site, it should have privacy. Better to use a secluded backyard than a conspicuous front porch where someone might interrupt you. When you are a bit more experienced and comfortable with going in and out of your trance, you may enjoy practicing in the warmth and freshness of a sunny day at the beach or sitting in a park.

Indoors will usually be best for most of you as you begin practicing. A bedroom, sewing room, den, or study may best suit you—especially if you have children. If it's difficult to find privacy in your home, try sitting in your parked car. Or, if you're at work, close the door of your office during lunch hour.

Do the best you can and, if it's possible, keep the lighting subdued. Most important, the place you select should feel as *comfortable, safe, and free from interruptions as possible.* Schedule your practice as a special time for yourself.

HOW LONG A TRANCE SESSION IS BEST?

Taking time to practice is essential to developing your self-hypnosis skills. It's helpful to recognize that the time you allot for your self-hypnosis trance is like time you deposit in a bank for making positive self-change. Both the amount of time and the quality of the time you invest in yourself create value. By this we mean that we want you to allow for variations in when and how long you might conduct your trance experiences.

For example, you may discover that midday is an ideal point in the cycle of your day to take a trance break. Whenever your midday occurs, it is a rest point between morning and evening and a time to both review and prepare for the balance of the day ahead. You can tell yourself a special phrase that reflects that notion, as an entrance suggestion and cue for your self-hypnosis induction, such as, "As I breathe and rest, I generate zest."

You may wish to allow yourself about 15 to 20 minutes for the first few times. As you become more skilled at entering trance, you may find you only need eight or 10 minutes. The more work you want to do in your self-hypnosis and the more complex your goals, the longer you may want to spend in your trance.

However, with practice, you'll require less time to become relaxed and develop the trance state. Eventually, the majority of your time in self-hypnosis will be spent working on suggestions and visualizations for specific goals and changes.

Many people focus on doing only three to four minutes per trance session and they do that several times per day. Repetition is a successful strategy; as you are able to enter trance more easily, you will find the experience gratifying and even easier to return to again and again for brief relief.

DEVELOPING YOUR EXPECTATIONS FOR RESULTS

Change is a natural part of our existence. Our entire universe is in a constant state of change. The seasons and tides change, all animals and plants grow and change. Cells in our bodies die and are replaced. Even rocks wear down over time. So, for us to expect change to occur within ourselves is quite natural.

As your expectations for change become more focused and you become more aware of your ability to influence many of the changes you are experiencing, you will be more effective in your life. Set your expectation right now that you WILL see results from your self-hypnosis. Change is part of nature and of your own nature.

BEGINNING SUGGESTION STRATEGIES

You can develop your own short, focused suggestion rhythm, sort of a trance mantra. For example, you might have an early day trance mantra such as, "Eating light, staying determined, enjoying awareness . . . all-through-the-day, eating light, staying determined, enjoying awareness . . . all-through-the-day."

That becomes the focus of your inner voice, using your imagery to see the words, sense the colors, breathe the words in, and keep your focus on your trance mantra. This can be an excellent way to develop a focus. (We'll talk more about developing a focus in Chapter 7.)

Another midday suggestion rhythm could be, "Relaxed and confident, what did I learn from this morning, relaxed and confident, what did I learn from this morning?"

And an evening trance mantra might be, "Breathe and let go, breathe and let go."

You may find value in long trance sessions that are extremely engrossing and stimulating. Or, you might come to find that brief, focused, repetitive trance and suggestion strategies work best for you. And of course, the blending of both those and other sorts of trance processes can also be valuable.

Many people find that before bedtime is an effective way to both invest in yourself with self-hypnosis and at the same time relax yourself for a good night's sleep.

SHOULD YOU SIT OR LIE DOWN?

Most people find that a relaxed sitting position is better than lying down. Lying down makes it easy to drift off to sleep when you are in a very relaxed state of mind. Of course, if going to sleep is your goal with that session, then lying down is fine.

Select a chair that is comfortable and has a back that supports your head somewhat or allows you to sit upright. If your head is too far back when you relax, it will have tendency to roll back even more. That can become uncomfortable after a few moments. A pillow might help.

Your chair may have armrests or not. Place your arms at your sides or on the rests of the chair if that's more comfortable, or let them relax in your lap. The most important feature is to be *comfortable*.

IS IT BEST TO HAVE EYES CLOSED OR OPEN?

Most of the techniques you learn can be practiced with your eyes open or closed. It seems that most people naturally close their eyes when relaxed because of the muscle fatigue in their eyelids.

However, many people skilled with their trance can enter and stay in trance with their eyes open. It really does not matter if you keep your eyes open or closed; whatever you are most comfortable with will work best. If you wish to keep your eyes open, you may want to fix your gaze upon some spot that has slow and regular movement or no movement at all.

Visual distractions such as busy people, traffic, or television may hinder your concentration. Concentration is important in developing a hypnosis trance. You may wish to experiment with this to see how you can experience eyes open trance.

For most of you, closing your eyes will be the easiest way to begin learning self-hypnosis. As in the learning of most new skills, you can start with the easiest methods and develop into more complex ones.

MAKING TRANCE EASIER EACH TIME

Whenever you do your self-hypnosis, remember to give yourself the suggestion, at some point, "I can return to this quality of focused awareness again with some deep and satisfying breaths." Such a suggestion helps to reinstate the trance experience more easily and quickly the next time. We will discuss this further in the chapter on posthypnotic cues.

4

Healthy Breathing and Relaxation Techniques

It's not surprising that most of us take for granted such basic aspects of ourselves as breathing and relaxing. We all know how to breathe—right? After all, we have been doing it since birth. We must be doing it correctly.

Relaxing? Some people think it's a piece of cake—easiest thing in the world to do. Some of us like to relax in a hot bath or lying in the sun by a swimming pool. Perhaps, coming home from work and putting your feet up and sinking into the sofa is your way. There are an infinite number of methods for releasing the stored tension and pressure within us. You likely have developed some favorite ones already. But are you able to completely, fully relax in a healthy, fast, and easy manner?

One method that works very well, requires no props or special conditions, and can be used anywhere is deep breathing. This is a very old technique used by yoga masters from ancient times to the present to develop an internal calm and tranquility. It is an enjoyable and useful way to begin your self-hypnosis.

THE DIFFERENCE BETWEEN DEEP BREATHING FOR EXERCISE AND FOR RELAXATION

There are different kinds of deep breathing. Rigorous exercise forces us to inhale deeply and quickly, so that we rapidly restore consumed oxygen and expel carbon dioxide. But deep breathing for relaxation is slow and occurs while we are at rest or, at least, free from physical exertion.

Normal, everyday breathing is rather shallow and rapid. It mostly involves the chest expanding and contracting. But the chest and ribs really don't have much capacity to stretch and expand.

Deep, diaphragmatic breathing is healthier and comes from the abdomen. As you inhale, allow your belly to move outward. Below your lungs is a wide membrane called the diaphragm. As your abdominal muscles pull the membrane downward, your lungs draw in air to fill the space.

Unfortunately, most of us, from our youth, were taught to throw our shoulders back and breathe with our chest—keeping our stomach tight and flat. "Stomach in, chest out," as they say in the military. While this may look good, it is very bad for proper relaxation breathing.

Try taking a deep, satisfying abdominal breath. Inhale slowly through your nose and exhale slowly through your mouth. Don't be concerned with the appearance of your stomach. This breathing is for your health.

Slow, deep, rhythmic breathing triggers a "relaxation response." Dr. Herbert Benson (1976), a renowned cardiologist, coined this term to describe the opposite of the "fight or flight" response—the flush of adrenalin we get when we are angry or frightened.

When you produce one part of the relaxation response, such as deep breathing, you begin a chain of beneficial physical changes in your body. Some of these changes are slower heart rate, increased blood flow to the extremities, and muscular relaxation. All of these bodily changes can contribute to better overall health and are useful for developing a self-hypnosis trance.

AN EXERCISE IN BREATHING

Begin by inhaling to the count of three. Hold your breath for a count of three. Then exhale to a count of six. Wait for a count of four, and begin the cycle again. Simple.

Notice that we suggest exhaling more slowly than inhaling. Breathing is a cycle that has both an activating part and a relaxing part. A deep and satisfying inhaled breath is activating; oxygen stimulates the brain and feeds the cells throughout the body. Exhaling is the let-go; tension is released, carbon dioxide is expelled and the muscles tend to relax during this part of the cycle.

You can enhance your relaxation by repeating the words "let go," quietly to yourself while exhaling. As mentioned earlier, you can develop your own trance mantra that can become part of your breathing cycle and pace.

We recommend you inhale through your nose—that will avoid drying your throat. Hold the breath for three seconds—that reduces the tendency to feel light-headed from the boosted oxygen levels to the brain. Then, exhale through your mouth—you are able to control and slow down the release of air this way. Your exhaled breath is best released so that it lasts about twice as long as your inhaled breath.

The counting cycle is flexible; as you develop your breathing technique, you may want to hold your breath longer. You may want to extend the exhaling period to triple that of inhaling. Be comfortable with it, however, and if you do begin to get light-headed or dizzy, stop for a while and then continue.

It's not necessary to breathe so deeply that your lungs hurt or burn. The inhaling should be comfortable and relaxing.

You will find that this kind of breathing can be done anywhere, any time you feel tense or under pressure. Experts in relaxation, such as Dr. John Mason (1980), recommend taking at least 40 of these deep breaths daily. Try to take at least four or five slow, deep, and satisfying breaths before beginning your self-hypnosis sessions.

A yoga and meditation technique for breathing is to close your eyes and use your imagery to visualize, feel, hear, or sense in whatever way you can your breathing cycle. You can learn to "watch" your breathing from within as a way of centering yourself and developing an inner focus of concentration.

PROGRESSIVE RELAXATION

"An anxious mind cannot exist within a relaxed body," said Edmund Jacobson (1964). He formulated scores of exercises designed to relax tensions and calm anxieties by developing muscular awareness. His system is called progressive relaxation, and it has a number of variations. The two most popular are passive and active progressive relaxation.

Essentially, progressive relaxation means focusing separately on all the muscle groups in your body, becoming aware of the tension stored in each and releasing that tension. First, we will look at a variation of the active progressive relaxation technique.

ACTIVE PROGRESSIVE RELAXATION

Sit or lie in a comfortable position. This technique operates by tensing muscles above their normal tension level and then releasing the tension. This action focuses your awareness on each muscle and the amount of tension it contains. With practice, you can do it quickly.

You can begin with your hands and arms. Make a fist with one hand, tighten the muscles, and feel the tension. Take a deep breath as you do this. Also, with your eyes closed, try imagining the tension in your body flowing to your fist like water or electrical current. Use whatever image seems most comfortable to you.

After holding this clenched fist position as you inhale and for a few seconds longer, relax the muscles of your hand as you slowly exhale. At the same time, visualize your tension, stress, and worries disappearing like smoke in a breeze.

Now, reverse the tension by extending your arm in front of you, spreading your fingers as wide as possible, and arching your wrist and fingers upward as if waving goodbye. Keep your arm and fingers rigidly extended for several seconds, as you slowly breathe in deeply.

As you slowly exhale, gradually relax the muscles in your fingers, hand, and arm and bring your arm to rest at your side. Feel the difference between the muscular tension before the exercise and after.

Do the exercise again with that arm. Then, repeat the process with your other arm. Or, you may choose to do both arms at the same time.

Use the same procedure with your feet and legs. Begin with the toes and curl them down as tightly as you can. Inhale, and hold your breath as you hold the muscle tension. As you release your breath slowly, also relax your toes. Feel the tension being let go.

Then arch your toes back toward your head as much as you can. Inhale as you do this. Hold the tension as before and release it along with your breath. Do this process as slowly as you can. The slower you go, the more effective it is.

Tense your calf and thigh muscles next, making your legs as rigid as you possibly can. Hold the muscle tension and imagine your legs are expanding with the pressure. Feel the tension from throughout your body flowing into your leg. As you exhale slowly, gently release the tension, allowing all of it to float away from you.

To begin, we suggest that you do this exercise twice with each muscle group. Repeat exercise of specific muscle groups as often as you wish to relax more deeply or release more tension.

Your shoulders, neck, and facial muscles store a great amount of tension. Pay special attention to these areas.

Shrug your shoulders up around your neck. Inhale deeply as you do this. Imagine you are gathering up all the decisions you've had to make for the week. Visualize them as flowers, stones, crumpled pieces of paper, or whatever image you like. You can gather the weight of these decisions by shrugging your shoulders as you breathe deeply. Then, release these worries and tensions as you might cut loose an anchor or shed a heavy, rain-soaked jacket while you slowly exhale.

Repeat this exercise several times to be sure your shoulders are free from the accumulated muscular tension. Then slowly rotate your neck around several times, first in one direction, then in the other.

To tense your facial muscles, create an expression of exaggerated surprise. Open your mouth and eyes as wide as you can and pull your chin down to your chest. Inhale deeply and imagine how surprised you can be to find yourself getting more relaxed than you ever thought possible. Hold that position for a few seconds as you hold your breath. Then, exhale slowly and release the muscles, gradually bringing your head up.

Do this exercise at least twice. Be aware of the muscles in your forehead each time. Allow as much tension as you can to be let go.

As you can see, this technique is one of tensing a muscle group as you slowly inhale, holding it for a few seconds, and then gradually releasing the tension completely as you slowly exhale fully. With each exhalation, be sure to force as much air out of your lungs as is comfortable.

Below is a list of muscle groups to exercise in this same fashion of tensing and relaxing. It may not be necessary to go through all of them each time you do your self-hypnosis practice. But if you are feeling tense and unable to focus your attention easily, go through all the muscle groups with active progressive relaxation. There is a script for this exercise in Chapter 11.

- Legs and feet
- Arms and hands
- Back, shoulders and neck
- Stomach and chest
- Buttocks
- Face and head

PASSIVE PROGRESSIVE RELAXATION

Passive progressive relaxation is a comfortable, easy method that does not require you to tense your muscles at all. You may find this technique easy to do in a quiet, peaceful setting, perhaps while lying on the grass at a park or while sitting in the sun next to a lake or at the beach. You can even try it sitting in your car or in your most comfortable chair at home.

In this passive technique, instead of deliberately tensing or flexing your muscles, you build on the natural feelings of relaxation you may have in one or another area of your body.

Begin by taking several deep, satisfying breaths. Close your eyes and imagine your tensions flowing out of you with each breath you exhale. Do this for three or four breaths. Allow any thoughts or worries to enter your mind, but direct them out with each breath. Imagine troubling thoughts as a current of water that can be channeled out of you as you slowly exhale.

After a few moments, begin focusing your attention on your toes. Think about how they feel. Think about the walking you have done today and about how your feet and toes can now rest. Imagine the tension and pressure of walking or running as being drained out, flowing out of your feet.

Try visualizing the flow of tension running down your calves. Feel the flow draining out of you like water out of a drain spout or like warm syrup out of a bottle. Find images that you can visualize clearly that convey this notion.

Move up your legs and continue your slow deep breathing. Imagine your legs as large rags that are wet and limp. Feel your legs get heavy and relaxed.

Continue this relaxation process, moving up through your buttocks, stomach, back, and chest. Feel the heaviness in your stomach as the muscles let go of the tension. Let the sinking feeling spread throughout your abdomen.

Allow any tension to gather and flow down your arms. Let it drain from your head and face and, like melting wax, flow down to your arms and hands and out of your fingers.

Roll your head from side to side and feel the tensions breaking loose and flowing down and out. Take a deep breath and, as you exhale, feel your arms and hands heavy with the flow of residual tension. Feel the tension draining out like warm butter. Imagine squeezing out the last bit of tension and stress from your shoulders down to each finger.

Take a deep, satisfying breath and go back over your entire body and search for any remaining tension. Examine your forehead, jaw, and neck. Carefully imagine stress and tension leaving the muscles of your back, buttocks, and genital areas. If there is any place you think might be trapping some residual tension, focus on it and allow it to feel warm and heavy.

Try visualizing or imagine feeling all the tension dissolving or evaporating like alcohol in an open dish. Feel the warmth dissolving the tension like warm water dissolving salt. Let it be washed away.

You may want to practice these techniques a few times to develop a pace for yourself and then record yourself as you talk your way through the exercise. Making a tape for yourself in this way can be helpful. We discuss making your own tape in Chapter 11.

Clearly describe the feeling of relaxation to yourself

Once you are satisfied that you feel as comfortable and relaxed as you can be, from whichever method you used, examine the feeling. Describe it to yourself in as many ways as you can. Remember this feeling of deep relaxation.

Feel it, perhaps as a warm glow, like coals radiating heat. Or see it as the shimmering of sand in the desert sun. Imagine yourself perhaps as a color, as orange or a warm pink, like an early morning sunrise or sunset sky . . . a nature painting.

The important thing is to find some image or experience with which you can identify this soothing, relaxed state. Each time you practice self-hypnosis, you can reinforce the image and memory of the feeling of relaxation. Eventually, with practice, just the image or memory in your mind becomes a posthypnotic cue and will produce the relaxed feeling.

Notice and remember which parts of your body seemed to have contained the most stress and tension. Each person can have special areas that store more tension than others—often the head, neck, and lower back. Next time, work on those areas a little longer. Be sure all the muscular tension has been dissolved.

Many stress-related symptoms such as headaches, stomach upsets, fatigue, and other pains and problems are the result of stored tension and emotional and physical stress. You can learn to STOP using your body as a receptacle for your tension and emotions. Healthy breathing and relaxation techniques are keys to opening the doors and ventilating yourself.

RELAXATION AND SELF-HYPNOSIS

The feeling of deep, pleasant, comfortable relaxation is an excellent point from which to begin self-hypnosis. The first few times you practice self-hypnosis, use one of these relaxation methods to prepare yourself. Later on it may not be necessary to go through a complete progressive relaxation exercise each time you enter a trance state.

Once you have practiced self-hypnosis a few times, you can develop cues—actions or events that start a response—for specific goals. We will talk more about cues in another chapter. For now, remember that deep breathing is an excellent way to cue yourself to regain the feelings of relaxation and to feel more at ease even outside of a hypnotic trance.

You will give yourself suggestions while in self-hypnosis that any time you desire to relax and feel less tense, several deep, satisfying breaths will cause this same feeling of restful comfort and relaxation to occur.

This reinforcing of the deep breathing cue while you are in your trance will extend and enhance the relaxation response and help you to employ it any time throughout the day when you feel the pressure and stresses of your job or of any situation building up.

REFERENCES

Benson, H. *The Relaxation Response.* New York: Avon Books, 1976.

Groves, P.M. & Rebec, G.V. *Introduction to Biological Psychology, 3rd Ed.* Dubuque, Iowa: Wm. C. Brown Publishers, 1988.

Jacobson, E. *Anxiety and Tension Control.* New York: J.B. Lippincott Company, 1964.

Mason, J. *Guide to Stress Reduction.* Culver City, California: Peace Press, Inc., 1980.

Salchidananda, S. *Integral Yoga—Hatha.* New York: Rinehart & Winston, 1970.

5
The Power of Posthypnotic Suggestions and Cues

Joan awoke from her hypnotic trance feeling refreshed and alert. She remembered everything the therapist had said. She also recalled all that she had spoken and thought.

She was using hypnosis to lose weight. With her psychologist's help, Joan had explored her childhood memories to better understand her use of food to respond to emotional turmoil.

The therapist had taught her to use self-hypnosis. In her trance, Joan had given herself the suggestion that whenever she wanted to reenter self-hypnosis, she would close her eyes and visualize a large, yellow, hot air balloon. When she took several deep breaths and counted backward from five to one, Joan would be in self-hypnosis.

That evening she went home and tried it. She imagined the yellow balloon and before she had counted to one, she felt herself relaxing and her hand beginning to get numb—one sign for her of a hypnotic trance.

Any image could have been used. But as a child, Joan had once taken a brief ride in a big, yellow balloon at a carnival. The balloon had gone up 100 feet or so, but had remained safely tethered to the ground by a large rope. Nevertheless, it had been quite a thrill for Joan. She remembered it vividly.

The yellow balloon and the counting backwards were posthypnotic cues. They triggered a prearranged response in Joan and helped her quickly reenter a trance.

The fact that Joan had already been successful at reaching a pleasantly comfortable state of absorption, imagination, and expectation of positive experiences was used as material for the posthypnotic suggestions.

WHAT IS A POSTHYPNOTIC SUGGESTION?

A posthypnotic suggestion is a suggestion given, while the individual is in a hypnotic state, for an action or other response to take place after the hypnotic experience. Just as Joan used her previous vivid memory of the balloon ride for reinstating a new and exciting state of mind, you can find many past experiences and present actions from which to create posthypnotic suggestions.

WHAT IS A POSTHYPNOTIC CUE?

Posthypnotic cues are any actions, thoughts, words, images, or events that initiate or trigger a posthypnotic suggestion response outside the trance. The response can be an action, a feeling, or an internal physical change.

For example, when Joan is at work and gets tense or feels stressful, she can relax herself by looking at the clock on the wall. It stimulates an image in her mind of a clock spring unwinding, which she associates with her own unwinding of tension. That cue, a posthypnotic association she suggested while she was in a trance, helps her feel relaxed and less tense. It reinstates the same feeling of calm and relaxation she felt when she was in self-hypnosis.

WHY DO YOU USE POSTHYPNOTIC SUGGESTIONS AND CUES?

Posthypnotic suggestions and cues are a powerful extension of your self-hypnosis work. They allow you to change or improve your behavior and responses anytime you desire, not just while you are in self-hypnosis.

If it were not for this remarkable effect, the value of hypnosis would be vastly reduced. One reason posthypnotic suggestions work is that your memories and past successes are used by your unconscious mind to provoke an action or a response that you have implanted while in self-hypnosis. The fact that it does work has been demonstrated countless times in clinical research.

Suppose your goal in self-hypnosis is to relax and lower your stress levels. While in a trance, you are calm and relaxed. But what about when you are faced with a stressful situation at work? You may feel your breathing getting quicker and your heart beating faster. You may not be able to tell your boss or a client, "Just a minute, please. I need to put myself in a trance for a few minutes. I'll be back shortly."

If you had given yourself a posthypnotic cue when you were in a trance, earlier, you could dissolve the tension without anyone even realizing it.

For instance, while in self-hypnosis you could have made an association between deep breathing and relaxation. The deep breathing would have become a cue. With several deep breaths, the feelings of relaxation and calm could return at any time.

Or, you might have used a cue such as straightening a paper clip. While in your trance state, you could have associated uncoiling a paper clip with relaxing your tense, coiled muscles. Then, later, when you untwisted the clip, that action would trigger the internal response of relaxation and release the stress in you.

Posthypnotic cues can also reinforce an action or other desired response. The cue of a refrigerator door can reinforce your resolve to avoid in-between meal snacks. You might suggest that you will feel full when you approach the door seeking unnecessary food.

Another example of how posthypnotic cues can work is in dealing with sleeping problems. Jerry, an executive at a brokerage firm, had trouble getting to sleep at night. He gave himself repeated suggestions that when he switched off the light in his room at night and yawned, he would then grow sleepy.

The first few weeks, he consciously remembered his cues. He continued regularly repeating his posthypnotic suggestions while in self-hypnosis. Gradually, his sleeping improved and he would go to sleep soon after retiring.

After a few more weeks, he reinforced the suggestion only occasionally. Later, he forgot about the light switch being a cue and he would yawn automatically after shutting the lamp at bedtime. Shortly thereafter, he would drift comfortably to sleep.

You need to repeat your posthypnotic suggestions in several trance sessions prior to the time you would like them to become enacted. The more you repeat a posthypnotic suggestion while in self-hypnosis, the more effective it will be.

CAN YOU RESIST A POSTHYPNOTIC SUGGESTION AND CUE?

Although it has some characteristics of a compulsive act, you can resist a posthypnotic suggestion if you choose. In self-hypnosis, you can remember having given yourself the suggestion—there is usually no amnesia in self-hypnosis. With repetition, the suggestion can become so ingrained that you may consciously forget about the cue. But your unconscious mind will respond to a firmly implanted cue even if you don't consciously remember it.

There are many examples of people in hypnosis not responding to suggestions. For instance, suppose a subject is asked to fetch a glass of water when a certain word is spoken. The person will very likely get the glass of water even though he is aware of why he is doing it. But he could choose to not respond to the suggestion. We all have the power to take action or not to act.

If while in hypnosis you were given a suggestion to do something that was against your best interests, you would wake up easily and spontaneously, drift into ordinary sleep, or state your refusal to comply.

What if you wanted to override a cue just once?

Suppose that one evening Jerry, from the previous example, turned off the light, yawned, but before he went to sleep the telephone rang. Would the posthypnotic suggestion for sleep be so strong that he wouldn't answer the phone? No, he would answer it. In fact, should he need to get up and help a friend or do something else, he certainly could.

With self-hypnosis, your unconscious mind understands your intent. Should you wish to cancel the effect or should an emergency or other situation require you to change your response, you can do so easily.

Once you work with yourself in self-hypnosis, you will develop a sense of trust in yourself. Your results will be satisfying and you can look forward to trusting that part of yourself in the future.

MOTIVATION AND LOGIC

To get the most effective use of posthypnotic suggestions and cues, be sure you are truly motivated to accept them. Additionally, make them as logical and relevant to your situation as possible. Experiment, find the most effective techniques for *you*.

For instance, in the example of Jerry's desire to improve his sleep, he had a strong motivation—the need to rest.

But if he had used a cue such as closing the garage door or washing the dishes, the effect might have been different. Those acts and sleeping have very little in common. There is no logical progression or connection between them.

Jerry's choice of the cues of turning off the light and yawning was appropriate to his goal—sleeping. He might also have used cues such as drinking a glass of milk, turning on the electric blanket, or taking off his robe. All of those could be consistent and related with going to sleep.

YOU ALREADY MAY BE EXPERIENCING POSTHYPNOTIC CUES

Many people have experienced the equivalent of posthypnotic cues without being aware of it. Writer and psychologist, Daniel Araoz speaks of negative hypnosis, where an individual has set up a pattern of behavior that reinforces itself in an unconscious and often unproductive manner.

Andrew is a case of negative hypnosis we have treated. Every time Andrew pulled into his driveway, he felt anxious about going inside. He knew he was supposed to talk with his wife about their financial problems, his two-year-old child needed attention, and there was work to be done around the house. He was tired from work and usually anticipated tension as soon as he approached home. He had developed a negative self-hypnosis and there were several cues to reinforce his feelings. The drive home was full of negative cues about the problems he would have to face. Pulling into the driveway was a cue to begin feeling anxious. Parking the car was a cue to begin thoughts of avoidance toward the unpleasantness awaiting him inside.

With self-hypnosis training, Andrew learned how to change the negative cues into positive cues and to add new cues for new responses. He altered his route home slightly, and this gave him a *different view*, both literally and metaphorically. The drive home became an opportunity to review his day and let go of work. He could see things differently and de-stress himself with slow deep breathing as he drove.

Soon, Andrew could imagine a more relaxed approach to his homeward drive. Like an airliner approaching a runway, he could land smooth and light in his driveway. He anticipated playing with his child when he first arrived home. This would be a time to play and change gears even more from the workday he had experienced. His conversations with his wife would be problem-solving opportunities. Even though he could still be somewhat anxious as he drove into the driveway, the anxiety could be from a positive expectation rather than from dread.

When he parked the car, Andrew could now feel he was landing or settling down into a friendly place. What had changed? First, his perspective: he could see the drive home, which he never before liked, as a time for himself. He told his wife he wanted to play with their child when he first arrived home (the little boy nearly always sought his attention anyway) and that he and his wife could talk later. He deliberately set this play time aside for himself as well as for his child. He had changed his view of this play time.

Andrew effectively took conscious control over the negative cues and altered them into positive ones by making some changes in both how he perceived his situation and how he performed certain actions. He changed his route home, he changed how the transition from work to home occurred with the play time, and he set aside the time to problem-solve with his wife, rather than simply tolerating her concerns and worries.

In a few weeks, Andrew looked forward to his drive home, enjoyed the play time with his boy, and felt more effective by problem-solving with his wife. She also felt better because she was being involved in the process of solving their situation instead of merely stirring her husband into worry.

You may examine your own life for instances of negative cues and explore how you can change those patterns into positive ones. The first step is to become more aware of such cues if they exist.

MAKE YOUR POSTHYPNOTIC SUGGESTIONS SPECIFIC

Suggestions should be specific to a situation. If you wanted to develop your ability to concentrate, begin with one specific type of concentration—for instance, playing cards. When you develop posthypnotic suggestions and cues for a goal, the more you focus on that goal, the more effective will be your self-hypnosis trancework.

As your skills for a goal improve, there will be a carryover into many other situations as well. From self-hypnosis for card playing, you will be able to increase your concentration in sports, work, or hobbies, for example.

Your suggestions for improving your concentration at card playing might be: "When I sit down to play a card game, there may be many distractions. The distractions are like the wind, rain, or snow blowing in through an open door and dispersing the cards. I can leave the door open or close it.

"The next time I enter a room or building with the intent of playing a card game, or any time I want to close out distractions, I will be aware of closing the door behind me. I may still talk, listen, and function as usual. But noises, voices, and sights that might have distracted me will be shut out like the wind and the elements are shut out by the door. I'll expect some distractions for contrast and even enjoy the added concentration that they make possible."

Create specific cues for each situation. The act of sitting down can be associated with resting and unburdening yourself of worries and distractions. As you sit down, your attention and concentration are sitting with you.

Be imaginative in finding or creating actions to use as signals for your cues. Perhaps clearing your throat will be your cue to clear out distractions. Straightening some part of your clothing can be a cue to align your attention. Baseball players often adjust their hats and clothing and could use those actions as cues to focus their concentration. Remember that it will be better if you find some connection between your goal and the cues you are reinforcing for achieving the goal.

VISUALIZING YOUR SUGGESTIONS

While you're giving yourself posthypnotic suggestions, as with all suggestions, visualize the scene, the action, or the feeling you desire. Be as vivid and detailed as you can. Expand each suggestion with the richness of colors, smells, sounds, textures, tastes, voices, and feelings that would be in the scene you are describing to yourself.

POSTHYPNOTIC CUES TO REINSTATE YOUR NEXT TRANCE

One of the most fundamental applications for posthypnotic cues is to help you develop future trances quickly. We recommend that you include in your self-hypnosis practice suggestions for easier entry into trance in future sessions.

For example, you might give yourself suggestions such as; "*Any time in the future I wish to reenter this comfortable and pleasant trance state, all I need to do is settle into a comfortable chair, breathe slow and deep for a few minutes, and I will easily and quickly return to this level of relaxed comfort and focused awareness.*"

Notice that the suggestion is conditional—that is, it is intended to occur when you WISH to reenter trance, not just anytime you sit down or breathe in this particular manner. Your intentions in trance matter considerably to how and when the posthypnotic suggestions and cues will function.

SUMMARY

1. Posthypnotic suggestions and cues are a powerful extension of your self-hypnosis. They are suggestions you give to yourself while in a trance to elicit a response you desire outside of self-hypnosis.

2. Be sure you are motivated to accept and act on the suggestions and cues you create. Though you can cancel the effect of a cue, you should have a strong desire to comply with your own suggestions.

3. Make your cues related to the action or event you want to respond to. Find or create actions that logically precede or are associated with the situation or event to which you wish to respond.

4. Give yourself four or five suggestions and cues for creating the change in behavior or emotions you wish to make. You may develop a series of cues that build and reinforce the change.

5. Repetition is the cement that bonds the posthypnotic suggestion and cue to your unconscious mind. Give yourself suggestions six or eight times, well before the time you expect them to become effective. For instance, if you want to use posthypnotic suggestions for relaxation and pain control before a dental visit, practice for a week before your appointment.

6. Make your suggestions and cues as specific as possible to the situation of change you wish to make. Broad, general suggestions are less effective than ones that focus in on precise and well-defined goals. Suggestions relating to concentration, for example, are more effective if they are related to specific situations requiring concentration.

   After your response to your cue becomes a habit, you will find that it can have the desired result at any time you wish and for other applications. That is, you can create concentration for playing cards, for instance, and the same process can work for you in another situation, through your cue response. Repetition can help make this possible. *As with any new skill, practice sharpens performance.*

7. As you conclude each self-hypnosis session, give yourself a posthypnotic suggestion to reenter a trance more easily and quickly the next time. Find some symbol for a cue, as Joan did, that is a vivid image for you. As you repeat this same suggestion with each practice, it will become easier each time to put yourself in a trance.

REFERENCES

Alman, B.M. & Carney, R.E. Consequences of direct and indirect suggestion on success of posthypnotic behavior. *American Journal of Clinical Hypnosis,* Vol. 23 (Oct.), 1980.

Araoz, D.L. *The New Hypnosis.* New York: Brunner/Mazel, 1985.

Araoz, D.L. *Hypnosis and Sex Therapy.* New York: Brunner/Mazel, 1982.

Duncan, B. & Perry, C. Uncancelled hypnotic suggestions: Initial studies. *American Journal of Clinical Hypnosis,* Vol. 19(3), 1977.

Erickson, M.H., Rossi, E.L. & S.I. *Hypnotic Realities.* New York: Irvington Publishers, 1976.

Hartland, J. *Medical and Dental Hypnosis.* Baltimore: Williams & Wilkins Company, 1971.

Kroger, W.S. *Clinical and Experimental Hypnosis.* Philadelphia: J.B. Lippincott Company, 1977.

6
How To Use Guided Imagery and Positive Visualization

Would you like to try an experiment with yourself? Close your eyes. Now, without looking, what is the total number of windows in your home or apartment?

The important question is not how many windows, but *how you arrived at the number*. A natural way to do it is through imagery. To accurately count the windows, if that number was not easily known to you, you had to remember and imagine each of them.

Almost all of us use some form of imagery. We use it to solve a variety of our daily problems. "The soul never thinks without a picture," Aristotle said.

IS IMAGERY ONLY VISUAL?

There is more to imagery than just visualization. We can use imagery to create or recreate emotions. We can also use imagery with our senses of smell, touch, hearing, and even taste.

Have you ever been hungry and remembered a special meal you once had? Perhaps you can close your eyes for a moment and remember a favorite dish. Your memory may be so vivid you can nearly taste it.

In fact, your mouth may water in anticipation from the thought and mental picture of the meal. If your mouth waters from the thought or mental picture, that is a physical response to a creation in the mind. That sort of response is one of the powers of imagery.

EYES, EARS, AND TOUCH—WHAT'S YOUR SPECIALTY?

Each of us is inclined to take in information and perceptions of the world differently. Though we use our five senses, we give each of those senses different values and importance. This is usually not a conscious process—it has evolved in our unconscious mind from early childhood.

Some people may be more aware of and sensitive to visual stimuli and only partially attentive to auditory (hearing) input. These people may be even less mindful of kinesthetic (touching, feeling) perceptions.

Of course, *no one operates in just one of these sensory modes.* We overlap input from our senses and we use all of them at various times. But most of us are more sensitive to one sensory input than to another.

Behavioral scientists find that a majority of people are visual in their perception mode. You may believe you are fairly equal in your sensitivities. That would be somewhat unusual, though the differences in your preferences may be too slim to detect.

Your imagery may be subject to these same tendencies. Visually-oriented people will tend to be most concerned with what their imagery "looks like." Auditory people will be "tuned in" and most sensitive to the sounds and voices of their images. Kinesthetic people will be most affected by the physical sensations and the ability to "sense or feel" the images.

Nevertheless, we all accept and process information and stimuli from all our senses and our images may contain *all* sensory perceptions, even tastes and smells. Therefore, the most *effective* imagery you can create incorporates elements that arouse all your senses.

There has been much written and studied about this phenomenon under the name of NLP. Richard Bandler and John Grinder have taken some of the work of Milton Erickson and fashioned it into a model of understanding communications and mental processing they call neuro-linguistic programming or NLP. These processes have been found to have value in understanding self and interpersonal communication patterns and will be discussed further in Chapter 10.

IMPROVING YOUR ABILITY TO USE IMAGERY

Each of us possesses the ability to use some sort of imagery, but we have varying degrees of skill. Depending on our life experiences and environment, we may have used imagery a lot or a little. Dr. Michael Samuels and Nancy Samuels (1975) devised some exercises to develop better imagery. Here is a variation of the exercises that can help you develop your imagery skills:

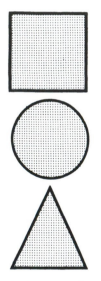

An imagery and visualization exercise is to gaze at one of these figures, then shut your eyes and try visualizing it.

1. Gaze at one of the geometrical drawings—a square, a circle, a triangle, or some such figure. Then shut your eyes and try to visualize it.
2. Examine for a few moments a three-dimensional object such as an orange, a glass of water, or a lamp. Again, close your eyes and imagine the object.
3. Visualize a schoolroom from your childhood.
4. Visualize your home or apartment. Move around in it, go from room to room.
5. Visualize a person you know.
6. Visualize your reflection in a mirror.

Practice these exercises every day for one month. It will take just a little more time to do the practice than it takes to read these directions. You may be surprised when you realize how vivid and creative your imagery can become.

Add to and expand these exercises with different places and objects as you gain in your imaging talents. Feel free to experiment with your favorite images, colors, smells, and sensations of touch, heat, and cold.

HOW IMPORTANT IS IMAGERY IN SELF-HYPNOSIS?

The images and visualizations you will develop along with your suggestions are powerful tools. In self-hypnosis, a mental picture is worth pages of verbal suggestions.

What makes imagery so powerful is that it comes from within you. You have created it. You have assembled the images from all your memories, experiences, and thoughts. *You are using the language of your unconscious mind to place requests for change.*

PERSONALIZE YOUR IMAGERY

Imagery of a suggestion can take an infinite variety of forms. If a hundred people were asked to imagine a walk in a forest and then to describe their images in detail, no two would be exactly the same. Their images of the scene would be a composite of recollections from their individual previous experiences involving forests and walks.

Use material from your own experiences and memories to form your visualizations and imagery. If you read a suggestion in this book, feel free (in fact, you're encouraged) to alter and reform it. Use your own words and mental pictures from your life experiences.

For example, if you are suggesting to yourself that your arm is feeling cold and numb, picture a time you really did feel cold and numb. Perhaps you will remember a time you were without gloves in the winter cold. Or you may remember a time when you dipped your hand into a cold mountain stream.

If you are suggesting a floating feeling in your arms or legs, find an image that represents to you a floating experience. Perhaps you'll recall a bubble of air floating up from the bottom of a pool of water you were once in; puffy dandelion seeds you've seen floating on the wind; or perhaps the sensations you had floating in an inner tube or a boat.

The important thing is to create images from your own experiences. Use the suggestions in this book to stir your memories for images that are *yours.*

IMAGERY AND DISEASE

There have been numerous experiments using imagery to combat certain diseases. Perhaps the best known clinical work of this kind is that of Carl Simonton, a radiation oncologist, and his wife, Stephanie Matthews-Simonton, a psychologist (1982). They pioneered the use of visual imagery as an additional treatment for cancer patients.

The Simontons first teach a patient to relax with a form of progressive relaxation. The patient is asked to mentally picture each muscle group and the releasing of the tensions in it (see Chapter 4).

After achieving a state of deep relaxation, patients are asked to picture their cancer cells as being very weak and their own white blood cells and immune system as being very strong. They are encouraged to see their own defenses as powerful, virile warriors, and the cancer cells and tumors as being various weak animals, such as snails and slugs, which powerful warriors can vanquish.

There is good reason to think that your unconscious attitude toward a disease plays a key role in mustering your internal forces to combat the virus, bacteria, or tumor associated with that disease. Imagery helps create a positive unconscious attitude toward getting well.

Two colleagues of the Simontons (1982), psychologists Jeanne Achterberg and G. Frank Lawlis, have done further scientific analysis of imagery combined with conventional therapy used by cancer patients. One of their patients was a man who had cancer of the pancreas, a cancer with a recovery rate of only five percent.

He imagined his cancer cells as armadillos and his white blood cells as white knights. The knights would charge through his system spearing the armadillos with their lances; each knight had a quota to fill.

At one point in his therapy, the patient mentally observed that many of his white knights were disappearing. A blood test confirmed that his white blood cell count was dropping. When he learned this, the man resolved to fortify his army of white knights. Shortly, his white count stabilized.

A while later, he reported that his white knights were having difficulty meeting their daily quota of little critters. They had to shake the bushes to scare up the creatures. An ultrasound examination the following week showed that the patient had no evidence of tumor.

Cancer is often a complex illness and a psychological tool like hypnosis may also be used to increase the patient's acceptance of his or her situation. It is frequently helpful *as an adjunct* to more standard approaches of treatment and to help a patient relax. *Self-hypnosis should never be used as a sole treatment for any cancer or related disease.*

How does imagery aid the body in the fight against disease?

It appears that we become susceptible to diseases when our normal balance becomes disturbed. Dr. Walter Cannon (1929) called this balance "homeostasis." Homeostatic imbalance can arise from many influences and may disrupt the body's chemistry.

One of these influences is stress. Research conducted by Dr. Hans Selye (1978), a leader in the area of stress, showed that excessively stressed rats secreted large amounts of corticosterone, a powerful hormone from the adrenal gland.

Normally, such hormones prevent inflammation in the body. That's wonderful if there is an infection or injury. But too much of this hormone for too long will reduce the effectiveness of the body's immune system.

Another change brought on by stress is a reduction in T-lymphocytes—white blood cells that help produce antibodies and trigger a defense against tumors. When these immune factors are lowered, bacteria and viruses gain an opportunity to multiply and create illness.

It is becoming increasingly clear that the mind affects and directs these immune processes through complex neuro-chemical processes. Ernest Rossi in his book *The Psychobiology of Mind-Body Healing* (1986) explains many of the theories about this phenomenon. This is an exciting new field of research called psychoneuroimmunology, which we will discuss further in Chapter 27.

Many clinicians believe that the better you are able to visualize your body and its problem areas, the better your unconscious mind can coordinate your internal defense forces. Your unconscious can wave the baton and, perhaps chemically, orchestrate the components of your immune system to function in harmony and with gusto.

TWO DIFFERENT WAYS OF USING IMAGERY FOR A GOAL

We will utilize two principal ways of using imagery to work toward a goal. One method is to visualize the process or actions of achieving the success you seek.

A second type of imagery for change creates mental pictures of the goal or result as if it has already occurred. Both *process imagery* and *result imagery* are useful in reaching your goals.

There are some goals—like that of the patient with pancreatic cancer—that are better approached through process imagery. The process was the patient imagining his immune system seeking and destroying the cancer cells.

Or, if you are trying to stop a throbbing, vascular headache, for example, you might imagine your hands and feet getting warm. Creating a warm sensation in the hands and feet may be accomplished by drawing more blood to those areas and away from the throbbing vessels in the head.

Your suggestions and process imagery could involve all your senses. You might visualize yourself with gloves on, sitting in front of a fireplace. You could imagine hearing the crackling of the wood, smell the pine burning. You could mentally feel the heat from the fire and "see" the glow of the hot coals. It has been found that many headaches respond to this treatment. Daniels (1980) reported excellent results in using hypnosis to increase hand temperature.

This is an indirect method of using imagery as part of a process to achieve a goal—headache relief.

"Result imagery" would have you picture yourself doing, appearing, or reacting in the way you wish as if your goal has already been accomplished. If you are working on more self-confidence, you might imagine yourself having boldly asked for a deserved raise in pay. Or, perhaps imagine yourself having confidently given a speech, hear the applause, and imagine the positive outcomes of your presentation, such as being elected to the post you were seeking or getting a raise in pay from your employer.

A process image for the speech goal just described might be to imagine yourself calm and relaxed as you pause at the end of one part of your speech and prepare for the easy delivery of the next topic.

Golfer Jack Nicklaus reports that he always imagines each shot well before he approaches the ball. He mentally pictures how a perfect shot will look. Then he "sees" himself making the swing that will create the result. A great combination of both end result and process imagery.

A study, by stress researcher Edmund Jacobson (1967), showed that visualizing an activity produced small but measurable reactions in the muscles involved in the imagined activity. When you conduct a mental rehearsal of something, you are implanting a learned memory of a successful action. You are also informing your unconscious mind what you expect it to achieve.

You can use this technique of mental rehearsal for any goal you are working on. If you're working on allergy control, for instance, picture yourself breathing clearly, even in the presence of what you are allergic to. Should you be trying to sleep better, visualize yourself in bed and deeply asleep.

Suppose your goal is to lose weight. You could imagine yourself as being thin. Visualize yourself fitting into a dress or suit you have seen that is the size you wish to become. Mentally picture yourself reflected in a mirror or in a window, trim and lean as you wish to be. This is result imagery. It is only one of several strategies for weight loss. You use imagery to lead you to the result you seek.

Within the same trance session, you might also want to use process imagery. You might imagine yourself eating smaller portions of food. You could picture yourself feeling full and getting up from the table with food still on your plate. You could visualize yourself closing the refrigerator door—between meals— with empty hands. These are process images. They reinforce the positive processes you need to go through to get to the result.

Process imagery can be used to implant posthypnotic suggestions—suggestions for how you will act after your trance—to extend your goal work and to set intermediate goals. By approaching a goal with *both* process imagery and result imagery, you will multiply the success rate of your self-hypnosis.

Imagery and self-hypnosis

You will probably use imagery from the very first time you practice self-hypnosis. It is an integral part of learning to relax and to focus your attention inward to develop a trance-state.

The imagery is your own; you need not share or reveal your images. So be creative, allow the positive images to flow from your mind and memories as freely as the wind blows.

Fill your images with colors, sounds, aromas, textures, and tastes. Become absorbed in your imagery as your scenes—like a convoy of trucks picking up new tools and momentum—evolve and move toward your goal.

Allow your positive visualizations to seem as real to you as you can. Your success with self-hypnosis will increase as you become better at using imagery. Take time to practice your imagery skills with the exercises at the beginning of this chapter.

You are developing communication with your unconscious mind. Learn to speak to yourself with greater clarity and richness through your mental movies and snapshots.

The mental pictures, while you are in a self-hypnosis trance, enter your unconscious mind much more rapidly and completely than at other times. During self-hypnosis you are not criticizing and analyzing each image to see how, where, why, and when it fits into your preconceived ideas of things.

The changes you will experience may be subtle at first. Make a commitment to yourself to work on a *program for change*—progress will follow.

Keep your visualizations positive. Leave negative thoughts and self-defeating images parked at the curb. Or better yet, junk them completely. In self-hypnosis negative thoughts can't help you at all. Your unconscious works best toward positive, affirmative goals.

Your imagery can be like booking passage on your own cruise ship, bound for anywhere you choose. The meals are as delicious as you can dream up. You can be as comfortable as you can remember and you can see yourself as whoever you want to be.

You are the captain and the crew. You can move with the care and deliberation of a diamond cutter or travel at the speed of light. Best of all, the cruise costs you neither cash nor credit. With your own abilities, you are learning to express more and change more; you only need expend a little effort and imagination to extend your limits.

REFERENCES

Bandler, R., & Grinder, J. *Frogs into Princes*. Moab, Utah: Real People Press, 1979.

Bandler, R., & Grinder, J. *Patterns of the Hypnotic Techniques of Milton H. Erickson, M.D.* Vol 1. Cupertino, California: Meta Publications, 1975.

Bandler, R., & Grinder, J. *The Structure of Magic*. Vol 1. Palo Alto, California: Science and Behavior Books, 1976.

Cannon, W.B. *Bodily Changes in Pain, Hunger, Fear and Rage*. New York: Appleton, 1929.

Crasilneck, H.B. & Hall, J.A. Hypnotic suggestions with cancer patients. in *Clinical Hypnosis: Principles and Applications* (2nd ed., ch.9). Orlando: Grune & Stratton, 1985.

Daniels, L.K. The effect of automated hypnosis and hand warming on migraine: A pilot study. *American Journal of Clinical Hypnosis*, Vol. 19, pp. 91–94, 1980.

Jacobson, E. *Biology of Emotions: New Understanding Derived from Biological Multi Disciplinary Investigation, First Electrophysical Measurements*. Springfield, Illinois: C.C. Thomas, 1967.

Korn, E., & Johnson, K. *Visualization: The Uses of Imagery in the Health Professions*. Homewood, Illinois: Dow Jones-Irwin, 1983.

Lenard, L. Visions that vanquish cancer. *Science Digest*, April 1981.

Maslow, A.H. *Toward a Psychology of Being*. New York: Van Nostrand, 1962.

Pratt, G.J., Wood, P., & Alman, B.H. *A Clinical Hypnosis Primer (Expanded and Updated)*. New York: John Wiley & Sons, 1988.

Richardson, A. *Mental Imagery*. New York: Springer Publishing Company, 1969.

Rossi, E.L. *The Psychobiology of Mind-Body Healing*. New York: W.W. Norton & Company, Inc., 1986.

Samuels, M. & N. *Seeing With the Mind's Eye*. New York: Random House Bookworks, 1975.

Selye, H. *The Stress of Life*. New York: McGraw-Hill, 1978.

Simonton, C. & S. *Getting Well Again*. New York: Bantam Books, 1982.

7
Putting Yourself into a Trance

Most of us can remember one of the first times we rode a bicycle. It was an unsteady but exciting experience. We soon learned we had some control over a new dimension of our own abilities—increased balance and coordination.

Of course, we already had balance and coordination, but this was something special: a delightful application of an enhanced skill. This is what you can expect from your first experience with self-hypnosis.

You already have many of the abilities you may be seeking to improve with the help of this book—for example, concentration and memory. And you already possess the basis for the changes you seek—pain control, stress management, habit control, physical changes, parenting skills, or other goals. Self-hypnosis is a natural skill; like riding a bicycle, it will help get you where you want to go.

GETTING COMFORTABLE

Ideally, begin by relaxing at a place you've selected with help from Chapter 3.

You may find yourself with feelings of expectation and anticipation of hypnosis. This is quite natural—just as with the bicycle.

Self-hypnosis is an individual, personal experience; therefore, you need to take an active role in formulating the best technique for yourself. We will provide a number of suggestions and examples. *You may want to choose one or another, or create your own combination of techniques.*

Read this chapter completely before you begin your practice session. Do the preparation recommended and later incorporate the suggestions in Chapter 10 on personalizing your suggestions. This preparation will give you delightfully surprising and satisfying experiences.

Take a few moments to relax with one of the relaxation techniques. Whether you use active or passive progressive methods is up to you. Develop as deep a relaxation for yourself as you can.

EYE FIXATION

We would like to point out here that many of the following explanations can become a script that you can adapt for your own purposes or even to make an audio tape.

Once you're in a relaxed, secure position and have taken several deep, comfortable, satisfying breaths—look in front of you. Find some small object or spot out in front of you and above your line of sight. This spot could be a mark on the wall, the tip of a plant leaf, a part of a picture, or anything that is stationary.

Focus all your conscious attention to the spot or object—gaze at it, examine it in detail. Continue slow, deep, satisfying breathing. Keep your attention on the spot and work all your thoughts toward it. The idea is to eliminate any extraneous thoughts and forget all problems, worries, and anxieties as much as possible. Don't worry if a stray thought or two slips into your mind now and then. That is difficult to prevent without practice, but that is precisely what you're doing—practicing. You'll get better at clearing your mind of distracting thoughts.

As other thoughts come into your mind, allow them to pass through you and return to thoughts about "your spot." Continue slow, deep, satisfying breathing. Begin telling yourself how relaxed you feel. Focusing on the spot you've chosen will help preempt other thoughts.

Begin giving yourself suggestions such as: "*With each deep, relaxing, satisfying breath I take, I feel relaxation spreading down from my shoulders and back, down through my legs and into my toes. The more I relax, the better I feel.*" Put these suggestions into your own words if you like. The exact wording is not important. If your goal—relaxation—is clear and your suggestions are positive, your meaning will be understood.

You may feel your eyes watering and blinking. Give yourself suggestions to encourage your eyes to close: "*As my eyes focus on the spot I've chosen, I may find that they feel tired. As my eyes water and blink, it is as if the more they blink the more they are clearing away all worries, concerns, and anxieties. My body is relaxed and at ease, and my eyes and my mind can be just as comfortable, relaxed, and at ease.*"

You may spend as long as 10 or 15 minutes with open eyes during the first few practice sessions. Or you may find that in only a few minutes your eyes become tired and heavy. You decide when you want to close your eyes. No one need decide that for you.

Continue with suggestions such as: "*I may notice that as my eyes continue to focus on the spot I've chosen, I can decide when I want to close my eyes. Just as I make decisions like when to go to sleep in the evening, I can decide when it is most comfortable for me to close my eyes.*"

As best you can, keep a steady flow of mental suggestions of this nature going to yourself. You can say the same things in many ways. Change the words slightly or change the order of the words. Find different ways of conveying the same idea of concentration on the spot, on relaxation, and on your eyes wanting to close.

Repetition of the suggestions and the monotony of the focus on one spot will shortly cause your eyes to *want* to close. If after 10 or 15 minutes they still feel wide open, don't worry, you can just close them gently.

Once your eyes are closed, continue giving yourself suggestions that you are relaxed and feeling safe and comfortable. The suggestions you give yourself may be similar to those you used in progressive relaxation. Even though you may feel very relaxed and comfortable, continue giving yourself suggestions to reinforce and generalize the feelings of relaxation throughout your body.

You can do the suggesting through your process imagery, result imagery and/or repeating your own words to yourself and focusing on your internal voice.

The guide to personalizing your suggestions in Chapter 6 will help you develop suggestions for expanding feelings of heaviness, lightness, coolness, warmth, or numbness throughout your entire body. Be aware of any changes you may notice.

UTILIZING YOUR TENSION OR ANXIETY FOR TRANCE

Throughout most of this book, we discuss relaxation and trance as a goal. However, it is not necessary to be relaxed to enter a hypnotic trance. If you are experiencing physical tension or anxiety and find it too difficult to let go of that tension to enter a trance, it is possible to utilize your stressed, anxious, or tense state to develop a trance state.

In his book "Trancework" (1990), psychologist Michael Yapko describes how to utilize anxiety and tension to develop a trance. You allow and accept the present state of mind, whatever it is—anxious, cautious, or even skeptical—essentially not creating any conflict over the present condition through noncritical acceptance.

Then begin thinking about a past experience in which you were so comfortably involved in an experience that you didn't pay attention to some things going on around you.

This technique in self-hypnosis is draw your alert attention to some past experience of comfort, or calm, or relaxation and absorption. This will allow your physiological responses to move toward matching your remembered feelings.

Another strategy is described by Ernest Rossi (1976), who chronicles how Erickson used the anxiety of his patients to develop a hypnotic trance. You can use a similar strategy for your own self-hypnosis. Focus on some visual target or even on your own physical experience of tension or anxiety as a point for absorption and distraction.

For example, as Rossi (1976) describes in "Hypnotic Realities," Erickson had a highly anxious patient focus on a clock: "*You might focus on the sweep hand of a clock. There is movement in the second hand that you can follow with your eyes. Allow your attention to become absorbed in this movement. Notice how your own experience of tension is felt in your body as you focus on the moving second hand. You can imagine how the gears in the clock are meshing and turning, imagine how the electrical current might be flowing just as energy is flowing in your own body at the same time.*

"*Wind yourself up into the focusing experience, and if you find yourself distracted by other thoughts, welcome those thoughts as you remain visually focused on the clock. You may notice that your heart is beating rapidly, you may even be able to discover a rhythm in the heart beat that is similar or close to the second hand movement. See if you can find a rhythm and absorb yourself in it.*"

This sort of approach will allow a trance to be formed and then let you lead yourself through a transition toward another focus or goal of your choice.

The next step is imagining or visualizing your suggestions.

VISUALIZATION AND SELF-HYPNOSIS

One of the best avenues for directing suggestions into your unconscious mind is to visualize them. Allow your imagination and visualizations to become as real to you as you can. *Create images for yourself that represent the suggestions of relaxation.*

Visualizations and imagination are closely related to your unconscious mind—imagery very well may be the language of the unconscious. Self-hypnosis focuses your suggestions to your unconscious. This is a perfectly safe, healthy experience similar to the images you may have while daydreaming. In this book we use the term unconscious, but another term for this concept is the subconscious.

Allow yourself to flow with your mental pictures or feelings. The more you detach yourself from your conscious, rational, logical thoughts, the more quickly you will enjoy the benefits of self-hypnosis.

SOME IMAGES TO EXPLORE

The images that follow are simply examples for you to explore with your imagination. Let this experience flow naturally from the relaxed state you have developed. Allow your suggestions to drift from ones of closing your eyes and heaviness to ones of relaxation and to images like those that follow. Do not feel restricted to only those presented here.

Create new suggestions and images using your own experiences, memories, books, or pictures from magazines or television which suggest relaxation to you. You can rehearse these visualizations beforehand.

For instance: *You may have walked through a busy area of your city recently and noticed a quiet store or shop. Or, perhaps you can recall a particular store in a shopping center that was quiet and unhurried. You too can have a quiet, unhurried experience each time you practice self-hypnosis.*

"*Imagine a child's rubber band model airplane, and perhaps you can even feel like a child playing. Conjure up the image of a large, knotted rubber band unwinding—use it to symbolize the release of tension in your muscles.*

"*Visualize a fallen leaf floating down a calm river. While you watch the leaf, mentally count backward from 30 to 1. Slowly, with each count, imagine the leaf drifting toward the mouth of the river or towards a quiet cove, a place where you are alone, with no one to bother you.*

"*As the leaf and your counting slowly flow downstream, feel your muscles releasing the stress and pressure that may have built up. Begin to feel yourself developing an undercurrent of relaxation, while in self-hypnosis and long, long after, whenever you take a deep satisfying breath.*"

Associate these mental pictures with your own experiences and make them as vivid and as realistic as you can. Involve as many of your senses as possible. Imagine the sights, the smells of the river, or perhaps of the ocean and the air. Imagine the sounds of water, wind, birds. Imagine the feel of the coolness of the water, the warmth of the sun, the wind against your face.

STAIRWAY TO RELAXATION

Below is a sample script of another type of mental image that can take you to self-hypnotic relaxation. We call it the stairway to relaxation.

It may be a place you are familiar with or once visited—a vacation spot, a place in the country or in the mountains. You can descend the stairs to a place that is real or that is fantasized.

Visualize yourself at the top of a long spiral stairway. Perhaps you are up in the foggy heights of the top of a mountain. There may be 50 steps to the bottom. At the bottom of the stairway is the most relaxing, most comfortable place you can imagine.

Suggest to yourself the following picture: "*As I take a deep, satisfying breath, I descend the stairway. Out of the fog and clouds of my busy day I move slowly toward a more comfortable, more relaxed place. Just as I can travel now with each step to a new place, a new experience, I may find that I am curious about what I will feel as I get closer to the bottom of the stairway.*

"*I don't need a train, an airplane, or a car to make this journey. I won't need a ticket, money, or baggage. All I need is my imagination, and I can take the steps necessary to bring me to my new and increasingly familiar experience of deep relaxation.*"

As you give yourself these suggestions, you may want to count down with each step. Or, you may simply visualize each step as you suggest to yourself that you are descending the stairway. It doesn't matter whether you count each step or just imagine each step. As you visualize yourself stepping down, you can feel your relaxation increasing.

Don't try to analyze your suggestions—let them flow. If you say something to yourself that doesn't seem to make sense, ignore it and proceed with another suggestion.

If one image is difficult to create in your mind's eye, don't worry—suggest a different one. Keep giving yourself a continual flow of words and images and symbols toward your goal.

CREATING A PHYSICAL RESPONSE

Creating a physical change in your perception of such sensations as warmth, coolness, or numbness in your extremities or elsewhere is a way to focus your attention even further. When you feel such changes while you're practicing, you will know that you have achieved some level of self-hypnosis.

When you feel like you are reasonably "wound down" and relaxed from the previous suggestions, direct your attention to your arm.

Right or left arm—it doesn't matter which—visualize it in your mind with your eyes still closed. Imagine your arm feeling cooler and cooler, or warmer, or heavier, or more numb. Give yourself a soothing flow of suggestions to one or more of these effects. If coolness is pleasant, visualize cold, icy water running over your arm and begin to feel a cool numbness in your fingers.

If warmth is pleasant, imagine the sun's rays on your arms, comfortable, relaxing. Let these feelings proceed naturally for several moments. Take this opportunity to feel more open and relaxed.

Gradually, continuing your concentration and attention on your arm, you'll notice a cool twinge, perhaps a numbness, or warmth. Fortify that feeling with more suggestions encouraging the numbness, coolness, or whatever the feeling might be. Here is an example of how your suggestions might proceed:

"As my hand rests gently, comfortably at my side, I may notice a new feeling. At the points where my fingers rest, I may soon feel a tingling. That feeling may be a cool tingling like touching the cold steel of a table. It may be a warm tingling like resting my hand on the warm sand of a beach or desert.

"It doesn't matter which of these feelings I experience. My hand may even feel numb. Or perhaps it will feel heavy, as if there were weights on the back of my hand pressing it downward.

"Perhaps the feeling may be one of lightness. My hand and arm may feel as if there are helium balloons attached to each finger, my wrist, and my elbow. The balloons make my hand and arm light.

"My hand may feel numb, as if growing lighter and lighter, and it may want

to float up off its resting place. It is a comfortable lightness, a detached feeling. It may be as if my arm is disconnected and wants to float up like the balloons."

This is a sample of the many feelings you might experience. Each person is likely to have a slightly different feeling. Whether the first sensation is coolness, warmth, heaviness, lightness, numbness, or some other response is not important.

Encourage the feeling, whatever it is, to spread from one finger or part of the hand to the next. Go as far as you can with these sensations. Take your time. You may experience some change right away or perhaps the second or third practice session. You'll soon be able to develop a numbing sensation from your fingers to your shoulders. Your hand or arm may even feel so light it will lift up and feel suspended on its own.

There is nothing mysterious about this new experience. *You have entered a self-hypnotic trance and have created a physical sensation through suggestions to your unconscious mind. This is self-hypnosis. Remember how it feels.*

However, do not inspect or analyze the experience right now. *Go directly to something else.* Think about the experience later, perhaps in a few hours.

The reason for not analyzing the experience right away is that the experience is in your unconscious mind. If your conscious mind begins to scrutinize the suggestions and the process, then the process of self-hypnosis may be disrupted.

CREATING AN INTELLECTUAL RESPONSE

One of the most difficult things to do for people who think a lot is to stop thinking so much. If you seem to have many thoughts on your mind that interfere with entering a self-hypnosis trance, we recommend you focus on the thoughts. Notice how they come in, seem to linger for a while, then depart. Notice how they overlap or how your thoughts can be focused by you. Try not thinking about your thinking. It is nearly impossible to NOT think about something that has been brought to your attention.

So, think about self-hypnosis later, think about your own thoughts even later. And certainly try and count them tomorrow.

As you may notice, this strategy is one of creating an inward focus on the thoughts first, then shifting to another inner experience. Specifically, inhale through your nose and on the exhale make the sound, "ohhhhhhh" all the way to nearly the end of your breath and then end with "mmm" sound. "ohhhhhhhhhhhhmmm." It's like saying the word home drawn out and without the "h" sound at the beginning. It is an ancient meditative sound that is said to be the answer to the Zen koan, "What is the sound of one hand clapping?" While most sounds are created by the contact of two objects, "ohhm" is the sound of air moving past a vocal chord, the metaphor of one hand. Think about that, later.

As you focus on this resonant sound from within you, you can become aware of the control you can exert on the movement of the "ohhhh" sound from your chest, into your throat and the back of your throat, and even into your nasal and sinus cavities. It you feel like doing 12 or 15 "ohhm" breaths, fine. Naturally you will feel more relaxed and very likely entranced.

Now, as you focus on your slow deep breathing and exhaling, begin to imagine a thought as separate from all other thoughts. Identify one thought, then another, another, and continue. As each thought is separated, you can file it away or discard it, the choice is yours. In a short while, you will notice how absorbed you have become in the process of focusing on your thoughts and you will have experienced perhaps your first self-hypnosis trance.

Practice with this until you are so familiar with the trance state that it will be easy to access.

CREATING AN EMOTIONAL RESPONSE

Some people find themselves immersed in an emotional focus that may feel so distracting that focusing on something visually is difficult. Also, some people may be so unknowingly preoccupied with an emotional problem that it prevents them from using imagery. If you are feeling a strong emotion right now, for example, sadness, grief, anger, or fear, you can utilize those feelings to help you enter a trance.

You have already read above that tension and anxiety can be used to enter trance and often that same feeling of anxiety is present with anger, fear, and other emotions. You might work with those strategies mentioned for tension and anxiety first.

However, if you still feel that your emotional state is preventing you from experiencing trance, learn this strategy. Start by getting as physically comfortable as you can. Find a place to be alone for a little while and close your eyes as you take several deep slow breaths.

Become focused on the emotion or emotions you are feeling at the present moment. Ask yourself what is happening in your life right now to contribute to the emotions you are feeling. Begin to develop an image, perhaps like a scene from a movie about your present or recent events. You are the star of your own movie and perhaps your life right now even reminds you of some character in some movie or television program you have seen.

Develop the sense that you are in a movie and allow your character to experience all the feelings you presently are having. Like a director of a movie, you can zoom in to focus on one part or another of the action, you can look into (you) your main character's mind and observe the point of view, the perspective.

Just observe and listen to the movie of your present situation. Become absorbed in your movie and soon you will discover that you have entered a trance state, you have detached yourself from your main character enough to become an observer. That state of detached awareness is also an entry into trance.

Continue the story and add new scenes for the main character (you) to release feelings. Imagine asserting your own wants and desires, expressing words of clarification and releasing the feelings.

Perhaps you will want to do this sort of actor/director/movie experience several times to feel more at ease with using your emotions to create an absorbed state of mental imagery. That is fine, take your time and when you are ready, then you can shift the scene of your movie at that point toward your goal work. You will then be ready to use other concepts and strategies from Section I of the book to expand your self-induced trance.

HOW LONG SHOULD YOU SPEND IN SELF-HYPNOSIS?

Most people will benefit from practice one to three times per day. In the beginning, it may take longer in each session to achieve a relaxed, calm state of mind than it will take later. It may require between 15 and 30 minutes to develop a trance at first.

Some people need more time, others less. There is no need for comparisons; accept the individual differences that make you unique. No two self-hypnosis experiences are exactly alike, either. Each time you practice, you will have a different level of tension that needs to be undone. Each session will have different distractions which you must utilize. You will find that each trance will be a unique experience, though there will be many similarities, also.

As we have recommended earlier, you may want to try very brief trance sessions—mini-trances. It is not so important how long you actually spend in a trance as it is that you do some trancework each day. Enjoy developing your skills.

HOW WILL YOU KNOW YOU HAVE SUCCEEDED?

The change from regular waking consciousness to hypnotic consciousness can be a subtle one. You might not notice it the first time or two you try. Be patient with yourself.

Three clues that you have achieved self-hypnosis are:

1. Noticing that the changes you suggested to create a relaxed state have come to be. For example, you become absorbed in a feeling of deep relaxation.
2. Noticing that your suggestion of physical sensations such as coolness, numbness, warmth, lightness, or heaviness somewhere in your body has produced one or more of these effects.
3. Taking notice of the time before you first close your eyes during the prac-

tice. Just before opening them at the end, guess how much time has gone by. When you open your eyes and check the time—did less or more time pass than you thought? Time distortion is a signal of an hypnotic state.

SUMMARY OF THIS METHOD

1. Relax yourself with progressive relaxation. Give yourself enough time to become completely relaxed.
2. Focus your attention on a spot in front of you.
3. Give yourself suggestions of fatigue and heaviness in your eyes and of deeper relaxation.
4. Visualize a real or fantasy place of peacefulness and comfort—a place away from all concerns and distracting thoughts.
5. Focus your attention and your images on sensations in your hands and fingers. Visualize feelings of coolness, numbness, warmth, heaviness, or lightness. When you detect one of these feelings, encourage it to expand with more suggestions.

REFERENCES

Bowers, K.S. & Brenneman, H.A. Hypnosis and the perception of time, *International Journal of Clinical and Experimental Hypnosis*, Vol. 27, 1979.

Erickson, M.H. *Healing in Hypnosis.* (Eds. Rossi, Ryan, & Sharp) Vol. 1, New York: Irvington Publishers, Inc., 1983.

Hartland, J. *Medical and Dental Hypnosis.* Baltimore: Williams & Wilkins Company, 1971.

Kroger, W.S. *Clinical and Experimental Hypnosis,* Philadelphia: J.B. Lippincott Company, 1977.

Rossi, E. *Hypnotic Realities.* New York: John Wiley and Sons, 1976.

Sacerdote, P. Teaching self-hypnosis to adults. *International Journal of Clinical and Experimental Hypnosis*, Vol. 29, 1981.

Yapko, M.D. *Trancework: An Introduction to the Practice of Clinical Hypnosis.* New York: Brunner/Mazel, 1990.

8

How To Deal with Distractions

One of the most frequently asked questions is, "What do I do when there are noises, distracting thoughts, pain, or even unsettling feelings that interrupt me from going into self-hypnosis?"

True, it is difficult to concentrate when a jet flies overhead or the sound of an "18-wheeler" comes barrelling down your street and ear canal. These kinds of annoyances are often impossible to avoid. No matter how deeply you have secluded yourself, nature and technology can chirp or grind their way to find you.

USING OUTSIDE SOUNDS TO HELP YOUR TRANCE

If you are being strafed from the air or pounded from the ground by airplanes, trucks, cars, trains—rather than fight the noise, use it. The adjustment you need to make first, though, is to see these unavoidable outside sounds not as obstacles, but as aids to your self-hypnosis. This mental switch-hitting is a necessary change in your perception.

Learning to see events and actions in your life from a new perspective is one of the key elements of your self-hypnosis experience. When you find unavoidable distractions in your trance setting, stop and think about them for a moment.

If the noise is of passing vehicles, you can imagine how they might be able to carry away your worries and problems. Give yourself suggestions such as: "*As the sound of the airplane approaches, I can pack all my tensions and worries into a bundle. As the sound passes closest to me, I can pitch the baggage of stress and problems up onto the plane to be carried away.*"

While you are giving yourself these suggestions, also visualize the airplane, truck, car, or whatever. Imagine your package of tension lifting up and away from you. Feel the relief of tension and pressure in your muscles as the sound of the engines retreats out of range.

Even though you may not yet be in a trance, begin giving yourself suggestions that incorporate the distracting sounds. Mentally speak to yourself.

You can use this technique as you are relaxing yourself with one of the relaxation techniques. Give yourself suggestions that use the sounds to help you relax. For instance:

"The sounds of children playing and people busy with their own lives are reminders that I, also, can take time to do things important in my life—such as the time I am taking right now, for self-hypnosis.

"The rumble of a trash truck can haul away more than just physical garbage. I can put my tensions, stresses, and problems in a box and the truck can haul them away too.

"The sounds of an air conditioner or heater are changing the nature of my air and environment. Those sounds can be a reminder of how I can use this time, in self-hypnosis, to change the internal environment of my body and mind.

"A clock ticking can remind me of my heartbeat. I can control my heart, with self-hypnosis, to unwind it from the hectic pace of the day."

Suppose you are within earshot of a feathered concert. Find traits in the bird's song that you can link with your goal of self-hypnosis. For example: "Just as the melody of the sparrows springs naturally from within them, I can find a natural relaxation arising from within me as I breathe slowly and deeply."

If there are outside sounds of people, you might give yourself suggestions such as: "I know that any time I take this opportunity for myself, there is no one that need disturb me. I may hear people coming and going about their business. I may hear the sounds of activity. But these sounds can give me the option of being distracted and then coming back to my relaxed state. I can leave my inner quiet to be aware of the outer noises and I can then better notice the changes that have taken place in me."

If there are sounds of people going up stairs or of elevator noises, you might suggest: "Any time I take time with self-hypnosis, I may better hear people coming and going in their lives. People climbing steps are like me, here, climbing or descending steps of my own. I can go higher, feeling closer to my goals. Step by step I can feel more relaxed.

"Just as the elevator takes people up to and down from their apartments, this quality of experience, in self-hypnosis, can take me to new levels of relaxation. I can imagine being on an elevator, going deeper and becoming less tense with each level I go down. I can feel more in touch with my muscles as I release the tension at each level my elevator stops."

From suggestions of this sort, you can then focus on changes in your body. Perhaps you can concentrate on feelings of lightness or heaviness in your hands. Maybe you can focus your attention on some object on the wall (eye fixation technique). Or, you can go on to use any other method of inducing self-hypnosis.

UTILIZING INTERNAL DISTRACTIONS

Once you have mastered the sounds from the outside, or even have begun to feel some sense of shift in awareness, it will be time to switch to utilizing your internal distractions. All of the sounds, noises, worries, pains, doubts that may have inhibited you from relaxation in the past can actually deepen your self-hypnosis.

The first thing to remember, just as it was for outside sounds, is to either allow the distractions to be or else become more aware of them. There is no sense in trying to talk yourself out of something that is actually present. Often, the more you try to ignore or push away something, the more you notice it.

For example, Sophie had chronic pain in her shoulder due to an auto accident. Her physicians wished to use a non-medical pain management approach because of the side-effects from her pain medications. She was a musician in an orchestra and the pain medication affected her musical timing and seemed to dull her other senses, too. It seemed that self-hypnosis was a way for her to reduce the pain while enhancing her musical concentration. She learned to enter self-hypnosis by first focusing on the pain, exploring the pain and examining it as if it were a separate thing from herself. She could take notice of how there were subtle variations in the pain once she stopped to study this distraction.

Then Sophie began to associate a color and shape to the pain, even descriptions such as sharp and deep or dull and throbbing. Her entire focus went to the painful area: How far did it encompass? Did the pain have a rhythm? Those were the sorts of questions she would focus on answering about her pain. As she focused more and more, she noticed how there were small changes and the more she examined those changes the more focused she became and able to shift her focus.

Sophie sensed the small variations in pain and imagined them as parts of an orchestra, with nerves as instruments, nerve impulses as notes and sounds. She was able to expand those images and consciously move them to images of how she could play music with the pain. She mentally rehearsed how she could play entire symphonic pieces in her work with the pain. She had discovered that as she distracted herself first to the pain and then converted to a more useful distraction, she was able to enter trance more easily. With more practice, she then used her self-hypnosis skills to directly reduce the pain even when she was going to play her instrument.

You can deal with inner distractions of overthinking in a little different way. Distracting thoughts are like cars crisscrossing a busy intersection, or pedestrians hurrying on their way. Let your thoughts be present and transform them into a counting process. Count your thoughts. Begin at one and count up to 40 or 50. Become very good at counting the thoughts. First, you must separate them so that you don't count only one when there are really three thoughts. Count carefully and accurately and notice how many different thoughts you have.

Then begin breathing slowly and regularly to a pattern of counting. Maybe counting in on each thought and exhaling with a different thought. Of course, you see what you are doing. You are counting yourself into trance. You have utilized your overthinking mind to help you focus on a positive goal that you have chosen.

Another example of internal distraction is worry or self-doubt. Here, as with pain, try to focus on the self-doubt to better understand it. See the worry or self-doubt as a place you are approaching. Become aware of the entrance to the feeling. Become very focused on how that feeling comes upon you or how you enter it.

Then listen to the inner voices or senses of self-doubt and worry. Avoid judging the inner critic or doubting voice. No criticism here, just listening as you gain some awareness of the experience of that worrisome or self-doubting feeling. You can actually show understanding and compassion for the doubting part of you, then begin letting it exit.

Take several deep and focusing breaths. Focus on your breathing and breathe out the worry, breathe out the self-doubt. Breathe in a cool focus on your inner friend. That is the part of you that has some specific goal you have in mind. Take four or five deep breaths to let go and relax until you are entranced by your breathing and can go with your self-induced trance.

WHAT ABOUT DISTRACTIONS YOU MAY NOT BE ABLE TO USE?

You may want to deal with some distractions more directly. These are disturbances to your trance that require a reaction from you: a child entering or knocking on your door, the doorbell ringing, an itch on the bottom of your foot, a crashing sound from the kitchen.

These sorts of concerns can be dealt with directly. Answer the the doorbell, the phone, or whatever and then return to your self-hypnosis. Sometimes it can be more distracting to try to ignore a noise and to wonder what could be the matter. If your nose itches at any time during a trance, by all means scratch it—then return to your self-hypnosis.

TURNING DISTRACTIONS INTO POSTHYPNOTIC CUES

Rather than distracting you, sounds can be turned into posthypnotic cues. If there are sounds that are frequently part of your environment, you can suggest to yourself that whenever you hear these sounds as you are preparing to practice self-hypnosis, they will cause you to relax.

For example, if there is a ticking clock in the room in which you practice self-hypnosis, you might suggest to yourself: *Whenever I take several deep, satisfying breaths and wish to enter self-hypnosis, I know the ticking of the clock can remind me of how steady and focused my own internal processes can be. Just as the spring in the clock gradually unwinds, I, too, can unwind and relax as I gradually enter a comfortable self-hypnotic trance."*

Distraction is your redirection of conscious awareness. For example, when you change your focus on physical sensations (warmth, tingling, etc.) to visual images (sunny days, swaying palms), you enhance your trance.

There is no need to worry about being in self-hypnosis. It is a completely safe, healthy, natural state of awareness. Remember that you are in control of your trance at all times. You can pay attention to the outside world whenever you need to. If an emergency arises that requires your immediate attention, you can respond quickly and clearly.

REFERENCES

Hammond, D.C. (Ed.) *Handbook of Hypnotic Suggestions and Metaphors*. New York: W.W. Norton & Company and American Society of Clinical Hypnosis, 1990.

Pratt, G.J., Wood, D.P. & Alman, B.M. *A Clinical Hypnosis Primer: Expanded and Updated*. New York: John Wiley & Sons, 1988.

9
Increase Your Motivation and Reach Your Goals

The first essential ingredient to bring to any self-improvement endeavor is the incentive to succeed. Self-hypnosis does not require belief in it to be successful—but motivation to succeed is crucial to your efforts toward self-knowledge and self-change. The more motivated you are to be relaxed and healthy, to be self-confident, to reduce pain, to fight skin problems, or to work toward any other goal, the more successful you will be.

Since you are reading these words, you are already motivated to explore self-hypnosis. Motivation is the primal force that gets us out of bed each morning. It seeps or floods into our every action.

When we are very motivated, we may arise early in the morning and jog a few miles. Others of us never get *that* stimulated, though we might drive miles from home for an ice cream sundae.

The greater your motivation towards a goal, the more open your unconscious mind will be to your positive suggestions. You cannot fool your unconscious mind easily. If you are not truly motivated to accomplish a change or achieve a goal, your unconscious will not be moved by insincere suggestions.

A noted researcher, physician, and hypnotherapist, Paul Sacerdote (1981), found a marked difference between two groups that he taught. One group was made up of patients, often chronic pain sufferers, who were seeking to relieve excruciating pain or escape the ravages of illness and disease or the discomfort of treatments such as chemotherapy.

The other group was made up of interested individuals, doctors, therapists, health-care professionals, and lay people, whose incentive was to increase their knowledge and understanding of hypnosis.

Which group do you believe learned the techniques most quickly and had the greatest levels of success?

The pain sufferers had the most intense desire and, not surprisingly, they learned faster and appeared to gain the larger measure of success.

HOW YOU CAN INCREASE YOUR MOTIVATION

As you begin to work on any goal, you are already bringing some motivation to it. You can increase that desire to succeed by better understanding *why you want to succeed.* What are the benefits to you in achieving your goal?

It can be helpful to make a list of your reasons for desiring to work toward your goal with self-hypnosis. Be detailed in making this list. For instance, if your goal is to control pain, you might have these reasons:

1. Relieve back pain.
2. Better sex life.
3. Sleep better.
4. Be less dependent on others.
5. Take less medication.
6. Travel in more comfort.
7. Do better at work.
8. Feel better about yourself.

Study your list and arrange the items in the order of their importance to you. Put all your reasons on the list, even if there are some you think are small or unimportant. No one else will see this list. You can benefit from writing your ideas and feelings about each reason.

Sometimes, it's surprising what you discover about your motivations and reasons for change. Often a reason for seeking a goal that may seem stupid can turn out to be very important to your unconscious. By bringing it out in the open, you may discover that it has more influence than you thought.

Being more aware of all of your reasons for working on a specific goal strengthens and increases your motivation toward it. Also, awareness helps dissolve resistance or blocks to increasing your motivation.

UNCONSCIOUS BLOCKS TO MOTIVATION

It is wise to clear any blocks or obstacles from the path of your motivation. A hindering trap of self-doubt or thoughts of failure can sabotage your motivation toward any goal.

When you look at your reasons and needs for achieving a goal, also explore for any obscured or subterranean reasons you might have for wanting to keep your *present* behavior. Certainly, it's best to acknowledge an obstacle or block and then to move on past it. Be honest with yourself—honesty is also a motivator. By being truthful with yourself about a reason for not wanting to actually achieve a goal, you better understand it and can set it aside.

Some changes that you might want to use self-hypnosis for are to remove habits or behaviors such as smoking or overeating. Often, these behaviors are firmly embedded in your daily routines. Altering them may be desired by your conscious, rational mind, but there can be unconscious reasons for continuing them.

Examine your motivations and cut loose any unconscious anchors that might hold you back. For instance, suppose you want to stop overeating so as to lose weight. That may be a very sincere desire at the conscious level. But unconsciously you may be overeating for an emotional reason. Or, you may be getting some unconscious payoffs for keeping the problem.

BREAKING THROUGH UNCONSCIOUS BLOCKS

One of the best strategies for breaking through unconscious blocks is giving yourself permission to have awareness of the reason or reasons for staying the same.

For many reasons, the blocks that have gotten in your way in the past are outside of your conscious awareness. Begin giving yourself conscious permission and developing conscious acceptance of that part of yourself. Now you may be asking what you are accepting, since the blockage is out of your normal awareness.

Accept the block just as it is, even without knowing exactly what it is. Accept that there could be something unconscious that is blocking your achievement of a goal. Accept that part of yourself that has not achieved what you consciously desire. Respect that there is a reason for the blockage. Self-protection from something emotionally intense may be the reason.

Next, develop a self-hypnosis trance for the purpose of opening yourself up to awareness of unconscious blocks. You may want to imagine watching a movie or a video of yourself in some activity that relates to your present way of being, relevant to your goal. Create a mental movie of yourself and watch as if you are an observer in the audience. Maybe you will actually create a movie theater in your mind, complete with popcorn you can imagine smelling or tasting. Watch how the star of the movie (you) acts, talks, relates, does, or doesn't communicate. Without judging yourself, allow yourself to observe and listen to your movie.

An unconscious block can serve to protect you from what you fear will be a negative outcome. Here is an example. Suppose you are insecure. By overeating and being overweight, you avoid situations in which your appearance would be complimented or where you would be considered attractive and appealing. Consciously, avoiding such apparently positive situations may seem ridiculous. But, unconsciously you may feel insecure and frightened at being in the spotlight. So it may be much easier to continue to be chubby and not risk being in that more uncomfortable situation. Watch and observe yourself in your movie. Avoid criticism or judgments. Acceptance of those parts of yourself is the key to this strategy.

Another example could be associated with pain. Suppose you were injured while at work. You developed low back pain as a result. There is little that can be done medically to help you. Pain medication has side effects and leaves you somewhat dazed.

Self-hypnosis can be very effective in relieving this sort of pain. However, if you are receiving workman's compensation, sympathy from family and friends, or easier working conditions, you might have unconscious reasons for keeping the pain.

Though your pain might be unwanted consciously—most people try to avoid pain as much as they can—unconscious benefits might prevent you from getting as much relief as possible. By watching your movie and, as a non-judgmental observer, being aware, accepting, and understanding that situation, you can begin to remove those blocks. You could dismantle those unconscious or hidden reasons for obstructing your progress.

You may need to explore such possibilities with yourself before trying to make a change. Before you attempt to modify a habit or work on some healing goal, read the chapter on self-exploration to help you see if there are any of these unconscious blocks to your success.

If you feel your unconscious is blocking your achieving your goal and you cannot get to the obstacle on your own, you may wish to seek the help of a trained hypnotherapist to assist you. There are times when a serious early trauma such as molestation, physical injury, or other experiences are best helped with professional help. Referrals in your area can be obtained from the American Society of Clinical Hypnosis in Des Plaines, Iowa.

Hypnosis is a very relaxing and renewing experience in itself. Motivation is what makes self-hypnosis dynamic in achieving a goal, a change, an enhancement. As you learn to care for and accept yourself, you will become more successful and those successes will create more successes.

Additional strategies for removing unconscious blocks are in the Thin Meditations chapter on weight loss.

MAKING YOUR GOALS SPECIFIC

You also need to examine closely your goals for self-hypnosis to make sure that they are clear and achievable. Having a specific, well thought-out, and attainable goal is essential to achieving it. Having vague, unsure, unattainable objectives can be like trying to see over the horizon through foggy binoculars. The clearer your goal and the clearer your suggestions, the more easily you'll see positive changes.

For instance, Jill, a student, wanted to increase her self-confidence. That in itself was an attainable goal. She had been giving herself suggestions that she would have increasing confidence and self-assurance at everything she did. Having given herself some good posthypnotic suggestions for that goal, Jill was disappointed that after many weeks she still noticed very little improvement.

The reason was that she really didn't have a well-defined idea of what self-confidence would be for her. She needed to find those specific areas in her life where she would like to exhibit more poise and self-confidence.

It was important for her to imagine specific situations or scenes in which she would demonstrate the exact qualities she wished to have. In Jill's case, she wanted to be able to deal with her parents in a more adult, mature way. She also wanted to be more assertive and confident in her work and at college—to stand up for herself when she knew she was correct.

Jill refocused her hypnotic suggestions and visualizations toward those specific goals. She created mental images of herself behaving in the way she desired. Also, she identified instances in which she saw someone reacting as she would like to react. She incorporated those role-model examples into suggestions and mental pictures.

Within a few weeks, she began receiving positive feedback from her family and work associates. She detected definite progress toward her newly expressed goals. *Her unconscious mind now had a clear picture of what she wanted to accomplish.*

CAN YOUR GOAL BE REACHED IN ONE STEP?

Another facet to setting goals for yourself is to make them attainable. This may or may not be possible without intermediate steps. Some goals are too big to reach in one stride.

For Jill, the self-confidence she sought was realistic and reachable. Had she desired the degree of poise and self-confidence necessary for seeking a public office, for example, she might have been seeking too much in one step. However, once Jill achieved her first level of job and school self-assuredness and family assertiveness, a goal of public speaking might certainly have been realistic.

Work at small steps. Use one small success to build to the next step. Even clear, well-described images and suggestions might be less effective if your unconscious mind knows you're attempting too big a step.

This is true with many goals. If they are great leaps of change, they are best approached in smaller increments. Just as a small hammer cannot drive a spike into a plank with one blow, many repeated taps will inevitably sink it. So it is with self-hypnosis. *There are seldom instant remedies.*

Suppose that your goal is to lose weight. You want to lose 80 pounds. Imagine also that you have had this extra weight for a long time—say eight years. This situation is not uncommon.

For you to give yourself suggestions of eating less and of finding certain foods unnecessary or unpleasant might easily be inadequate. General suggestions of losing weight might be even less effective.

A more reasonable way to approach the target of 80 pounds is to break it up into increments of achievement. Try three pounds a week, or 15 pounds in eight weeks.

Notice that these goals are more reasonable and have set a specific time objective. With major weight loss, it is always best to check with your physician to get advice on safe amounts of loss for your physical condition.

Your unconscious mind can accept and work toward a reasonable goal, such as 15 pounds in eight weeks. Plus, you will enjoy the satisfaction of your intermediate successes. They will strengthen your stamina and resolve to succeed at each subsequent level. In this way, cycles of accomplishment replace previous cycles of disappointment and failure that may be present with any problem of long duration.

When you create specific, personalized, motivating suggestions, your *unconscious mind* will more easily see why the action is needed and how to implement your desires. Your *conscious mind* can also see what the rewards will be from the time and effort you put into your self-hypnosis program. This will help you keep practicing. Self-hypnosis works only when you work at it.

It is your own abilities that create change. Self-hypnosis is only the vehicle which drives you to your goal.

REFERENCES

Hartland, J. *Medical and Dental Hypnosis.* Baltimore: Williams & Wilkins, 1971.

Kroger, W.C. *Clinical and Experimental Hypnosis.* Philadelphia: J.B. Lippincott Company, 1977.

Ruch, J.C. Self-hypnosis: The result of heterohypnosis or vice versa? *International Journal of Clinical and Experimental Hypnosis,* Vol. 23, 1975.

Sacerdote, P. Teaching self-hypnosis to adults. *International Journal of Clinical and Experimental Hypnosis,* Vol. 29, 1981.

Soskis, D.A. *Teaching Self-hypnosis: An Introductory Guide for Clinicians.* New York: W.W. Norton & Company, 1985.

10
The Language of Hypnotic Suggestions

"Language is the blood of the soul into which thoughts run, and out of which they grow."

—Oliver Wendell Holmes

We speak to ourselves in a language that has special meaning to us based upon our previous experiences. For example, what do these words and images bring to your mind: a sunrise, a cross, a dandelion, a frog on a lily pond, a crackling fireplace, a puppy dog?

It is very likely that these words will stimulate some images or memories that have unique meaning for you. In other words, your past experiences in life will influence what comes to mind, what you feel emotionally and physically, and even what your senses perceive.

A MATTER OF STYLE

Your unconscious mind can best relate to suggestions that spring from your own well of experiences. For this reason, when you are developing suggestions for yourself, it's best to put them into your own words and to use symbols you are familiar with. Therefore, we recommend you develop your own style of suggestion language that will have the most powerful meaning and effects on your trancework.

Take notice of how you communicate with others. Are you a primarily visual person who likes to see things and picture concepts or ideas? Perhaps you are more auditory and favor the way things sound to you, and listening and hearing ideas is more effective for you. You may discover that you like to touch something to get the feel of it by using your kinesthetic senses. Remember, as we discussed NLP in Chapter 6, most of us use several modes, but have one that is predominant.

If you want to discover your predominant mode of communication—visual, auditory, or kinesthetic—here is a helpful idea. Listen to your own speaking style by tape recording yourself in a conversation and then playing back and listening for key words. You may notice that you tend to use more words that are associated with one or another sense.

For example, words such as "look, see, picture this" are visual even when used abstractly. You might say something like, "I can see your point," or "Picture this, he got real angry when I asked for a raise, and then . . ."

Or, you may notice you will say something such as, "I hear that the best car for gas mileage is . . ." or "It sounds like the economy is headed for higher interest rates."

A kinesthetic person will notice more tactile words used, such as, "It feels like the economy is headed . . ." or "I just can't get a handle on why she . . ."

There are other ways of determining your predominant NLP communication style that go beyond the scope of this book and interested readers are directed to Bandler and Grinder's work (1979) and that of others in the chapter references for more detailed information.

Researchers, such as Michael Yapko (1981), examining hypnotic suggestions, have found that when suggestion language is matched neuro-linguistically to the individual's communication style, the suggestions are acted upon more effectively. So, in developing your own suggestion language, begin by using your most favored style—visual, auditory, or kinesthetic—and then you can intersperse words from the other modes as they may fit toward your goals.

Visual, auditory, or kinesthetic words and symbols can be powerful tools in your self-hypnosis suggestions.

WHAT ARE SUGGESTION SYMBOLS?

A symbol is anything that represents something else. Your suggestions will be more effective when you use symbols to represent your goals. Positive symbols from your memories and past experiences can tickle your unconscious mind and cause you to respond as you did before.

For example: *"When I imagine the blue of the sky and the gentle flowing of the clouds in the warm, relaxing breeze, I can feel myself less pressured, less tensed, like when I was young, lying in a soft patch of grass and looking up at the sky. Not a care or concern to bother me.*

"The sky, cushioned with billowy white clouds reaching down to the horizon, reminds me of my youth. I am just a few deep breaths away from that time, young and growing. Now I am growing into a self-controlled, relaxing state of mind."

You can find images and symbols of relaxation from your own life. Symbols are plentiful in our lives, past and present. Tie those words, images, and feelings that make up symbols with the goal you are trying to achieve.

Leaves falling off a tree as the season changes can represent the unburdening of problems or can symbolize the changes we all go through. An image of productive ants quietly marching along the ground can be a metaphor for more industrious concentration at work.

Often the same image or symbol can be used for many different goals. A hard-working ant can also suggest how an individual is able to accomplish great feats through teamwork.

The words you use to express a suggestion are less important than the mental picture or feeling you create and the meaning that exists behind the words.

"*I am as relaxed as a strand of overcooked spaghetti.*" The symbol of relaxation—the limp spaghetti—is effective if your unconscious mind can easily understand the comparison.

"*I am as flexible and relaxed as the rag doll I had as a child or that I can imagine now.*" Many people can quickly picture a flexible rag doll's movements; hence it is a useful, general symbol. To a dollmaker, this may be an especially powerful image. He or she knows from daily experience how relaxed the limbs should feel and appear. On the other hand, how effective would this comparison be for men who had never played with dolls?

Try to find suggestion symbols from your own work, hobbies, memories, or even dreams. The more vivid the symbol is, the more likely your unconscious mind will act to accommodate your request.

Consider for a moment Sally, an office worker. She plays guitar to relax herself and to entertain friends and her family.

It would be possible for Sally to relax and enter self-hypnosis using suggestions such as: "*I am unwinding like a clock spring.*" That is a symbol she sees every day at work.

Perhaps a more effective suggestion for her could be: "*As I breathe deeply and exhale slowly, my body releases tension and stress just like the strings on my guitar slacken when I turn back the keys.*"

How easy it would be for Sally to visualize in her mind the guitar string loosening as the tuning key is unwound. Someone who has never played a string instrument might not relate to it nearly as well.

Material for creating your personalized suggestions is all around. You can find things with which to relate to your goals everywhere—in your home, in your yard, at the store, driving down any street, at work, in books and magazines.

The next time you drive up or down your street, take notice of the wind blowing the trees or shrubs. That can symbolize the refreshing winds of change that you can bring to your life.

Your foot on the accelerator is one way to symbolize your control over your car. It can also represent the control you can exert over your own life. The self-confidence you have in your ability to safely drive the car is a symbol of the control and self-confidence you can have in other areas of your life—control over allergies, pain, bad habits, or fears.

CREATING YOUR OWN SYMBOLS

Before beginning a self-hypnosis session, spend a few minutes writing down your specific goal or goals for that session. Also, think of several images for each goal ahead of time.

Seize this opportunity to plunge into your own creative mind and take charge and direct yourself. The rewards you will get in self-hypnosis from your efforts will be like planting a garden, watching it grow, and then harvesting the delicious rewards of your work.

Below are some hints for material from which you can develop your own suggestion symbols. Put them into your own words and use images from your own experiences and memories. This is an opportunity for you to be as creative and imaginative as you feel. It is like having your own private garden where you are the gardener, able to plant and grow whatever you wish.

Rain softly washing away pain, stress, and self-doubts.

The contrast of stormy weather and summer days is like the contrast of activity and quiet, or concentration and daydreaming, or stress and relaxation.

Turning on and off a light switch can be like starting and stopping a desire for a cigarette or food.

The tea pot lets off steam when the pressure builds up, just as you can let off more pressure or stress by exhaling slowly.

Are you getting the idea?

A flock of birds gliding, soaring toward their destination is like you soaring and winging toward yours.

A flower blossoms in its eagerness for growth, just as you can blossom and grow with more control over your allergy, or with growing control over your fears.

The telephone pole wires carry energy and vitality charged with potential, just as you are charged toward your goal and have more energy to play tennis or volleyball.

The water flows briskly from the bathtub faucet in a soft but steady stream, just as your energy flows.

With clock-beat regularity, the sun and moon and stars regulate themselves in many ways, as you can regulate yourself in a variety of ways.

Just as looking through binoculars brings closer objects that seem far away and unclear, you can use self-hypnosis to bring goals that seem distant near.

Bees can choose which flower to alight on and you can choose to eat less at regular mealtimes or choose to avoid cigarettes after eating.

Now you may really have the hang of it. You can add an appropriate goal suggestion for comparisons that are most vivid for you. Spend a few moments to find new material for comparisons and metaphors. Imagine the scene in your own way—make it real for *you*.

Be specific in your suggestions

A general or ambiguous suggestion such as, "I will relax, I will be less tense," may be weak. The unconscious mind may accept it, but lacking specific degrees or contrasts it may have difficulty knowing what to relax first or how much to relax. The more specific and familiar the suggestion is, the more readily it can be acted upon.

By doing the previous exercise and looking for metaphors and comparisons to couple your suggestions to, you can narrow the scope of your suggestions. A goal of simply having more concentration is vague. But to concentrate your attention while you are reading *as a funnel concentrates a flow of water* is more specific. Suggestions can be directed toward your exact goal.

You can put this image into a suggestion such as: *"While I sit reading and studying, my mind will be focused on the words and thoughts in this book. Just as a funnel can direct and concentrate water flowing into it, my eyes can channel and focus my concentration on the words and concepts in this book."*

Suppose your goal is to lose weight. An objective to simply eat less is vague. A more specific suggestion would be: *"I will feel full with one portion of food at my mealtimes, three times a day, at eight, one, and five o'clock."* That is specific and achievable. The more specific you make your suggestions, the more force they will have.

Find several suggestions for the same goal

Even suggestions with Pulitzer Prize winning symbols should be reinforced with three or four different specific suggestions to your unconscious mind.

There can be blocks to some suggestions, causing them to be less effective than others. Perhaps there are blocks or negative associations to certain words that inhibit your absorption of them and you may not be consciously aware of such blocks. It is best to develop several different suggestions for each goal. The more suggestions you offer yourself, the more opportunities you have for creating the catalysts and actions for changes you desire. This is particularly important if you have tried one suggestion repeatedly with little or no success.

RELAXATION GOALS

Suppose your goal is reducing stress. You could suggest that your body is unwinding with three different approaches. *Unwinding your muscles like a* knotted rubber band. *Soft and relaxed muscles like bread dough. Unstressed and unpressured as a deflated balloon.* If one or two symbols are weak, having three makes it more likely that at least one will be acted on.

Remember that the best suggestions are built from examples you are familiar with. For instance, suppose one of your interests is in auto or motorcycle mechanics. You could develop suggestions that relate to an engine idling or coasting.

"I breathe smoothly and effortlessly as I relax, just as an engine draws in fresh air and burns it smoothly and easily while idling. Just like a motor needs calm, idle time to cool down after a long haul up a steep grade, my muscles and my mind need a period of relaxed, idle coasting to cool down from the stresses and tensions of the day."

Suggestions such as these, for a person familiar with mechanics, allows the unconscious mind to become involved, as if to say, "Hey—I know what that's all about—relax like an engine idling? No problem."

But for the same person, a suggestion to unwind like Mozart's Piano Concerto No. 5 in F minor might cause the unconscious to put on the brakes. That comparison and metaphor would not relate to someone whose favorite music was rock and roll.

Music that you can relate to is very good for symbolizing suggestions for relaxation or other goals.

ATHLETIC GOALS

Suppose your goal work is to increase your concentration for playing tennis, golf, or some other sport. You can select several different images and metaphors to suggest your target goal.

Each one can be paired with a separate posthypnotic suggestion. The cue you develop might be any action you routinely take just before or during your tennis play. For example:

"Whenever I lace up my shoes before a game or workout, I may notice that my mind cinches up in its focus, also. As I tighten the laces on my shoes, perhaps I am also tightening my concentration on my game to come.

"As I walk onto the court, I will see the net dividing the area. The net can prevent the ball from passing from one side to the other. I will find that the concentration of my attention is able to screen out distractions just as the net stops poorly hit balls.

"I will grasp my racket firmly and confidently. The racket is designed for a specific purpose—to play the game most effectively. As I grip the racket, I may bring that same kind of concentration and purpose to my game."

Notice that some of these suggestions are permissive; that is, they gently persuade your unconscious with "I may" and "perhaps I." In other suggestions, you are more direct and commanding with "I will."

By using both indirect, permissive, choice-oriented suggestions and direct, commanding ones, you insure that one or both kinds will be accepted. However, if you find you respond better to one over the other, use it.

You can see that each suggestion is different. Yet they all progressively lead you toward more focus, toward screening out distractions, and toward more attention to your game. Also, they can continue to provide posthypnotic reminders for your goal throughout the play.

The tying of the shoes, the gripping of the racket, and seeing the net would all become posthypnotic cues. They would prompt your reaction even outside of the trance-state.

More will be discussed about athletics in a later chapter. But remember that recreational athletics are for recreation and exercise. You can achieve your goal of playing with more concentration for recreation and exercise and still win and lose games.

Look for success toward your goals in gradual steps. Your continued work with self-hypnosis builds on itself. See if you are doing better at your game after two or three weeks of suggestion work, rather than after one or two days.

MAKING SUGGESTIONS POSITIVE

There are reasons why most people react poorly to negative, "NO" statements. Each of you can look to your own reactions to see the validity of this concept. Which request are you more likely to accept: "Do not close the door" or "Would you please leave the door open?"

From childhood most of us have heard many more "NOs" than "YESs" and often we have developed a conditioned response to negatively worded statements. They can bristle the hairs on our neck. Though we react less severely to telling *ourselves* "NO," nonetheless a negatively worded self-suggestion has a smaller chance of being accepted.

"I will not smoke cigarettes anymore" is a negative command that might easily be ignored by the unconscious mind. A more effective suggestion would be a positive statement interlaced with a positive concept. An example would be: *"As I smoke fewer and fewer cigarettes, I feel healthier and more satisfied with myself."*

Wherever you can, connect a positive suggestion with a realistic benefit to come from it. The rewards you will get from positive images, words, and symbols will help your suggestion become adopted as action.

At first, it may seem difficult to eliminate "NOs," "NOTs," "WON'Ts," and other negative words from your suggestions. Put your mind at ease about it. You'll get better with practice. A few "NOs" or "NOTs" creeping in here and there are harmless if you're balancing them with plenty of "I WILLs," "I CANs," "I MAYs," and "PERHAPS TODAYs."

PREPACKAGED OR PERSONALIZED?

Some people have success with prerecorded self-hypnosis audio tapes and others do not. We believe that you will have the most success with self-hypnosis when you take the time to personalize your suggestions as this chapter discusses. Certainly, if you find some of the words suggested in this or other chapters relevant to you, use them. However, modifying a few words to evoke positive personal memories or images for you will be worth the time it takes. You can learn to utilize both personalized self-hypnosis sessions and prerecored tapes to maximize your opportunities for positive changes.

REFERENCES

Bandler, R., & Grinder, J. *Frogs Into Princes.* Moab, Utah: Real People Press, 1979.

Hartland, J. *Medical and Dental Hypnosis.* Baltimore: Williams & Wilkins, 1971.

Kroger, W.S. *Clinical and Experimental Hypnosis.* New York: J.B. Lippincott Company, 1977.

Selye, H. *Stress Without Distress.* New York: J.B. Lippincott and Crowell, 1974.

Yapko, M. The effect of matching primary representational predicates on hypnotic relaxation. *American Journal of Clinical Hypnosis,* Vol. 23, 1981.

11
Nine Varieties of Self-Hypnosis Techniques

Presented in this chapter are a variety of methods which you can use to develop a self-hypnosis trance for yourself. These are examples of techniques which you can change and adapt for your own use. In practice, there are hundreds, even thousands, of methods of trance induction. The ones presented here are varied and effective.

You can take these scripts and use them just as written or you can modify them in any way that will make them more comfortable to use and more relevant to your situation. You may wish to read the scripts to yourself. Or you can record them on tape.

MAKING TAPES FOR YOURSELF

Making a tape recording of self-hypnosis scripts from this book and of the suggestions you create for yourself can help you practice self-hypnosis without feeling as if you need to create suggestion words and symbols at the moment you are developing a trance-state. This offers you a passive way to enter self-hypnosis and to make changes that you have already designed and thought out. You can change the tape and add or alter suggestions easily and quickly.

Whatever way suits you best is just fine. Try all of the methods at least once and see which you find most effective for you. All of them have been used thousands of times in clinical settings and have been selected as the most popular by our patients and students over the years.

Coupled with what you have learned about self-hypnosis and the suggestion process from the preceding chapters, you will likely find success in entering self-hypnosis with any of the following techniques. As you become more comfortable with your self-hypnosis, you can include suggestions for progress toward specific goals. You can also interject posthypnotic cues for goal work and for easy reentry into self-hypnosis for later practice sessions.

In many of the scripts, there are places where you might blend in suggestions of your own. But you can interweave other goal suggestions and posthypnotic cues where you wish. By preplanning or scripting your posthypnotic suggestions and cues as shown in Chapters 5 and 10, you can create your audio tapes easily.

PREPARING FOR YOUR SELF-HYPNOSIS

Here are some specific instructions to help you get the most from this chapter and from your self-hypnosis experiences:

1. Write down a list of your goals and be specific and detailed. Be clear with yourself as to what you want to work on, why, and for how long.
2. Write down what you'd like to say to yourself, from beginning to end. You may want to write out a script for your own self-hypnosis. You can use the material from chapters in this book on progressive relaxation, stress management, or any of the goal-work chapters. You can develop your own personal combination that *you* are comfortable with. Experiment.
3. Write out several different kinds of suggestions for each goal.
4. Develop some material for using visualization and imagery.
   Such suggestions could guide you to a quiet, relaxed setting and blend in some metaphors for changes that you wish to make. For example: *"With my eyes closed, I can picture an open meadow in the mountains . . . similar to the one I saw on my vacation last year. I may be able to feel the warmth of the sun on my face as I lie relaxed in the grass and watch the leaves fall slowly from the trees . . . Those leaves falling can remind me of how I can let go of old problems and worries . . . and let them fall away from me . . . just as the old leaves fall from the trees to make room for new growth . . . new changes."*
5. You might imagine going down some steps in order to deepen your trance-state. Visualize yourself going down in an elevator or floating down a stream or river, and the farther down you move, the more relaxed and the deeper into your self-hypnosis you can go. If you feel more comfortable and get better results by imagining moving *up* an escalator or river, then feel free to direct yourself in that manner.
6. You can include any number of varied suggestions toward whatever goal you wish to work on. However, try to work on only one or two specific goals per trance session. With more than that, your efforts will become diluted and less effective. But you can give yourself many different suggestions toward the same goal. For a goal of more concentration in a sport, you could include suggestions for before, during, and after play.
7. It may be soothing and relaxing to record some background music along with your suggestions. You might want to experiment with metronome ticking or any other sound that you can use as a focus for your concentration and attention.
8. Toward the end of your trance, always include some suggestions for reentering self-hypnosis the next time you practice. For example: *"I know that the benefit I get from this trance experience is a positive, healthy experience, and any time I wish to enter this quality of time, all I need to do*

is relax in a comfortable position, take several deep breaths, and imagine a warm pleasant color (or any cue that reminds you of the relaxation of self-hypnosis). Whenever I take several deep breaths and imagine that color . . . I will notice that I can return quickly and easily to this deep level of relaxation and comfort."

9. If you're going to tape record the script, speak at a pace that begins in your normal tone of voice and at a relaxed speed. As you progress with the recording, slow your pace and soften the tone of your voice slightly, if you can. By the time your tape concludes, you may be speaking in a much slower cadence and much more softly than when you began. This will provide an audio cue for you to slow down and relax as you enter self-hypnosis regardless of which technique you use.

As you begin your practice, find a place that is quiet, and free yourself from potential disturbances as much as possible. Let any people around you know that you will need 20 to 30 minutes of privacy.

TECHNIQUE #1: SELF-HYPNOSIS THROUGH PROGRESSIVE RELAXATION

Sit down and make yourself as comfortable as you can. You will be allowing yourself to relax and to reach a self-hypnosis state by tensing and relaxing one part of your body at a time.

You can begin with the top of your head and work your way down to your feet, or begin with your feet and go up in the other direction. Where you begin is up to you.

The following script will begin with your feet, but you can create your own script and include suggestions and images from your own experiences.

The script

Feet and Legs:

As I begin, I'm going to experience the tension in my feet. I'm going to stretch them out and hold the tension there for 10 or 12 seconds. As I hold them there, I'm going to squeeze my feet, right now. I'm going to push down and hold the tension and force my toes to curl as tightly as I can.

While I'm holding this tension I can recall that my feet do a lot of walking for me . . . a lot of supporting . . . and now I'll let go of the tension and let them relax.

I'll take a deep breath . . . to become more relaxed . . . and in just a few moments I'll find that I am more comfortable . . . more relaxed as this experience continues. I'll stretch my feet out again, hold the tension there . . . be aware of the tension . . . push my toes out, push my heels up . . . and be aware of the part of my body that supports me so much . . . I'll hold it . . . hold the tension.

Then I'll relax my feet and feel so much more comfortable, so much more at ease . . . as I exhale my breath . . . I am exhaling the tension. I can feel so much more relaxed from knowing that I'm beginning a process that's going to change my state and allow me to give myself suggestions for changes all through the day, and all through the week.

Now I'll work on my calves. I'll feel the tension in my calves. I can make my calf muscles tense and hold my calves tightly. I'll be aware of all the tension as I tense those muscles and take a deep breath and hold it. Naturally I know that my calves do a lot of walking . . . a lot of working for me. Now I can exhale and release the tension in my calves . . . while I exhale.

I can bring the tension back into my calves as I bend my feet, my toes, upward towards my head and hold the tension in my calves . . . hold it there . . . as I take a deep breath. I can be aware of any tension that may have been hiding in my calves.

Then I can exhale and relax my calves. As I do . . . I may shift my position and I can become even more comfortable.

Now I can move my focus into my thighs, my quadriceps, the biggest muscles of my entire body. I'm going to make my thighs stretch out and feel the muscles . . . feel the tension . . . and be aware of all the weight that this particular part of my body carries. As I take a deep breath . . . and hold it . . . I'm becoming aware of the tension stored in my thigh muscles.

Both my right side and my left side together . . . can feel the tension. I'll hold it there . . . I'll be aware of it . . . and then I can relax. As I exhale . . . I can release the tension in my thighs and exhale tension and stress in my breath . . . as well.

As I'm relaxing the lower parts of my body . . . more and more of me is becoming comfortable and feeling more at ease.

Back, Abdomen, and Chest:

Now I can relax my waist and my lower back together. I'll pull my stomach in and I'll hold the tension there. Many times I carry around too much tension in my stomach and abdomen. Now I can hold it there extra long . . . feel the tension . . . be aware of it as I pull in . . . and I'll take a breath and really exhale.

Maybe I'll take a couple more deep breaths for this particular part of my body. Then again . . . to my stomach and even my lower back . . . pushing in . . . pushing out at the same time . . . just trying to become more aware of the tension . . . holding it there . . . feeling it . . . becoming more aware of it.

Then I can relax again . . . as I take a deep breath . . . and relax . . . and feel myself becoming more comfortable . . . more and more at ease.

I know this is a wonderful way of taking care of myself. I know that this has worked for tens of thousands of people all over the world. It is a very effective technique that is helping me now, and every time I use it, and for days after I use it.

Now I'll pay attention to the middle of my back and chest. I'll try to bring the tension to the middle of my back . . . I'll try to push back in my chair, pushing against the middle of my back. I'll feel the tension there . . . I'll be aware of it.

Maybe I know I've had too much on my back lately, and then I'll take a deep, satisfying breath . . . and blow out the tension . . . as I feel more and more relaxed.

Then again I'll bring tension to the middle of my back . . . maybe pushing on it . . . holding the tension there . . . being aware of it . . . perhaps for 10 or 12 seconds . . . and then a deep . . . comfortable breath. I can feel overall more relaxed . . . overall more comfortable . . . overall more at ease . . . and closer to a self-hypnosis state . . . where I can accept the suggestions for change I will give myself.

Hands and Arms:

Now I'll go to my hands. I'll make a fist with both of my hands at the same time. I'm holding the tension there . . . I'm closing my grip tightly . . . taking a deep breath . . . holding it . . . getting a better grip on things. I am sure that I'm squeezing my fists as tightly as I can . . . holding my fists in this clenched fist position . . . being aware of all the tension . . . squeezing just as tight as I can.

Then I'll let my fingers open slowly . . . extending . . . opening as I exhale slowly. I may notice that my fingers have a slight tingling . . . perhaps they feel cooler . . . yet my hands are more comfortable.

And again my hands squeeze tightly . . . getting a grip on things . . . feeling the tension . . . I can imagine that all the tension in my body is draining right into my fists. I'll be aware of this as a valuable technique for weeks . . . months . . . even years from now. All the tensions in my fists as I deeply inhale . . . and I am more aware of that tension now . . . holding it . . . focusing on it.

Now I can exhale and extend my fingers outward . . . relaxing my palms . . . spreading my fingers . . . feeling this relaxation spreading like a wave of warmth all through my body.

Next I can feel the tension pushing my arms straight out in front of me. Pushing my arms straight out, and holding the tension as I inhale and hold that breath. I can feel the tension in my biceps . . . my triceps . . . my forearms . . . holding the tension there. I can be aware of every bit of tension . . . that's right . . . aware of the tension.

I can now relax my arms as I exhale . . . releasing the tension . . . letting it go. As I relax them . . . I'm becoming more comfortable . . . more at ease.

Again I'll stretch out my arms . . . holding the tension . . . aware of the discomfort . . . aware of the squeezing . . . counting to 10 or perhaps 12 . . . holding the tension there naturally.

Then I can relax . . . exhale the tension and stress as I release the muscles in my forearms . . . letting the tension go.

Shoulders, Neck, and Head:

Next I can focus on my upper back, my shoulders, and my neck at the same time. I'm going to lift my shoulders up toward the top of my head and squeeze tightly the back of my neck, my back, and my shoulders. I can squeeze these muscles . . . take a deep breath . . . hold it . . . hold the tension . . . focus on the tension . . . collect it . . . know that I can get rid of it.

Then as I exhale . . . I can relax those muscles . . . release the tension there . . . let go of the stress that has built up. I can let my shoulders sink down as I exhale completely.

Then I'll lift my shoulders up . . . take a deep breath . . . I'll feel my neck and my upper back tensing up again . . . I can become more aware of the stress and tension . . . aware of every bit of it. I can hold it . . . I know there are often pains in the neck and I know I want to get rid of these. I can picture anything that's troubling me . . . bothering me . . . that's right.

Now I can let it all go . . . exhaling . . . I can let go of the tension . . . let go of the stress . . . let go of the pains . . . the troubles . . . and the problems. I'll feel even more relaxed . . . I can feel more at ease . . . I can notice a tingling sensation in various parts of my body. Perhaps in my toes . . . perhaps in my fingers. I can notice how totally relaxed I can feel.

I will next concentrate on my facial muscles. This is an area where I carry a lot of logical tension and rational thoughts and stress. First I'll hold the tension in my mouth . . . be aware of the tension . . . squeeze my lips together. I can clench my jaws . . . squeeze them tightly . . . hold the tension as I draw in a deep breath between my teeth . . . hold the breath and the tension.

I'll then exhale . . . releasing the tension as I release my breath . . . letting go of the stress . . . letting go of the tension as I exhale. My mouth which smiles and talks and frowns and laughs . . . can feel relaxed.

Again I can squeeze my lips . . . take in a deep breath . . . clench my jaws . . . hold the tension . . . focus on the muscles. I can be aware of the tension . . . hold it there. Then I can exhale and relax.

Now I can squeeze my eyes together. I know my eyes have muscles, they feel tension just like other parts of my body. My eyes can now be tensed and then relaxed just like those other parts of me. Closing my eyes tightly . . . aware of the tension . . . aware of the feeling of tension in my eyes . . . and I take a deep breath . . . holding it . . . holding the tension.

Then I can release the tension as I release my breath and exhale. I can feel the relaxation spreading over my face like the sun warming my body on a summer's day.

Next I can lift my eyebrows up toward the top of my head . . . lift them up and feel the tension in my forehead. This is a part of me that thinks far too much . . . my frontal muscles . . . aware of the tension . . . taking a deep breath . . . holding it . . . holding the tension there also.

And I can let go of the air in my lungs . . . let go of the tension . . . release the stress . . . and feel the relaxation flowing over and through me. I know that it's impossible to feel tension and relaxation at the same time. I know that the more relaxed I feel right now . . . the less tense I become. As I make myself aware of the tension and work on it . . . acknowledge it . . . then let go of it . . . I relax even more.

I know that as I practice this technique more that changes will evolve . . . changes as my body becomes more relaxed . . . my mind may still be active . . . yet I can notice there are physical changes.

My heart has slowed . . . my blood pressure has regulated . . . my mind and my body are far more relaxed now than before I began this relaxation exercise. I may notice that my fingers feel numb . . . perhaps they even feel lighter or heavier than before.

Reaching this state may be the most relaxing way for me to experience the changes . . . for me to know that I control my own changes . . . my own restfulness . . . my own tension . . . my own relaxation. And as I recognize this . . . I'm suggesting how I'd like to feel the rest of the day.

I can change how I feel about tomorrow and the rest of the week. The changes can be felt inside me just like the sense of calm and relaxation I feel right now . . . or the changes can be outside of me like a warm wave that flows over my body . . . or a cool breeze that leaves my fingers tingling or even numb.

I can learn this control . . . this comfort . . . this natural regulation. I can now suggest any other changes to myself that will bring me closer to my goals . . . and these suggestions will be more effective . . . I will listen to myself closer now.

[*Insert your goal suggestions*]

And the next time I wish to enjoy this quality of time . . . this relaxing . . . healthy time . . . I can experience this quiet state of mind even more quickly. I can return more easily . . . now that I know the path . . . now that I know the feeling I want to return to.

In fact, whenever I want to feel more at ease . . . more calm . . . more relaxed . . . all I have to do is take a deep . . . comfortable . . . satisfying . . . relaxing breath [*insert your own suggestions for returning to self-hypnosis*]. I have an ability to relax that I can take anywhere. I can enjoy this ability and make positive changes . . . forever.

To sleep now I could drift easily by counting backwards from 20 to 0, one or two times, and as I go down one step for every number I count backwards, I'll drift into dreams and a night's rest . . . or if I want to awaken refreshed right now, I'll count from 1 to 10 and go back up to conscious alertness one step at a time to 10 when I can open my eyes, stretch my muscles, and feel well rested, like I had napped.

$$1 \ldots 2 \ldots 3 \ldots 4 \ldots 5 \ldots 6 \ldots 7 \ldots 8 \ldots 9 \ldots 10$$

TECHNIQUE #2: THE INDIRECT LANGUAGE METHOD

This technique uses indirect, permissive requests and suggestions. The language of the suggestions is flexible and you will suggest to yourself that you *may* do something or that *perhaps* you'll notice such and such a change.

Find as comfortable a position as you wish for yourself to relax. Take a few minutes or as much time as you need to relax your mind as well as your body, perhaps with an amusing thought or a pleasant memory of a vacation spot. Take as many deep, satisfying breaths as you like before you begin your suggestions.

The script

Now I'd like to notice how much more comfortable I might feel by just taking one very big, satisfying, deep breath. That's fine. I may already notice how good that feels, how warm my neck or my shoulders can feel.

Sometimes the warmth begins at my feet and works its way up. Other times the warmth begins at the top of my head and works its way down. Of course it doesn't matter if it begins in the middle of my body, or where it begins. I may enjoy all the changes I'm experiencing during the same time.

It is always helpful to become more comfortable. I may notice how very easy it is to take four more very deep, very comfortable breaths. And as I exhale . . . I can notice how comfortable my eyes can feel when they close.

When my eyes close, I can let them just stay closed . . . that's right. I may notice how when I exhale . . . I can feel the relaxation beginning to sink in . . . just as my eyes can begin to sink . . . sinking, absorbing . . . receptive . . . open . . . taking-it-all-in feeling.

I may already notice how much more relaxed I can feel. I wonder if there are more places in my body that can feel as relaxed as my mind wants. I wonder if there are places in my shoulders and my neck that can feel similar to the relaxed places in my legs or arms.

Perhaps I can feel many places . . . inside of me . . . beginning to relax. I wonder if the deep . . . relaxing . . . restful heaviness that sometimes comes in my forehead . . . is already beginning to spread and flow. That heaviness and soothing comfort may flow down . . . across my eyes . . . down my neck . . . deep and restful.

A wave of comfort can wash over me like an ocean wave washes over a sandy beach. I can feel as relaxed as I feel in the warmth of the sun on a sandy beach. The wave of comfort and relaxation can feel so good . . . and feel so relaxing.

There are no rules or requirements or regulations of any kind. There's no one to bother me. There's no one to disturb me . . . there's no one to take care of.

I may notice the heavy, restful, comfortable feeling . . . spreading down into my shoulders . . . into my arms. I wonder if I may notice one arm feeling heavier than the other.

Perhaps my left arm feels a bit heavier than my right arm. I don't know . . . it probably changes from moment to moment . . . from trance to trance. Perhaps both arms will feel equally comfortable . . . equally heavy. It doesn't really matter.

The feeling may even be one of lightness . . . or floating. It changes . . . it matters little whether I feel heaviness or lightness. It's all to my advantage . . . for changes today . . . may have already begun . . . or may be about to begin . . . or are beginning right now.

Perhaps I can notice that even as I relax . . . there may be a tingling in my fingers. Breathing comfortably . . . more slowly . . . more deeply. I know that it doesn't really matter if I feel . . . a tingling in my fingers . . . or perhaps a part of my fingers . . . or perhaps around my mouth. I may notice that the relaxation continues to spread . . . growing more comfortable.

How easy it is to understand in this quiet, relaxed state . . . to make changes in myself . . . and to note changes that I want to make. I know that nothing really matters . . . except perhaps . . . the enjoyment of my experience . . . the comfort of my relaxation with nothing to bother me . . . nothing to disturb me.

Now, as often, is the time to suggest the changes . . . and images . . . and feelings . . . and thoughts I wish to give myself. The best way may be a variety of changes . . . or a succession of changes. Or the best way may be just allowing whatever is known to help to be . . . and to trust myself.

[*Insert your goal suggestions*]

I can trust myself . . . my experience. I have trusted myself many times before. Perhaps for small changes and perhaps for bigger changes. I wonder how many different ways I can trust myself.

I can trust the changes . . . the goals . . . the variety of answers to a variety of questions. But no matter, the variety of my experiences can help me to feel pleased . . . comfortable and relaxed.

I can remember or not remember what I've suggested . . . so that the most effective way is experienced. I can remember something all at once . . . so that memories move quietly into the back of my mind. Certainly in the back of my mind in a very fundamental way . . . is the experience of that deep . . . satisfying breath that can always bring back this level I'm enjoying, right now.

As I've taken this time out for myself . . . I can continue to find it much easier or a little easier any time I wish to reenter any helpful trance state . . . like this natural state. I may find I can reach a deeper state at times.

In a moment . . . not yet, but . . . as soon as I'm ready, I'm going to count from 0 to 5. At each number . . . each step . . . I can take all the time I need . . . after all, time is relative. I can feel myself slowly and comfortably returning to alertness with each number . . . with each step. Or, if I want to sleep fully, deeply, I can go the other way . . . from 5 to 0 . . . down some steps, to my world of imagination and freedom.

To awaken . . . and to be more alert . . . I go up the steps. One step for each number. When I reach 3, my eyes can be almost ready to open. When I reach 4, they may have already opened. And when I reach 5, I can be alert, awake, and refreshed.

Perhaps I will awaken as though I have had a nice nap, refreshed and alert. I can feel alert and quite well, perhaps surprised in a pleasant way, feeling very well. Now I have all the time I need as I begin to return to alertness.

> 0 . . . 1 . . . 2 . . . feeling more alert . . . 3 . . . my eyes
> opening . . . 4 . . . 5 . . . alert, awake and feeling well.

TECHNIQUE #3: EYE FIXATION METHOD

This is a technique of entering a trance by focusing your visual attention and concentration on some spot or object in front of you. You allow your conscious mind to become absorbed in gazing at a spot while you give yourself suggestions to relax and develop your trance.

Locate some spot on the wall across from you or some small object upon which you can fix your eyes. Call that spot the target and continue to stare at it. Your suggestions can be like these:

The script

As I stare at the target, I will become more relaxed. After a few minutes, it will be easier to focus, yet appear to move slightly and even appear to change in some color slightly . . . yet I will continue to stare at the target.

I will continue to stare at it even if it does something or nothing. I will feel more relaxed the more I focus on it. My eyes will focus and they will become more and more tired . . . sometimes blinking . . . sometimes watering . . . as I continue to stare . . . I become more relaxed.

The target I've chosen will help me to go into a hypnotic trance . . . a self-hypnosis state . . . self-directed . . . self-contained, and very helpful. I am directing it . . . I will be aided by it and I will learn from this self-hypnosis experience.

I will be open to learning and knowing more information . . . more about myself . . . than I do right now. I will be as open to these new insights as I can be. It's all my information . . . it's all self-directed.

Just staring at that spot is a self-directed choice. I will stare and become relaxed and perhaps feel my eyes glazing . . . and drifting . . . and yet still focusing. Sometimes I will become aware of my feet and how my legs feel . . . and even a sinking feeling in my shoulders . . . as I continue to stare.

I will begin to count backwards . . . to myself . . . from 30 to 0. When I begin . . . I will feel my breath exhaling . . . getting rid of any air that's no longer needed. I will feel the inhaling of new . . . fresh air . . . and I will know that my system inside . . . has a filtering system to give me the best possible breaths . . . naturally.

As I continue . . . I will feel more and more relaxed . . . and my eyes will get heavier and heavier. If my eyes have already closed . . . just from staring and focusing . . . .and experiencing the target . . . that's fine. I will just find myself getting more deeply . . . more comfortably relaxed with each number that I count.

If my eyes are still open . . . I will continue to stare and focus until they close on their own . . . or until I reach 0.

I will allow myself to do whatever feels most natural . . . most comfortable, to enter this self-hypnosis state. And as I count backwards . . . I will feel as if I'm walking down a step for every number I count . . . and the closer I get to the bottom . . . the more relaxed and comfortable I will feel.

I may feel as if I'm going down on an escalator . . . or an elevator. Sometimes I will choose to imagine myself walking down some steps. I will feel as if at the bottom I will get to a beach . . . or to a grassy field . . . or at the bottom I will find myself floating . . . comfortable . . . relaxed.

I will feel as deeply comfortable and relaxed as I like. Now as I begin to count backward . . . I will feel each step taking me further and further down. I will feel the weight of my body and my eyes. I will feel the heaviness of the feeling . . . all over . . . from top to bottom.

Now I'll begin at 30 . . . I'm feeling more and more comfortable.

29 . . . an odd number . . . and all the odd numbers will help my body become more deeply, more comfortably relaxed.

28 . . . an even number . . . all the even numbers can help my mind to drift and wander and become more available to my unconscious abilities . . . to the powerful person inside of me . . . for mental, psychological, emotional, and physical changes that I will work on.

27 . . . relaxing, down another step. 26 . . . comfortable, at ease. My eyes are feeling heavier . . . my head is drooping just a little.

25 . . . more and more relaxed, more comfortable. I will learn more and more about myself. 24 . . . heavier and heavier, my legs feeling heavier and more relaxed. My arms . . . feeling heavier . . . my jaw is relaxing.

23 . . . comfortable changes. 22 . . . my breathing is deeper, slower, more

natural. I will feel more and more of what I want. 21 . . . comfort, relaxation . . . more and more.

20 . . . a third of the way down and I will feel as if I've gone down even further, because I know I have and I know I will.

19 . . . more and more heaviness . . . 18 . . . my arms and legs are so relaxed . . . 17 . . . deeper and more comfortable. 16 . . . I will hear sounds outside that will help me to further my relaxed state . . . and allow me to feel even more deeply comfortable.

15 . . . halfway down . . . one eye closing more than the other. Both eyes closing together . . . already closed . . . I will allow whatever is going to happen, to happen.

14 . . . relaxing more. 13 . . . deeper and deeper relaxed. 12 . . . my feet may feel as if they're part of the floor or they may feel light and tingling. 11 . . . 10 . . . two-thirds of the way down.

9 . . . closer to the bottom . . . closer to even more comfort and relaxation. 8 . . . my jaw is loose, my face is relaxed . . . my arms and legs are heavier and heavier. My hands may be just as numb as my feet.

7 . . . relaxing . . . feeling the changes in my hands and feet . . . I will allow the feelings to spread. 6 . . . almost all the way right to where I want to go . . . to more comfort . . . to a place where I will be working on the most effective changes that I want to make.

5 . . . I am already making changes in myself . . . in more comfort . . . more relaxation. 4 . . . deeper and heavier. 3 . . . almost there, more relaxed. 2 . . . closing or staying closed . . . staying receptive to suggestions . . . yet deeply, deeply relaxed . . . staying open to my suggestions . . . yet very, very comfortable.

1 . . . 1 . . . 1 . . . 1 . . . 1 . . . as many times as I need to say that. I will feel myself using this state.

0 . . . 0 . . . 0 . . . 0 . . . 0 . . . 0 . . . 0 . . . 0 . . . all the way . . . totally relaxed . . . at the place I call self-hypnotism . . . naturally self-hypnotized.

[*Insert your goal suggestions*]

I can return to this state of deep relaxation . . . any time I wish . . . simply by counting backwards from 30 to 0. By taking some deep, satisfying breaths and counting backward from 30 to 0.

I can return to a refreshed and alert state by counting from 0 to 5. As I get closer to 5 my eyes will open . . . I will feel more refreshed and more alert.

0 . . . 1 . . . 2 . . . 3 . . . 4 . . . 5 . . . I am awake, alert and feeling good.

TECHNIQUE #4: GUIDED IMAGERY TECHNIQUE

This method of self-hypnosis encourages your mind to form mental pictures, sensations, images, and visualizations of various scenes. Your ability to use imagery is a powerful tool in self-hypnosis. Refer to Chapter 6 for an explanation of the role of imagery and for exercises to better develop your skills.

Find a sitting position with your arms resting comfortably and your legs flat on the floor or propped-up and uncrossed. If you wear eyeglasses remove them, and loosen any constrictive clothing. Adjust your position and become as relaxed as you can. Close your eyes.

The script

To experience even more comfort and relaxation, I'll begin to breathe deeply, maybe I'll take three or four deep, satisfying breaths. As I do this, I'll pay particular attention to the various sensations I experience as I exhale and the air leaves my body.

Every breath brings in new air and every exhale gets rid of old air. Like a bellows . . . healthy winds flow . . . into me. I can let myself feel as comfortable as I desire with every breath I take in . . . and I can feel even more comfortable with every breath I exhale.

Each outgoing breath gets rid of stress . . . gets rid of worry . . . gets rid of discomfort. I can imagine a tea kettle that is boiling water and see in my mental picture how the steam escapes and relieves the pressure in the kettle. I can let my breath escape in a hissing sound . . . just like the tea kettle . . . releasing unnecessary . . . unneeded pressures and tensions.

I can feel the muscles in my body relaxing. I may notice them first moving downward from my head . . . through my face . . . through my shoulders . . . down my arms . . . through my chest . . . all the way around my back to my waist. With each breath I exhale, I exhale more tension . . . exhale my troubles all the way out.

As I naturally continue breathing, comfortably and deeply . . . and in rhythm . . . I can begin to picture in my mind a staircase, any kind of staircase I choose. Perhaps it is a spiral staircase . . . maybe a staircase from a home I have been in . . . it might even be a staircase from a movie or television program I have seen. It doesn't matter what shape or what it looks like.

I can form an image of it now, in my mind. I can see the banister, carpeting, and all the details clearly. It may be a staircase from my childhood or one that I completely makeup in my mind right now.

The staircase can have any number of steps on it. Perhaps it has 10 steps. I can see myself at the top of the stairway. And as I stand there I may be able to notice the smells and the sounds around me. I may hear birds or the sounds of the outdoors, as people move about in their natural daily life . . . just as I am taking time out now, for myself . . . naturally.

And if I hear a car pass by or a plane fly overhead . . . I know that I can imagine all my tension . . . all my stress has been packed into a suitcase or a bag. As the car or plane passes . . . I can imagine that package being flung by me and landing on the back of the car, truck, train, or airplane. And as the vehicle passes, and the sounds drift farther away from me . . . I know that my tension and stress is leaving with it.

So in a moment, not yet, but in a moment I'm going to begin moving down the imaginary staircase. I'm going to count each step as I move down. And as I probably already know . . . or may even anticipate . . . as I count each number down, I'll become more relaxed . . . more comfortable with each step.

One step for each number that I count. The larger the number the farther down I go. I may find that there are even more steps than I thought. The farther down I go, the more relaxed and more comfortable I get.

Whether I feel as if my feet are sinking into the carpet, perhaps so deep and so soft, or whether I feel supported by the railing . . . with my hand keeping me steady as I move . . . I know that I will be more relaxed . . . more comfortable with each step.

I'm going to get ready to begin. Clearly in my mind, right now, I can see or sense the staircase, feel the steps . . . I'm getting ready.

I'm ready now to begin . . . with each step I can feel more relaxed more comfortable.

10 . . . the first step down the staircase. I can be pleasantly surprised to find myself getting rid of even more tension. As the first step in any journey . . . this is often an important one . . . relaxing.

9 . . . the second step and I can move as if I'm taking a walk on a comfortable, clear day. The more I walk, the more steps I take, the more I can feel comfortable and distanced from any worries or concerns.

8 . . . in this state, the tension loosens and the warmth and coolness can take their place. There are various numbers of images that may be helpful for me, rivers . . . fields . . . mountains. This staircase can be like one of them.

7 . . . I may also see many colors. Perhaps the colors of the staircase or of the walls . . . or of the sky or pictures on the wall. The colors may vary from a gray shade to a deep navy . . . but no matter what shade of blue I find myself imagining, I know the color can bring about different things . . . different feelings. The grey can bring about a cool breeze blowing past my body. The brilliant blue can bring the warmth of the sun directly on me.

6 . . . I'm halfway down the staircase. I may see other colors. I may see greens like the grasses outdoors. I may visualize reds or pinks and yellows. Gold, brown, and even black or white can all intermingle . . . mix or stay clearly separate. Whether in a kaleidoscope or individually, I can feel myself using these memories of colors and images to feel as comfortable and as deeply relaxed as I'd like . . . colorful rainbows . . . sails on boats . . . paintings . . . and even balloons. More and more relaxed.

5 . . . and as I descend more, I can feel the relaxation sweep over me, so comfortably, so safely that I know that I can enjoy this experience and return to it again. I know that I can travel wherever I wish. Into the future . . . or into the past . . . with colors or without. I can feel sensations in my fingers . . . I may enjoy feeling the cool wetness . . . perhaps a tingling or a numbness. I may feel a numbness around my mouth, like a river with cool waters and this is perfectly natural.

4 . . . feeling more and more relaxed.

3 . . . nearing a new level of the stairs. I can feel the warmth in my body and perhaps even coolness. All through me like I'm in a painting or part of the landscape . . . all around me . . . so personally designed.

2 . . . almost there.

1 . . . I can feel more deeply relaxed. I can take a deep, satisfying breath and feel more calm, more relaxed than maybe ever before. It is as if I have arrived at my peaceful setting. Perhaps I can even imagine a more peaceful setting now, in my mind.

Maybe I'll see some shapes . . . circles . . . triangles or squares. I can even color in the shapes. So I'll color in a circle or a triangle. And whether it's an ancient image of me or a circle that balances me, or whether I can see in my mind's eye the changes in shades and the subtle changes in the shapes or not, it's all there . . . and here . . . and available . . . and healing . . . just by being here now.

I can use my mind's eye to see the changes that I suggest to myself. And as I get ready to do this, I can take a couple of deep . . . satisfying . . . breaths. And I may notice how light or how heavy my body can feel. I might even feel my hands and arms . . . maybe my left . . . or maybe my right, get lighter and feel as if it can float . . . like a leaf . . . safe . . . supported being in nature . . . for a while . . . comfortable . . . secure . . . alive and open . . . in a flow.

I might imagine balloons tied to my arm. Colored balloons filled with helium like those I had as a child. The balloons make my arm feel lighter and lighter. My arm may feel as if it wants to float up . . . like a balloon.

Let me see how vividly I can imagine the balloons. I can picture them now. Clearly and colorfully tied to my arm and tugging gently. My arm may even float up a bit off my lap or off the armrest. But whether my arm floats up a little or a lot is not important. I know that the feeling I have right now is of deep comfort and relaxation.

And in just a couple of minutes . . . I'll know that I can make changes in me . . . positive changes that I want to make. I can begin to feel the energy that's been with me all this time . . . beginning to move upward and downward.

[Insert your goal suggestions]

In a couple of minutes, perhaps sooner than I might expect, I can feel the satisfaction of knowing that I am treating myself to a wonderful experience. I know that I can return to this level of comfort and control anytime I wish. Just by taking a few deep, satisfying breaths . . . and using my imagery . . . all of it . . . or just part of it . . . I can visualize the stairway and take several deep . . . comfortable breaths and return to this level of relaxation.

Each time I practice this form of deep relaxation it will be easier for me to return. Each time I return I can become more relaxed, more deeply comfortable, more controlled. Because I enjoy this feeling of comfort and control, I will find it easier each time.

If I want to drift off to sleep or dreams . . . that might be my intention as I count from 0 to 20 or 30. Or, I can return to a refreshed, alert, awake state merely by counting from 0 to 5. As I count, with each number I count, I become more awake, more alert. 0 . . . 1 . . . 2 . . . 3 . . . more evenly and gradually alert . . . 4 . . . 5 . . . fully alert, refreshed and awake when my eyes open.

TECHNIQUE #5: THE DIRECT LANGUAGE METHOD

What marks this technique as different from the indirect method is the commanding, directive language of the suggestions. That is, the language of the suggestions is stated in a way that directs you to the suggested goal in a straightforward manner. Your suggestions to yourself are more in the form of commands to be followed.

Begin by getting comfortable in a chair. Take several deep, satisfying breaths and relax. You may start with your eyes open, but you will want to close them shortly.

The script

I'll breathe quietly . . . in . . . and out. And now I know that I want to concentrate on my feet and ankles. I will let them relax . . . let them feel totally comfortable and limp.

I will begin to feel heaviness in my feet. They will feel just as heavy as lead. I will even feel them sinking down, down into the floor.

My eyelids will become heavier and heavier . . . and they will begin to close as they get tired. My eyes will want to close. As soon as I feel them close . . . I will just let them stay closed. I'm letting go . . . safely and comfortably.

I can let go of my muscle tension completely. The muscles of my calves and thighs will go quite limp and comfortable. I will let them go . . . let them relax and they will feel even more and more comfortable.

My eyes are beginning to feel more tired and may even become watery. They will feel so heavy that they will want to stay closed. I'm letting myself go completely and comfortably.

I can give myself completely to this pleasant, drowsy, comfortable, relaxed feeling. I will let my whole body become heavy and wooden-like.

Now I will begin to picture in my mind a staircase with 10 steps. I am at the top and I will begin to get ready to go down the stairs. I will go deeper . . . and feel heavier with each step.

Shortly I will count out loud or to myself from 1 to 10. I will see myself stepping down one step for each number I count. I will notice how much more relaxed and comfortable I will feel at each step.

All right . . . I'm ready to begin. 1 . . . the first step down the staircase . . . to entrance myself . . . toward the first step in positive self-change.

2 . . . the second step down the staircase. I'm beginning to feel more deeply relaxed as I will feel myself becoming more and more comfortable.

3 . . . at this third step . . . I can notice how much more relaxed I will feel . . . and how much more relaxed I do feel right now. I am noticing places in my body that are more relaxed than others. Deeper and deeper relaxed . . . I am becoming . . . in all parts of my body . . . all over . . . everywhere . . . a feeling of deeper states and deeper steps.

4 . . . I will continue to go deeper and become more comfortable the further down I go. I will feel different parts of my body sinking . . . feeling heavier and heavier . . . like lead . . . heavy.

5 . . . I am now halfway down . . . enjoying how much more relaxed . . . and how much deeper I feel. I will allow everything to become part of my experience in noticing a deeper state . . . all of me . . . heavier . . . in a trance . . . in my own trance . . . my own direction . . . my own relaxation.

6 . . . I will notice the heavy . . . restful . . . comfortable feeling spreading . . . down my shoulders . . . into my arms. My arms and legs will feel very heavy . . . as I go deeper and deeper.

7 . . . I will breathe more comfortably. I will take a deep, slow, comfortable breath. I will notice a pleasant . . . relaxed feeling . . . spreading more and more throughout my body . . . inside . . . and outside.

8 . . . I am feeling increasingly heavy . . . more and more comfortable as I become deeper and deeper relaxed. I will continue to breathe slowly and comfortably.

9 . . . I am almost to the bottom of the staircase. I'm continuing to feel more and more comfortable . . . more and more relaxed. Heavier and heavier I feel as I get more and more comfortable.

10 . . . Now I am almost at the bottom of the staircase. I will continue to go deeper with each breath I take . . . sinking farther and farther down. I am so deeply relaxed . . . I will enjoy the comfort that I am feeling. Deeper and deeper . . . heavier and heavier . . . I will continue to relax· very . . . very deeply.

Every feeling that I am experiencing will make me more and more comfortable. Every thought that wanders or travels through my mind will make my body more and more comfortable.

Everything I can imagine, feel, or experience . . . will help me to feel deeper and heavier and more comfortable. I have reached the bottom of the staircase. I have reached the place I want to be. All the muscles of my body are heavier and heavier . . . my breathing is deeper . . . more comfortable . . . more relaxed.

The sound of my voice and even the words from my thoughts . . . will be easy to understand. I will feel comfortable talking mentally to myself, or if I want to speak to myself out loud . . . either is just fine.

My words will be clear . . . the images will be clear. I will feel more and more relaxed as each moment passes. I will not need to remember everything . . . I only need to concentrate on total relaxation.

As I continue to enjoy my comfort and relaxation . . . I can notice that the heaviness in my arms and hands will turn to a tingling or to a numbness. The deeper and deeper my sensations . . . the deeper is my feeling to follow all my instructions . . . exactly as I have planned.

My instructions and suggestions will be followed just as I say them to myself. Each moment passing I will go deeper and feel more comfortably relaxed. Any time I count from 1 to 10, I can return to this feeling of deep relaxation.

I can picture myself going down the stairs and I will be able to reexperience in a slightly different way . . . my own abilities to relax myself. These abilities are my own . . . and I can help myself with them.

While I'm in this deep state of self-hypnosis and relaxation . . . I can give myself other suggestions to work on other goals I have.

[Insert your own goals]

I know that whenever I wish to return to this relaxed state of self-hypnosis . . . all I need to do is take several deep breaths and count from 1 to 10 . . . and will return to this same deep level of relaxation.

In a few moments I'm going to count from 10 back to 1. When I do this . . . I want to begin climbing back up the staircase. I will feel myself going up, and I will become more alert the closer I get to 1.

When I reach the top of the stairs . . . I will awaken feeling refreshed and alert. The closer I get . . . the more awake I will feel and the more refreshed I will become.

   1 . . . 2 . . . 3 . . . 4 . . . 5. Just like I've taken a long nap, I can begin to
      awaken and feel well rested, clear, alert, refreshed.
   6 . . . 7 . . . 8 . . . 9 . . . 10. A deep refreshing breath, an awakening breath,
      I feel clear and alert.

TECHNIQUE #6: USING DREAMS FOR SELF-HYPNOSIS

Begin this technique, like all the others, by getting as comfortable as you can. You will want to take several deep, satisfying breaths to let go of any tension that might exist in your body . . . like at night when you're dreaming while sleeping . . . This is the same sort of experience but yet different at some levels.

You may want to do some progressive relaxation first, if you feel especially tense or stressed.

The purpose of this dream method is to reach a comfortable state of self-hypnosis and to gather some information from your dream-state to use in creating positive suggestions.

As with some of the other methods, you may want to create your own script for this technique and perhaps make a tape recording to play for yourself. Like the others also, this is a script you can modify and put into your own words if you wish.

The script

As I begin, I know that the purpose I have in mind is to reach a natural state, to use it to experience change in the direction of my goal. Whether my goal is to relax and develop posthypnotic cues for relaxing any time . . . or some other goal . . . I can feel very relaxed right now. My whole body can dream . . . with my mind . . . with warmth just like the colors that hint warmth.

I can move myself around . . . shift my position . . . and get as comfortable as I desire. I know that this relaxed state . . . is like a dreaming state . . . it is as natural as other states that I could possibly experience. I know that people go in and out of dream-states all the time.

I may be aware that people can have a brief daydream every 12 minutes or so . . . all day long . . . where their minds just naturally wander into a thought that's unrelated to the experience of the moment . . . to drift . . . to float, like a cloud . . . in the sky, like on a magic carpet.

I also may know that dreams in the nighttime . . . nocturnal dreams . . . are normal for people to have all through their lives . . . and this is a way . . . right now . . . for me to have one of those kinds of dreams. Yet this time . . . I may be able to remember my dream . . . use it . . . change from it.

So I may have noticed in other self-hypnosis experiences . . . that I've already been experimenting with . . . that my mind has wandered quite naturally anyway. This dream technique is just taking what always happens for me . . . and focuses on it . . . and uses it to make changes in myself.

As I continue to breathe . . . comfortably . . . easily . . . I can take more deep, satisfying breaths . . . at any time . . . to become more relaxed . . . to become more at ease. I can feel myself swallowing . . . I can feel my eyes closed and comfortable . . . as I begin almost every technique with my eyes closed . . . and comfortable.

Already, the *rest* of my body wants to join my eyes . . . and become more relaxed. My feet . . . my legs . . . all through my body . . . from the top of my head . . . through my neck . . . my shoulders . . . all of me is cooperating . . . getting as comfortable as possible . . . like magic dust, relaxing dust . . . sprinkled on me, misting softly.

I may want to count *slowly* backward to myself . . . from 20 to 1, and inhale on the odd numbers and exhale on the even numbers. Or, I might imagine myself going down an elevator to be as relaxed and as comfortable as I'd like.

Then . . . soon . . . but not yet . . . after I go all the way down into my relaxed self . . . I am going to have a dream . . . a dream in which I can go to a favorite place that I remember from childhood . . . or from adulthood . . . or from a fairy tale . . . or any pleasant image.

Or . . . I might dream of a favorite place. I can be with people that I enjoy being with . . . or I can be by myself. But I know one thing . . . I can create a sequence of events . . . an experience of comfort . . . where my mind wanders to a place and to people . . . and this wandering is directed by me and is as comforting and soothing as I choose and is most natural . . . such as this state . . . can be.

As I continue . . . the dream can begin. The dream can be of an ocean or a lake . . . or of a place I have visited . . . recently or long ago. It can be of the mountains . . . or of the seasons . . . perhaps snow . . . maybe the warmth of summer . . . floating . . . freely wandering.

I may enjoy spring . . . and the readiness for growth . . . both of the spring and . . . for myself. No matter what the place . . . the season . . . the location . . . the experience . . . the people . . . or my thoughts . . . the dream may continue and the benefit . . . of this quality of time . . . is to reach this soothing . . . relaxing . . . state on my own . . . and to bring positive . . . creative . . . experiences into my self-hypnosis.

And with these experiences . . . I can now associate the positive dream . . . to a positive feeling . . . with my goal. The goal I have in mind is as natural . . . as comfortable as a pleasant dream.

I carry with me the capacity . . . to daydream . . . all of the time . . . and I can also use that ability now. And the dream I'm having in this state . . . perhaps more than one dream . . . all helpful for the changes . . . I want to work on . . . and am working on and creating.

Now . . . like all dreams . . . there may be distractions . . . of sounds . . . voices . . . cars . . . or people . . . and with those distractions . . . I may add those elements to my dream. I can add people . . . or I can travel myself . . . to other places.

But all the shifts in my experience are subtle . . . positive . . . and enhancing.

I may want to write my dreams down . . . I may want to remember it . . . just as an image . . . to reinstate the experience . . . to re-experience the pleasant sensations . . . and the comfort of self-hypnosis. And when I complete my dream and my self-hypnosis . . . I will be able to remember the dream only if I want to.

[*Allow some time to drift into a dream sequence.*
Insert your goal suggestions.]

And as I continue . . . I know that I can finish this experience . . . as I finish many others. And I know that the next time . . . I wish to enjoy this same quality of time . . . this same relaxed experience . . . I can reenter it . . . perhaps more quickly . . . maybe even easier . . . whenever I take several deep, satisfying breaths . . . and desire to find this same level of relaxation.

I can digest new ideas . . . float to new levels . . . and create positive change for life . . . unconsciously and . . . consciously.

I can move around . . . slowly . . . ready to drift into sleep if that is my intention . . . or to awaken from this trance with a refreshed . . . wakeful feeling. Perhaps I'll climb back up some steps . . . or I'll count back up from 1 to 20 . . . I'll direct myself and stretch out . . . and feel as if I've awakened from a dream, comfortable . . . refreshed, very naturally, at my own pace.

TECHNIQUE #7: THE ERICKSON HANDSHAKE TECHNIQUE

This method for developing trance was popularized as a clinical hypnosis technique by Dr. Milton H. Erickson. We call it the "handshake" in recognition of Erickson's hypnosis technique and from the position your hand is in at the beginning of the practice.

Start by extending your arm (it doesn't matter, right or left) out in front of you as if you're about to shake someone's hand. Keep your arm suspended there in this comfortable yet somewhat unusual position.

You can fix your gaze on a part of your extended hand or close your eyes to begin, the choice is yours. If you begin with your eyes closed then form a mental image of your arm in front of you.

The script

I'm going to bring in new air and exhale old air. I'm going to create as comfortable a state as I can . . . with my arm and hand extended out in front of me . . . my hand from the wrist down just feeling as if it's dangling in mid air . . . a comfortable feeling . . . a relaxed feeling . . . as I continue to breathe easily.

Now I can notice my shoulder working to support my hand and even to support my arm . . . and at the same time as my hand and arm are feeling comfortable . . . I can pay attention to my feet. I can pay attention to the back of my legs . . . and all the time I notice how much more comfortable my breathing is becoming.

I may now choose to count backwards from 20 to 0 . . . to myself . . . I may feel as if for each number I count backwards my arm is becoming heavier and heavier . . . so that in just a few seconds from now it will fall limply and heavily to my side, if it hasn't already . . . while other times my trance will take it up . . . in the air . . . lighter than light and of course . . . heavy is fine, too.

An indicator to me that my self-hypnosis trance has begun . . . such as my arm begins to feel lighter . . . with each number I count . . . as if each number is another helium balloon tied to my arm . . . and my arm is lifting higher, upward toward the sky with each additional number and each additional balloon . . . that will be fine also. And as my hand floats up and touches my forehead or my facial area, or anywhere like that at all . . . I'll know that this is also an indicator of the beginning of my trance. (*Count backward to yourself and visualize your arm moving either up or down as you count slowly and breathe deeply and slowly.*)

Whether one time when I practice the counting I create a heaviness or whether another time my arm lifts upward and feels lighter and my experience creates a floating quality . . . it matters little which direction my arm goes. In fact, sometimes it may feel like just staying right where it began. Right in the same position . . . arm out in front of me . . . comfortable and relaxed.

Any movement in my arm at all from this position is going to be very helpful, as my whole body seems to feel the same thing my arm feels. All my thoughts may be in my fingers . . . in my wrist . . . in my palm . . . even in my forearm.

At times in this technique my mind may wander far away . . . it may wander far from this experience. Other times I may feel as if I'm very close to my own experience and the closer I get . . . the more at ease . . . the more comfortable I can pleasantly be surprised to feel.

But no matter what . . . I know . . . I've begun this experience in a certain position . . . I can finish the experience in either that same position or any other position that feels comfortable to me. Any movement, change . . . of course leads to more comfort. Any change can create the kind of openness and sensitivity to me . . . to allow me much more of an opportunity to create a whole river of change . . . a whole valley of change.

So, whether it's a great big area I'm working on . . . or some succession of changes . . . it's much like the movement of my body as I become more and more comfortable. The movements are all part of my experience. And just as I know that there is an outer experience . . . there's also an inner experience . . . and I can recognize the difference between the two . . . by doing . . . by feeling more able to work on each separately . . . or one at a time . . . or even together.

I can suggest changes for the outside and changes for the inside of me. I can feel more open to the movement of tensions or distractions moving out of my fingers . . . moving from where they originate in my back . . . my head . . . or my legs . . . my toes . . . the top of my head . . . my fingers and the bottom of my feet become exits for discomforts and tensions.

[*Insert your goal suggestions*]

Just as I know that even the slightest movements are going to be helpful . . . for me to remain in the state of deep relaxation and work on my goals . . . and even the changes . . . so I can return to this state . . . more comfortably each time . . . any time I choose to count backward from 20 to 0. If I want to sleep, rest, be totally and fully relaxed, I can count backwards again from 20 to 0 . . . easily, or I can now return to an awake state. I can feel refreshed and renewed . . . perhaps count back up to an alert and wakeful state by counting from 0 to 10 and I know how healthy and beneficial this quality of time can be for me . . . very satisfying and very enjoyable . . . when I reach the number 10.

TECHNIQUE #8: SELF-HYPNOSIS WITH MUSIC

Have you ever noticed that you can become absorbed and "lost" while listening to some piece of music? That experience is a common one.

Find a record, compact disc, or tape that is relaxing and comfortable to you, one that in the past has been relaxing, comfortable, and absorbing. This could be classical music with a variety of instruments or new wave music with a continual beat. You may find that reggae music or jazz works best.

It doesn't matter if it's active music or soothing, quiet music. Anything that *you* become absorbed in is fine. Feel free to be creative and to experiment with different kinds of music, if you wish.

Begin by getting into a relaxed state without the music. Give yourself some suggestions of how you'll feel when the music comes on and how the music has affected you in the past. Suggest how this same effect can happen even *more* with self-hypnosis.

You can use the music as a vehicle to get into the trance-state and you can give yourself suggestions while in self-hypnosis that will be far more effective than any other time you might give those same suggestions. Perhaps 10 to 15 minutes of relaxation without the music will be sufficient.

Start the music and spend about 5 minutes talking to yourself quietly. Allow the music to become part of you and you to become part of the music. This absorption and increased imagination helps you to reach a state in which the goals you are working on are more available and the changes are more comfortable.

Allow the music to help you to develop suggestions. Imagine the instruments as voices that you can direct to convey your suggestions. If there are lyrics in the music, let the words become positive and encouraging suggestions. What the words are saying is not important; what is important is what you want to get out of your trance experience. That may be relaxation and a release of tension or some work toward a specific goal.

As you reach the absorbed trance-state and as you give yourself goal suggestions, you can also let the music itself become a cue. For example, when the music gets louder and more forceful, that can be a cue to *acknowledge* your tension or any situation in your life and become more *aware* of it.

When the music gets softer and more soothing and the pace changes, you can use that space to release the tension or release any unwanted feelings and exhale the pressure you may have built up. Notice the changes in your body sensations that have occurred. Perhaps your fingers have become cool or warm. Your hands might feel slightly numb or heavy. Your toes might tingle. Any change you feel can be an example of the changes brought on by your change in concentration and awareness.

When the music ends, you can continue to give yourself positive suggestions toward more relaxation and toward achieving any goal work you wish. Interweave some posthypnotic suggestions and cues for reentering self-hypnosis. For example: *"Whenever I want to relax and feel this deep level of comfort in the future . . . I can get into a comfortable position and listen to this piece of music. When I listen to this music and take several deep, relaxing, comfortable breaths . . . I will return to this same feeling of calm and peacefulness."*

Give yourself several posthypnotic suggestions for experiences that you'd like to achieve. Use this time to give yourself suggestions for specific other goals such as pain control, weight loss, or habit changes.

Be focused like a creative music director, bandleader, or even singer. Know the music. Know the rhythm. Know your intentions, your wants, your ability to extend your limits.

You can experiment with different kinds of music and different suggestions. Most of all, enjoy the experience and feel positive and rewarded with the change in your awareness of yourself.

This technique is always available to you. And just as you can change the channels on a radio, you can also change the music in your mind, or how you mind the music. If you need to relax, stop taking yourself so seriously, and gain a healthier perspective, change the tune, the words, make them work for you, in rhythm, your own inner rhythm.

TECHNIQUE #9: SELF-HYPNOSIS DEEPENING

A very effective way of deepening or developing new qualities of trance-state at any time is to bring yourself out of trance and then quickly reenter. This seesawing in and out of self-hypnosis increases the depth of your trance. Each time you reenter the self-hypnotic state in this exercise, you can reach a deeper level than you experienced before.

Use this script along with any of the other methods, to develop a deeper level of trance.

The script

As I begin, I know that the purpose I have in mind for this session is to give myself as deeply relaxing a time as I possibly can. I know that I'll be in this relaxed state, and that I'll also be able to leave this self-hypnosis state and then return again.

So like other practices and experiments with my own self-hypnosis, I'm going to take a couple of deep, satisfying breaths. I'm going to move my legs around, and my arms . . . I'll also make my head and the rest of my body as comfortable as I can.

I know that in this relaxed state, as I enter self-hypnosis, I may remember some activities and recognize those as completed or finished for the day or for the time being. I may picture myself in those various situations and activities and then leave them behind me as I move on to where I am now, relaxed . . . comfortable, at my own pace.

I've already found it useful to feel as if I'm going down some stairs, or perhaps in an escalator or elevator. Now I'm getting ready to imagine going down from the fifth floor to the first floor. The fifth floor is a floor full of carpeting, full of padding, that I can roll on and move on until I find a position that's just right. I know that I can talk to myself in this level. I can ask myself how relaxed can I feel right now.

As I repeat the question a number of times, I can begin to feel my words affecting my body . . . I can begin to feel my body affecting my words.

Sometimes I can feel a wave of warmth or a cooling wave spreading all through my body. I know that my body is naturally regulated and that this is an opportunity to influence myself positively, comfortably.

I can feel as I talk . . . as I listen and experience, how I can change from breathing comfortably to becoming more relaxed. I can feel a change from feeling heavier to being more comfortable. I can feel a floating sensation . . . lighter and more comfortable and relaxed.

As I continue to talk to myself, soon I'm going to count from 5 to 1, not yet, but in a few moments. And when I do, I find that as I get closer to 1, I'll become more and more relaxed and perhaps even distant from my surroundings. I may feel as if I've traveled in my elevator or escalator to a vacation spot. A place where I can feel the most relaxed.

And now I'm going to count and feel my elevator or escalator or staircase taking me down to that relaxing, comfortable place in my mind.

5 . . . 4 . . . 3 . . . 2 . . . 1 . . . I can feel more relaxed now than before. I can feel the waves of comfort . . . wash over me like the waves of sunlight flowing

over me in summer. Perhaps I can even feel a floating sensation as if I am in a balloon . . . floating over a green meadow.

[Insert your goal suggestions]

Now I'm going to go back up the staircase or elevator or escalator. As I count back up from 1 to 5 . . . and feel as if I'm going back up the escalator with every step . . . every number I count . . . I'll feel more wakeful . . . more alert . . . more aware of my own external surroundings.

And when I reach the number 5 . . . I'll open my eyes, recognize my experience and just for a moment . . . I'll be aware of everything around me. Then I'll close my eyes again.

And as I close my eyes again, I'll count backward again from 5 to 1. I'll imagine the changes that can take place in my body, as I felt them before.

Slowly, comfortably . . . by counting backward and going down to the deep level . . . I can lift my index finger, or perhaps one of my fingers, when I get to 1 and then slowly lower that finger down again . . . comfortably . . . to signal to my unconscious, that I am so relaxed.

And gradually, I'll move back up . . . to a light, alert, more wakeful and relaxed state . . . 1 . . . 2 . . . 3 . . . 4 . . . 5 . . . eyes open and alert. I can become aware now of the changes from what I felt a few moments ago.

I can return again now. Moving back down . . . 5 . . . 4 . . . 3 . . . 2 . . . 1 to a meadow or a sandy beach or maybe a mountain forest. I can travel in this state . . . with my mind . . . to any state . . . to anywhere I choose. I can explore.

So as my experience continues to unfold and I feel more relaxed . . . I may want to go to a clear . . . grassy area . . . where the wind is blowing softly against the branches of the trees.

The wind in the trees may whistle like the birds whistle. The mountains in the distance are perhaps even nearer than I think, and are a symbol of strength . . . a symbol of age . . . wisdom . . . they can be a comfort to me in this state.

My mind may wander to any image I wish . . . from mountains to fields. From railroad tracks to airplanes. From bright colors to various shapes.

And just as the train moves down the tracks . . . there's a time when it, too, needs to rest. I may find my own station to relax in . . . perhaps a station like the one I'm in right now. I know my momentum will be more comfortable . . . enthusiastic and motivating as I take off again from the station.

I know where I'm headed . . . the changes I have in mind. I know my goals . . . the places I want to stop. I can even picture the places I want to visit and visualize them as stations that I'll be moving to and recognizing when I experience them . . . all within my control.

[Insert your goal suggestions]

And now again . . . I'll begin to count up to 5 and begin to slightly awaken myself to move into a more alert state. Again I will become aware of my surroundings . . . more aware of the external world as I count up to 5 . . . perhaps going up that escalator.

1 . . . 2 . . . 3 . . . 4 . . . 5 . . . and now I can open my eyes and I may move just slightly to make myself even more comfortable.

Then I'll close my eyes again and count backwards from 5 to 1 and feel myself deepening . . . feeling heavier and more relaxed. 5 . . . 4 . . . 3 . . . 2 . . . 1 . . . to a place where I can take time out . . . where there is no one to bother me . . . no one to disturb me at all . . . and no one for me to take care of.

I have as much of an opportunity as I'd like to create for myself in this experience . . . to find my own images that are relaxing and comfortable. I can find my own place that I enjoy . . . and give myself suggestions of positive changes.

I can find my own place to rehearse situations in which I would like to be more effective. I know that my relationships with people will improve with this practice . . . because my relationship with myself is improving now also.

So as I continue . . . naturally my own experience will change. I can experiment with different goals and suggestions for changes I want to make in myself and in my life.

I can use any outside noises or sounds as enhancements, as helpers to me to feel more relaxed and comfortable. I can somehow fit those sounds and distractions, using my imagination, into effective signals for me to relax even more.

I know that any time I take a deep, satisfying breath . . . I'll bring about my comfort and a deep relaxation. I know that any time, now or even later while I'm at work and I feel tension . . . I can squeeze my fist . . . clench it and hold the tension there, in my fist.

Then I can be aware of the tension or stress . . . gather it up in my fist and slowly open my hand and spread my fingers out to release and let go of the tension.

I know that I can take better care of myself . . . perhaps better than I ever thought was possible. And every time I practice with self-hypnosis, I reconfirm this thought and enjoy the comfort and relaxation I'm giving myself right now.

[*Insert your goal suggestions*]

And as I count back up from 1 to 5 . . . and become more alert with each step . . . I know that the next time I want to take this sort of time for myself . . . it will be even easier for me to return to this level of comfort. I know that each time I practice self-hypnosis it becomes easier to reach this level of relaxation and control.

Whenever I wish to reenter this state of comfort and control . . . all I need to do is take several deep, satisfying breaths and take the elevator ride down to this level of relaxation.

Now as I return to wakeful awareness, I may wish to repeat this cycle and count myself back down . . . perhaps even deeper than I am right now. Or I may wish to go on with my daily activities . . . refreshed, renewed, and alert. It doesn't matter which I choose. I am ready to return to an alert, wakeful state. With each count I will take another step towards a refreshed, alert awareness. 1 . . . 2 . . . 3 . . . 4 . . . 5 . . . refreshed and alert and with my eyes open.

COMMENTS

The techniques and scripts presented in this chapter contain many forms of image and suggestion material for gaining relaxation and developing a calm, renewing, self-hypnotic trance. After reading this chapter, you may have a good notion of how to improvise your own monologue of suggestions without a written script. That is fine.

You may need to practice several times with any technique before you are completely successful at entering self-hypnosis, or you may find you easily enter a trance the first time you practice. Whether you develop a self-hypnotic trance the first time or after several practice sessions has no bearing on how effective self-hypnosis will ultimately be for you. Be patient and enjoy the relaxing time you are giving yourself.

Section II
WORKING TOWARD YOUR GOALS

Now that you've learned to develop a self-hypnotic trance, you probably want to begin working on one of the specific goals in this section. While Section I was intended to be read through entirely, you may now want to turn directly to the chapter concerning a goal you're particularly interested in.

When you begin your work toward any goal, remember these general principles to benefit most from your self-hypnosis:

1. Examine your motivation toward your goal and dismantle any underlying blocks to your success. Make a list of the motivating reasons for the change you wish to make. This may be your first goal.
2. Make your goals specific and attainable. If your final objective requires a major change for you, set up specific intermediate goals.
3. Design your suggestions using symbols, metaphors, and images that are personal and relative to you. Draw from your past experiences, dreams, work, play, and memories to develop effective personalized suggestion language.
4. Use your imagery and visualization to add power to your suggestions. "See, feel, hear, smell," and "taste" your suggestions and the results you seek.
5. Develop posthypnotic cues whenever possible, to extend the effects of your work with self-hypnosis beyond the trance experience.
6. Be patient with yourself. Change takes time and effort. Set aside some time every day to practice a few minutes of self-hypnosis. It is not so important how much time you invest— what's very important is your intention, during that time. The energy and time you are devoting to self-change are investments in yourself. You will be enjoying the valuable, positive dividends for a long time.

The skills you develop in self-hypnosis are lifelong. You need only practice them to keep them sharp and effective. Your talents can grow and expand as you use and experiment with them. Enjoy your new capacity for self-change and better health.

12
Stress Management: Relax Anywhere

Bill is a company manager with a budget proposal deadline staring him in the face. His chief aide has been out sick for the last week and two days ago his own wife was hospitalized with a serious illness that had been troubling her for some months.

Bill's blood pressure has shot up. He hasn't been eating or sleeping well and his boss has noticed that Bill's concentration is lagging. He is becoming irritable and withdrawn. Bill is not the enthusiastic, high-spirited man he used to be. Unless he learns a new way to cope with his stress, he could be headed for an ulcer or a heart attack.

Unfortunately, this is not an isolated case. A majority of executives and business people consider stress a significant problem in their lives.

Of course, stress occurs in every occupation. In many cases, factors other than work itself contribute to stress in a big way. Family discord, financial troubles, child rearing—the list of stressing agents is long and varied.

Whether arising from a job or from other causes, excessive stress results in lower and poorer production and frayed relationships with coworkers, friends, and family. It can also mean absenteeism, tardiness, lack of concentration, on-the-job accidents, and job burnout. Many company staff psychiatrists and physicians believe that about 80 percent of employee emotional problems are caused by excessive stress.

At home, stress can create problems with children, lead to marital conflict, and result in depression and illness. We may be more likely to notice the problem in others, while failing to recognize it in ourselves.

Even if you recognize that you have a high stress level, do you know what to do about it? There are healthy and unhealthy ways of stress management.

Overusing alcohol, tranquilizers, and other drugs can be a damaging way to manage stress. Exercise, meditation, and self-hypnosis are much better ways.

The reason we talk about stress management rather than stress removal is that a certain amount of stress is good—indeed, it is necessary for life. Absence of all stress would be death. Some stress is produced by nearly every action or reaction we have. It is excessive, prolonged stress that is damaging.

THE PHYSICAL SIDE OF STRESS

The effects of stress are so broad that it's possible that stress may play a role in nearly every illness and disease. Excessive stress affects the equilibrium of the body's chemistry.

In the nineteenth century, the French physiologist Claude Bernard observed that healthy bodies maintain a fairly constant internal environment (Kroger, 1963). Blood pressure adjusts to daily demands, oxygen levels and blood chemistry are regulated within limits, and other variables are balanced to maintain optimum life.

Some time later, another physiologist, Walter B. Cannon (1929), added to Bernard's findings. Cannon studied how the body reacts to sudden changes. He found that fear, anger, and pain cause the body to react quite remarkably. These emotions trigger the "fight or flight" response.

When this response is triggered, Cannon noted, adrenaline, a powerful hormone, is immediately pumped into the bloodstream. Another reaction stimulated by certain emotions, called the "sympathetic nervous system," causes the release of a very similar hormone called noradrenaline.

These hormones set up a number of potentially lifesaving changes in an organism. They speed up the blood circulation and dump into the blood more oxygen and more energy-producing sugar. At the same time, blood clotting processes are fortified. Breathing is accelerated, muscles are tensed and strengthened, and the senses become sharper. Digestion is temporarily halted. The body becomes energized and prepared to either fight or take flight.

The design of this reaction system was, however, for emergencies. Cannon noted that these survival reactions are triggered by fear, rage, pain, injuries, lack of air supply, or intense emotional situations. Normally these are not a constant occurrence.

Our bodies can safely maintain this sort of response for only a short period of time. If this reaction is allowed to continue for too long, the imbalance begins to cause problems.

Hans Selye (1978), endocrinologist and specialist in stress research, used the term "distress" to describe damaging or excessive stress. He found that when continued for a period of time, the powerful hormones that are secreted to trigger the fight or flight response wear down the body's immune system.

Selye described the body's overall effort to adapt to distress as the general adaptation syndrome (G.A.S.). This is a process which attempts to cope with "nonspecific" stress—as opposed to specific short-duration stresses such as injury, the flu, or momentary fear.

It is the chronic, non-specific pressures of work, financial, and domestic concerns that hurt us most.

The G.A.S. has three stages: (1) the alarm reaction; (2) a period of resistance; and (3) the exhaustion stage. It is during the resistance and exhaustion stages that the body's immune system progressively breaks down. Whatever organ or part of the body is the weakest tends to break down or become diseased first.

Stress can affect the foundations of your immune system and may set up your body to be infected by agents of disease you could normally withstand.

You may ignore a tension headache. You can take antacids for an upset stomach. But if you continue to disregard your body's early warnings, the next stage could be ulcers or much worse.

However, you *can* learn to manage your stress levels. You can stop headaches and other early symptoms, and you can prevent future illness and disease.

COPING DEVICES

When we are subjected to long bouts with stress-causing situations, most of us develop some coping mechanisms. Unfortunately, many of the methods we choose are either inadequate or harmful.

Many people try to alter the excessive demands of their work, family problems, financial concerns, or illness. Perhaps they seek a better job, go to family counselling, or take steps to directly deal with the stress-producing situation. Perhaps they also increase their recreational exercise, take a vacation, talk with a close friend, punch a punching bag, or find some other appropriate way to blow off steam. These methods are healthy and wise.

However, many people find that even these ways of coping are insufficient. Stress is a contributing cause in the epidemic of alcoholism in America. Drug abuse, legal and illegal, is rampant. The anxiety reducers Valium and Xanax are two of the most widely prescribed drugs in America.

In business, management has increasingly recognized the need for stress management programs for employees. The American Institute of Stress, a nonprofit clearinghouse for stress research in Yonkers, New York, has related studies showing that more than 66 percent of all visits to primary-care physicians are for stress-related problems and that job stress costs American industry more than $150 billion yearly in absenteeism, lost productivity, medical coverage, and accidents.

Government studies cited by The American Institute of Stress indicate that over 70 percent of companies with 750 or more employees offer programs of stress control. The trend now is for specialists to do an assessment of the companies' stressors, as perceived by the employees. Then company specialists develop plans that address specific problems. Sometimes, different employees within a company will receive different stress management programs, depending on what is most needed. Many methods have shown effectiveness, including meditation, biofeedback training, assertiveness training, psychotherapy, physical exercise, and dietary changes.

The National Institute of Occupational Safety & Health considers stress in the top 10 leading workplace hazards to health.

One technique provides for deep relaxation, both at the moment you are practicing it and whenever you experience a stressful situation in the future. That method is self-hypnosis, which we know to have many of the benefits of meditation and biofeedback, yet with the added power of posthypnotic responses.

REDUCING YOUR PHYSICAL STRESS WITH SELF-HYPNOSIS

Self-hypnosis offers you the ability to dissolve the immediate stress you feel. It can also provide a tool—posthypnotic suggestions—for handling stress outside of your self-hypnosis. The relaxation and deep breathing of the trance-state unravel your muscular tension and set up what is called "the relaxation response."

Herbert Benson (1976), cardiologist and noted stress researcher, believes that the objective of all stress reduction is to enhance this relaxation response. It is the opposite of the fight or flight reaction. Some characteristics of deep relaxation are:

1. Your breathing becomes slower and deeper.
2. Your heart beats slower.
3. Blood flow increases to your hands and feet.
4. Your muscles relax.
5. Your metabolism slows and normalizes.
6. Your hormonal activity becomes balanced.

What is important to understand is that **if you can create one portion of the relaxation response, the chain of other responses will follow.** Deep, slow breathing may be one of the easiest of these effects for you to learn because it is already in your conscious control.

You have begun learning to lower your tension and stress levels by simply putting yourself into a self-hypnotic trance. The trance state itself is usually very relaxing.

When you first prepare for self-hypnosis by taking several deep, satisfying breaths, your deep breathing initiates the relaxation response. Here is an example of how you might suggest relaxation to yourself:

"As I focus my attention on my hand, on a spot on the wall, on a sound or color, I may encourage my body to relax even more. I might visualize the stress and tension that builds up in my muscles as constricting bands or layers that can be peeled away. Deep breathing breaks the bonds of the outer layer of stress.

"A numbness, coldness, warmness, or any feelings that follow in my hands, arms, or feet can serve to further reduce the tension of my muscles. Perhaps I'll choose to progressively relax each muscle group in my body.

"Layer by layer, I can unravel the tightness of stress. My heartbeat may

decrease, and with further relaxation many other changes will occur. These are positive feelings that promote good health and increase the quality of my life."

Using your own feelings of stress to relax

Rather than trying to deny or prevent feelings of tension or stress, once they have built up, acknowledge them. Pay attention to those sensations of muscular tension in your forehead or stomach, or to the clenching of your jaw, or wherever you may be feeling it.

Take a few moments to mentally examine where your tension has accumulated. Try to gauge how much it is on a scale of 1 to 10, for example.

You might try closing your eyes for a few seconds and imagining a speedometer reading. Use whatever image feels comfortable to get a fix on how much tension you are feeling. Determine in your mind the level of intensity.

Then apply additional tension to the troubled areas for a few seconds. Deliberately tense those areas—your forehead, stomach, jaw, or shoulders. Take a deep breath while you are doing this. Hold the breath for a few seconds along with the additional tension.

Then slowly exhale and release the air and all the stress that has build up.

Another method of reducing tension is to vigorously shake your arms and your legs, to move around, and to stretch. Take a deep breath and exhale as you shake out all the tension and stress. Of course, this technique may be more practical in some situations than others.

SELF-HYPNOSIS TO RELAX YOUR MIND

You may find times when in addition to physical tension there seems to be a "something on your mind" type of stress. Most people can attest to the fact that the mind never sleeps, like we know that sharks never seem to sleep.

Recent research (National Geographic, 1975) has shown us that sharks do sleep (but usually keep their eyes open) and that the mind does rest. In fact, the brain gets replenished during certain cycles of sleep. If you feel that it is difficult to shut off your mind from thinking, worrying, concerns, then you may want to incorporate the following into your self-hypnosis.

Begin your self-hypnosis by focusing on your breathing, being sure you take a really satisfying breath. Then, carefully experience the exhale of each breath, four or five times, noticing the let-go from the air escaping and your body letting go of tension, your lungs letting go of air, and a let-go of thoughts for only a moment or two.

As you continue to follow yourself through slow, deep-breathing let-gos, softly exhale to make a gentle humming sound from as deep in your throat as you can

. . . really let it vibrate as slowly and as soothingly as you are able. Hum softly as you exhale for four or six slow, deep breaths.

Next, let yourself watch your thoughts as they begin to come back to you, one at at time, as you might watch clouds drifting by on a gentle breeze. Develop the skill of having one thought at a time, observe it, or hear it, or sense it in your own way. Then allow it to be replaced by another thought.

You may sense the thoughts as clouds, or as birds, or as leaves floating on a stream, or a person walking by, or any image you are comfortable with.

Learn to distance yourself from your thoughts. Drift with your ideas, thoughts, concerns . . . one at a time. Let go of each one along with a slow exhaled breath . . . perhaps hum it along in your own unique way. Make way for the next thought as you let go of the present one.

Finally, to relax your mind, notice an emotional feeling you may be experiencing. Whether anxious, or sad, or excited, or fearful, or happy, or upset, just become aware of your emotional state of mind. Experience the feeling, express it (out loud, write it down, say the feeling to yourself, etc.), or even hum it. Give it an expression.

Allow the feeling to move out of you just as the thoughts can be let go of and float out. Accept the feelings as you accept the one-by-one thoughts, observe them approach, experience them as they pass over you, then watch or sense them exit, depart you.

Imagine how you can do this as often as you wish. Perhaps you will want to practice this technique several times a day, maybe once every hour for just a few minutes. With some practice, you will be able to utilize your thinking to enter a trance state and convert the stressful thoughts into a relaxed trance-state using your breathing as a cue and your thoughts as individual markers of breathing and counting and focus.

Perceptions of stress

In a recent study (Stanton, 1989), 40 high school teachers participated in four weekly group hypnosis sessions focusing on the cognitive (thought) process about the stressing situations they were in. This hypnosis group did significantly better, at a 12-month follow-up, than did the control group who did not receive the hypnosis training.

You may have noticed that situations that stress you very much do not seem to affect others. Or, conversely, you may find a situation easy to deal with while a friend, coworker, or spouse may be stressed-out in the very same environment.

It has been found by researchers like Aaron Beck, David Burns, and others who have studied and written about cognitive therapies that our thoughts about an event or situation affect our feelings and behaviors. It was the thought patterns that were influenced with hypnosis in the study of the 40 high school teachers mentioned above.

SELF-HYPNOSIS TO CHANGE STRESSFUL EMOTIONS

Here is an example of a self-hypnosis technique to enable you to manage stressful emotions by controlling your thoughts and perceptions about potentially stressful circumstances.

Jenny was in a relationship with Rick, a man who seemed to ignore her a lot. Rick loved her, she knew, but there were times when he would be preoccupied with reading, a project, a telephone conversation, or other such distractions and didn't give her much attention. There were other times when he did show a great deal of attention to her, such as when they were out to dinner together, when she had a problem to talk about, when they were making love, and so forth.

However, when he wasn't being very attentive, Jenny said, "I feel very tense and stressed, thinking he may not love me or that something was wrong between us."

At these times, Jenny would become distraught within and sometimes even erupt in an irritable, unreasonable way toward Rick. Afterward, she would sometimes feel worse for having let her emotions get her so upset.

Using self-hypnosis, Jenny learned to gain awareness of such situations as they occurred and then take conscious and unconscious control of her thoughts in a focused way. For example, when she noticed that her emotions were beginning to feel insecure or doubtful of Rick's love, those feelings became the post-hypnotic cues for her to STOP—*Start to Observe Purposefully*—and examine if there was any evidence in reality for these feelings to indicate change in her relationship with Rick.

In most situations, Jenny discovered that her feelings were not based on anything evident in actions; rather, her perceptions of insecurity seemed to come from the feelings. Once she could STOP—*Start To Observe Purposefully*—in the middle of those feelings-turned-cues, Jenny developed ways to "talk herself up" from those feelings and into more reasonable perspectives.

The purpose of observing the feelings and thoughts is to compare them with tangible reality. Jenny would say to herself, "He didn't say anything about the new plant I bought for the living room, but does that mean he's upset with me or ignoring me for some reason?" Often she would directly ask him if there was anything wrong?

Other times, she would remember past evidence and say to herself, "I know he loves and cares for me because there are times when he tells me so, when he remembers my birthday, and other special times, and he enjoys our quiet time together. Just because he is preoccupied at times does not mean he's drifting away. This has happened many times in the past and he's later shown how he does care."

In these ways, she "talked" herself toward more reasonable perspectives. She noticed that eventually the uncomfortable feelings she had would leave and that the less time she spent analyzing her feelings the less time she spent feeling uneasy.

DEALING WITH STRESS OUTSIDE OF TRANCE

With self-hypnosis you can program yourself to relax, without apparatus or equipment, any time you are exposed to stressful situations. By giving yourself posthypnotic cues—suggestions that are activated outside of your trance state—you can turn a stressing event into a relaxation signal.

You can turn a sign for stress into a cue for calm. If you become tense and feel pressure when your pay your bills, you might convert the opening of your checkbook into a cue and turn on some favorite music, or sit in a comfortable chair, or have a glass of water, or carry out any positive actions you might want. Those actions become posthypnotic cues when you imagine them in your trance images.

How posthypnotic suggestions can help you handle stress

Phyllis worked in administration at a large hospital. Her boss, the administrator, was seemingly forever making snide quips about her work. He would tell her that her desk was a cluttered mess. Or he would comment on how slow she was in finishing a report.

She knew in her heart that she was not lacking in her job skills. Her boss was also rude and insensitive to others in the office. Nevertheless, Phyllis would seethe inside whenever her boss would criticize or berate her. She was having headaches and crying spells and was ready to quit her job.

Instead of leaving her well-paying job, she tried hypnosis to cope with her stress. After learning self-hypnosis, she gave herself cues for reacting positively in the face of aggravating comments from her boss.

For instance, while in a trance at home, she made these associations: "*I know that Mr. G (her boss) often is childish and uncaring when he criticizes me. I may find that when he comments rudely on my work or actions, I can feel forgiving and not take it personally. I can take a deep breath and go to the pencil sharpener and grind away the callousness of his remarks. I may find that as I grind away the pencil I have also ground away the source of stress and tensions that I might have felt.*"

By finding an action that she could take at the time she felt the stressful event, Phyllis was able to release her stress before it built up into an irritating problem. She also found other posthypnotic cues to use as signals, such as noticing the poisonous inflection in Mr. G's voice that accompanied his sarcasm. That was another cue for her to let his venom pass over her and not poison her.

Along with the words and symbols of her suggestions, while in her trance, Phyllis visualized specific situations she expected to encounter and visualized herself behaving and feeling differently. She practiced self-hypnosis five times a week with this particular goal. In about two weeks, she noticed that her pulse rate remained steady even after one of Mr. G's tirades. She did go through a lot of pencils, but that is a small price to pay for an increase in health and peace of mind.

Finding posthypnotic cues in your own situations

We each have unique circumstances that give us stress. Though the sources may be similar, the particulars change from person to person and even from one person's work-place to home. Like Phyllis, you will need to select stress reduction cues that are pertinent to your own environment.

This will be easier to do than you may think. A cue for releasing tension in a stressful situation can be anything that can be routinely associated with that moment. You can even *create* an action as Phyllis did with the pencil sharpener.

The closed drawer cue

Don is a salesman for a large printing company. His tensions and stress arise from a number of sources through the day. "I'd really like to go into a trance about eight or 10 times on some days," Don reported. "Most of the problems hit me when I'm in the office. Now I have this drawer on the lower left of my desk for those problems."

Don has given himself cues while in self-hypnosis that whenever a problem comes up that stresses him, he will put his stress in that drawer. "I write down the name of the person or account or the supplier, or sometimes just a word that describes the problem. Then I take two deep breaths, open the drawer, and put away both the slip of paper and the feelings of tension. Sometimes I also visualize putting away the throb in my head that means a headache is on its way," Don said. "When I close the drawer I leave it all in there."

Once a week he throws out the old slips of paper and makes room for new calm and relaxed reactions. He also has a folder in his briefcase for situations that occur when he is out in the field.

You may want to adapt this technique for yourself. Choose a drawer in your dresser at home or in your desk at work. Make a place to deposit your tensions and stress, and when your close the drawer, leave your unnecessary stress there. Use your imagery and visualization to reinforce the feeling of distance between you and the stress.

REHEARSING OTHER STRESSFUL SITUATIONS

Often a stressful event is one that could benefit you. But you avoid it because it seems too difficult to face the tension you know it will cause. You might have avoided going out on a date or going to a party where you might not know any-one. Job hunting, especially, can be a gut-wrenching experience.

Instead of going ahead with these kinds of activities, some people hold back. They are not quite ready for the tension these situations will put them through. Also, there may be more holding them back than just the fear of stress—perhaps a fear of rejection or feelings of insecurity. But self-exploration with self-hypnosis often uncovers how these problems can be eliminated, too (see Chapter 16, on self-exploration).

First, put yourself into a relaxed comfortable trance. Then imagine yourself asking someone out for a date, going to a party, or doing whatever you have wanted to do but avoided doing. Visualize yourself in the scene as best you can. Put in as much detail as possible—even dialogue. Make the mental picture as real as possible.

Allow yourself to feel the tension, the tightness in your stomach, or the quiver in your voice. Experience your tension in this vivid but detached way. It can be as if you are watching yourself in a movie. Perhaps the movie is being filmed from your point of view or perhaps from the sidelines—it's not important which.

While in your trance, suggest that your hand may feel tingling, warm, or cool. Take your hand and place it over the areas of your tension, one at a time, perhaps first over your stomach, then over your forehead. Be aware of each place the tension has built up. Allow the sensation from your hand to transfer to the place of tension—let the warmth or numbness flow from your hand to your stomach, or other place of physical tension. Feel the relaxation, the comfort.

Talk to yourself at the same time. Describe your feelings to yourself in your own words. "*I can feel the tension, the twisting feeling in my stomach. It feels like a washing machine sloshing back and forth.*" Mentally examine all the areas of your body and experience the tension that might be in each.

Then go back and unwind and untwist each. Use your hand transference as before, if that feels comfortable. Or, if you are nervous, imagine your mouth opening up and releasing the butterflies from your stomach. Perhaps see your muscles as ropes all twisted up in stress—allow them to untwist as you would hold a twisted rope by one end and let it fall loose.

Use your imagination to find ways of vividly undoing the tension you feel. Be as direct or imaginative as you please. The idea is to express the tension and then to relax it in a variety of ways.

Become accustomed to the feelings of both tension and relaxation in your rehearsal. Learning the entrance and exit of a stress experience is helpful in controlling it. Imagine the stressful situation coming on and then imagine it dissolving. Like an engine that you can start up and then turn off, allow a feeling of stress to start and then feel it turning off.

Recreate your visualized scene several times, first feeling the anticipated tension, then releasing it. Using this sort of mental rehearsal, you can experience the entrance and exit of the stress or tension. Developing more mastery over the entrance will also provide you more control over the exit. After you try this in several self-hypnosis sessions, then imagine yourself in the scene first without the tension, then with it.

Always finish your self-hypnosis with a successful outcome, however. This will help you achieve your results sooner. In a short time, you will find that you only need to enjoy the positive points of your experience.

In a week or perhaps less of this type of rehearsal, you will notice that you can readily control your tension and stress. The fears you had will dissipate.

REFERENCES

Benson, H. *The Relaxation Response*. New York: Avon Books, 1976.

Burns, D. *The Feeling Good Handbook*. New York: Wm. Morrow, 1989.

Cannon, W.B. *Bodily Changes in Pain, Hunger, Fear and Rage*. New York: Appleton, 1929.

Collins, R.E. Managing Stress on the Job. *Blue Print for Health*. Blue Cross Association, 1974.

Groves, P.M. & Rebec, G.V. *Introduction to Biological Psychology*, 3rd ed. Dubuque, Iowa: Wm. C. Brown Publishers, 1988.

Guenther, R. *Wall Street Journal*, series on stress in business, Sep. 30, 1982.

Kroger, W. *Clinical and Experimental Hypnosis*. Philadelphia: J.P. Lippincott Co., 1977

Mason, J.L. *Guide to Stress Reduction*. Culver City: Peace Press, Inc., 1980.

National Geographic. Strange World of the Red Sea Reefs. Sept., 1975.

Ricklefs, R. *The Wall Street Journal*, series on stress in business, Sep. 29, 1982.

Selye, H. *The Stress of Life*. 2nd rev. ed. New York: McGraw-Hill Book Company, 1978.

Stanton, H.E. Hypnosis and Rational-Emotive Therapy—A de-stressing combination. *International Journal of Clinical & Experimental* Hypnosis, Vol. 37, Apr. 1989.

Waldholz, M. *Wall Street Journal*, series on stress in business, Sep. 28, 1982.

13

Freedom from Fears, Phobias, and Anxiety

Snakes, spiders, eels in the ocean, or things that go bump in the night—it is safe to say that most normal, healthy people are fearful of something.

Many of our fears have a survival element in them. Fears of things like heights, snakes, and burning buildings are fears of things that could actually threaten our existence. There is little reason to remove such fears unless you are a high-rise construction worker, a herpetologist, or a firefighter. Only when a fear or phobia interferes with your daily life need it be a concern.

The difference between a fear and a phobia is mostly one of degree. A phobia is something that causes you to change your way of living to avoid the object or situation. A phobia of flying is not just fear in the air; it is trembling at the sight of the airplane, or being gripped by fear even when sitting in a plane still on the ground, or perhaps even suffering anxiety from just thinking about taking a flight.

A fear can be something only mildly interfering; it does not control your life to any great degree. For instance, you might be fearful of bees. That is a common fear and not one you might choose to change. After all, how often do you encounter bees? Besides, there are some valid reasons for avoiding them.

But if fear of bees kept you from enjoying a walk in the park or anywhere that bees might appear, that could signify a phobia. There are many rare and unusual phobias, such as extreme fear of snails. Many such phobias are laughable—except to those stricken with them.

ANXIETY AND PANIC ATTACKS

Severe anxiety and fearfulness can take many forms. Individuals may experience a high level of anxiety that seems to persist for hours or even days at a time. Other anxiety sufferers have brief episodes of intense anxiety or a feeling of panic that comes on quickly and lasts for only minutes. Often these panic episodes feel like attacks; hence, the common term, panic attack.

A book written by two former agoraphobia sufferers, "Free From Fears" (Seagrave & Covington, 1987), provides a detailed background and explanation of panic attacks and anxiety.

Panic attacks have a cluster of varied symptoms that can include several or more of the following:

- shortness of breath or smothering sensations
- dizziness or unsteady feelings or faintness
- racing heart
- shaking or trembling
- unusual sweating
- choking feeling
- nausea or stomach distress
- numbness or tingling sensations
- hot or cold flashes
- feeling unreal or out of touch with your body
- chest pain or discomfort
- fear that you are dying or will die imminently
- fear that you are going crazy

Any four of these during an attack usually indicate a panic condition. Of course, you would be well advised to check with a physician to rule out any underlying physical disorder. However, many sufferers from panic or anxiety have consulted physicians numerous times, or even gone to hospital emergency rooms, only to be told there is nothing physically wrong.

Another form of anxiety is less time-limited and more generalized. It can include many of the same symptoms of panic, but also can include:

- feeling keyed up or on edge
- very easily startled
- problems with concentration or mentally "going blank"
- sleep difficulties
- irritability
- restlessness
- muscle tension or soreness
- easily tired

Again, when physical causes have been ruled out, these symptoms may mean an anxiety condition is troubling you. This form of generalized anxiety is often present for hours, days, weeks, or even longer periods of time with little of no relief.

PHOBIAS

One example of a phobia that can be quite severe and restricting is agoraphobia. This depressing and unnerving condition afflicts hundreds of thousands of Americans and is no laughing matter. Agoraphobics, in the most extreme cases, are afraid of the outdoors. They fear leaving their own homes. Only about five percent of agoraphobics are housebound; most work, go to school, and function reasonably well by all appearances. However, they may have frequent or occasional panic attacks or feelings of severe anxiety when in certain situations or places.

If your life is limited by feelings of apprehension or fear of having anxiety or panic attacks, then you may be suffering from a form of agoraphobia. This condition exists on a continuum of severity, from mildly limiting to so severe one is housebound our of fear that panic attacks or anxiety will result in embarrassment or humiliation.

Other phobias include fear of heights, closed spaces, flying in airplanes, certain animals or insects, public appearances (severe stage fright), and the dark.

USING SELF-HYPNOSIS TO GAIN CONTROL

The first thing you need to do to deal with a fear, phobia, or anxiety condition is to gain more control over other aspects of yourself. Anxiety conditions can be a learned response to their environment for people who are predisposed. Such individuals seem to be generally intelligent and sensitive, but often with some family history of anxiety condition. Many anxiety sufferers are less aware of their bodily responses, particularly responses to stress, and are therefore less able to control them and often have not learned adequate relaxation skills.

Begin by developing control over some physical sensations in your body. You may wish to read again Chapter 12 on stress management to better understand the body's responses to stress. Developing the ability to physically relax is a first big step to overcoming anxiety, panic, and fear. From the early chapters of this book, you will have learned how to develop some control over your heart rate, breathing, muscular tension, skin sensations, and other internal processes. Also, you will have learned to develop your skills in visualization and imagery.

The next step is to imagine some activity that you can mentally accomplish which is unrelated to your fear. Imagine taking a trip to a park, or taking a warm, soothing bath, or preparing a tasty meal. Any nonstressful activity is fine. It is important to develop your ability to see and experience positive aspects of a situation. You should not begin working on the fear immediately because the emotions raised by the fear or phobia might block your attempts.

Visualize and experience with your imagination the positive features of an activity. Explore your actions in your imagination. Perhaps remember a good time you had while engaged in that activity the previous time. With the skills you are developing, you will later be able to work on the fear or phobia situation. At the present, you are developing the internal foundation for your self-hypnosis work.

For example, suppose in your imagery you prepare and eat a favorite meal. You might concentrate on the visualization of baking, grilling, or steaming your favorite food. You might imagine the aroma of the natural juices steaming up, the sounds of the butter and lemon simmering under the food. Then you could imagine the tender taste of the food as you chew it. Feel the crispness or softness and textures and smell the warm rolls and butter (or margarine). Are you hungry yet?

Perhaps you once shared a meal like this with someone special. Remember how warm and close you felt with that person, how content you were when you finished the dinner.

With imagery of this kind, you have controlled your perceptions, memories, and feelings. You have allowed only the positive aspects of the experience to be created in your imagery. In this way, you are learning to enjoy and control more aspects of yourself.

Albert Ellis (1986), a well-known author and therapist, uses a general relaxation technique similar to a direct induction, as we have provided in Chapter 9. Ellis combines hypnosis and his rational-emotive therapy. He suggests that the hypnosis be along the lines of strong self-talk that may sound like a loving and directive teacher or parent. *"Anxiety will not kill me, there are lots of unpleasant things in the world, but I can stand them. I don't have to get rid of all of them to feel in control. I control my emotional future. I like being non-anxious and there is no logical reason why I must be excessively anxious. I would prefer to be more relaxed, even in difficult situations. I control me."*

This direct approach can be repeated in self-hypnosis and offers continual support and new structure in self-hypnosis and afterwards. You can then link these suggestions to specific posthypnotic cues. For example: *"I can be in control and relaxed by focusing on my breathing and slowing my breathing down, consciously. I can remember that I can stand anxiety, by remembering that I have experienced anxiety before, I am able to survive it, I can close my eyes for a moment and remember a peaceful setting, and breathe deeply whenever I begin to feel anxious. It can be like turning a switch on . . . or off . . . even like a dimmer switch . . . more . . . or less . . . I control it . . . from my unconscious . . . inside me . . . I control my goals."*

CHANGING NEGATIVE SELF-TALK TO POSITIVE SELF-HYPNOSIS

If you are experiencing anxiety, panic, or fears that interfere with your life, it is very likely you are engaging in negative self-talk. Here is a case that illustrates the extent to which self-talk plays a part in agoraphobia.

Wendy suffered from panic attacks associated with agoraphobia, she described her self-talk in this way: "I would tell myself that if I go to the movie theater or to a large shopping mall, or whatever, and I get a panic attack, I would be so embarrassed I wouldn't know what to do. I kept telling myself, 'what if' this or 'what if' that. I would get anxious just considering what ifs."

Wendy related: "I noticed that the negative dialogue that I had going in my mind kept me from doing things I enjoyed; in effect, I was afraid of the fearful feelings. I had been talking so negatively and so fearfully to myself for so many years that I had talked myself into doing less and less outside my home."

Through self-hypnosis training, Wendy learned to recognize and replace negative comments with positive suggestions, such as, "If I go to the theater and have a panic attack, I know I'll live through it, I know from past experiences that the feelings of panic last for a few minutes, maybe four or five, and then when I breathe slowly and regularly the uncomfortable sensations subside and I can enjoy the movie again."

With practice, Wendy identified each negative comment to herself, wrote it down, then created a positive suggestion or two to counter it. She repeated that suggestion over and over in her self-hypnosis at the same time that she would mentally rehearse breathing through an imagined experience like a movie, or shopping, or going in an elevator, or any fearful situation for her.

Wendy allowed the negative words in, then would use them as a cue to respond with two positive self-hypnosis suggestions. She soon found the negative words and thoughts were occurring less and less. She imagined it was like small fires and she was a firefighter recognizing them and extinguishing them one by one.

APPLYING THE TECHNIQUES TO FEARS

Once you are able to gain some control over your physical self and your imagery by using self-hypnosis, you are ready to begin work on your fear or phobia.

You will not be trying to eliminate all your fears at once. Instead, identify several stages of success. Work toward and achieve intermediate goals. Remember how long you have been suffering with your fear. Quite likely, you've had the fear a long time compared with the short time it may take to overcome it.

Here is a case that demonstrates how the techniques of self-hypnosis are applied to desensitizing a fear (weakening the bond between the fear stimulus and the fear response).

Betty is a 38-year-old woman who suffered from agoraphobia for a great many years. She was afraid to go out of her house and did so only with great difficulty.

Whenever it was necessary for her to go somewhere, one of her children or her husband had to take her and be with her. Betty had become the baby of the family.

She had gone through two years of psychotherapy at a local mental health clinic. This had included some forms of behavior modification. Although she felt a little more confident and was able to get out alone once in a while, she still felt in the grip of her agoraphobia, specifically her fear of having a panic attack in public.

With self-hypnosis, Betty first established some internal control. She practiced giving herself suggestions for relaxation. She began practicing in the most comfortable and safe room of the house for her—the bedroom.

In a few days, she was able to go into trance in the kitchen, her next most comfortable room. Practicing in the living room was a little difficult because that was a room unfamiliar people came into—her children's friends, sales people, and such.

After a week of daily practicing in the living room, she was able to relax and go into a trance more easily. Next she tried the backyard. That proved to be even more difficult.

Notice that, progressively, Betty was able to go to each part of her home and practice self-hypnosis. Her only goal, initially, was to relax completely and make some physical changes internally. This first stage of developing more comfort and confidence took about a month of daily practice.

Betty's next goal was to *imagine* walking to a neighbor's house. She visualized each movement, from opening her own front door to entering the house next door. Visiting her neighbor was an action which, in reality, she had mustered the courage to do only once before. Now, in her trance imagery, she rehearsed that trip and others.

She rehearsed in her mind for three weeks without leaving her home alone. She imagined a walk to the corner of the block. A drive to the park, and to the supermarket for a shopping trip. Betty learned the positive mental rehearsal of self-hypnosis and always finished her imagined outings with a "Thank you" to her unconscious and an acceptance and a trust of her whole self.

Those who have never experienced an extreme fear such as agoraphobia cannot appreciate the feeling of accomplishment that Betty felt when she finally made a trip on her own. It was nearly three months since she had begun her work with self-hypnosis. She got in her car, drove down to the shopping center, and returned after making a purchase.

With further practice and trance rehearsal, she was able to expand her travel outside the home. Within a year, with continued practice of these techniques, Betty was leading a relatively normal life again. Betty also used daily journal writing to help her become more aware of her feelings, both positive and negative. The process of getting her feelings out of her mind and body and onto the paper was also reinforced in her self-hypnosis sessions.

FEAR OF FLYING

Another fear that seems to be fairly common is that of flying in an airplane. In our highly mobile society, that can be a very inconvenient phobia.

Certainly, there are some very good reasons for not flying at specific times—during thunderstorms, in very snowy conditions, and in other hazardous situations. Normally, scheduled flights are cancelled under those conditions anyway.

Statistics bear out the fact that flying is actually safer than driving on the freeways. To completely avoid all commercial flight is to give in to an irrational fear. Unfortunately, it is a fear that prevents thousands of individuals from traveling for business, vacationing, and visiting with friends and relatives.

George, a 42-year-old businessman, was terrified of flying. Though he made other arrangements for travel whenever he could, he had to take the "white knuckle" flight occasionally. Those flights were invariably the long stretches, four, five, even six hours.

He had tried all sorts of therapies and remedies—tranquilizers, alcohol, sleeping pills, biofeedback, progressive relaxation, and every conceivable position and seat on the airplane. Nothing worked.

For George, relaxing was not hard. He had learned to do that quite well. His problem was how to get on the plane and not feel panic once they closed the door and started the engines.

He had already learned to gain control over various parts of his physical body and processes. So he began by learning self-hypnosis and developing posthypnotic cues for relaxing when he became panicked.

Clenching his fist and then relaxing it became a cue to bring all the tension into one part of his body and then release it. Rubbing the back of his neck with one hand was another cue to help him let go of panic and fear, along with any pain-in-the-neck worries. Certain warm colors and sounds were also developed as signals for George to take a deep breath and release the tension he might be feeling. These cues enabled him to gain the same degree of relaxation and stress relief he had while in a self-hypnotic trance any other time he chose.

Because he was doing so much travel between time zones, George used a method of time distortion to aid him in getting over his fear. He would imagine, *while in a trance*, the face and hands of a variety of clocks—old, big, small. By learning to advance or retard the movement of the minute and hour hands, he developed control over his perception of the passing of time. He was surprised by the changes he felt, but realized that when sleeping or daydreaming or just being absorbed in an activity, he experienced time as being just as distorted.

While his eyes were closed, George imagined that 30 minutes appeared to take actually 10 minutes to pass. He would see the hands of the clock move very slowly. By concentrating on the tiny movement of the clock hands and seeing them creep ever so slowly from one minute to the next, George developed the ability to compress several hours' time into seeming like only one. George's focus moved into non-time or free flight, similar to the view he would have from far away, like up in the sky or another planet. An hour on earth would look like a moment, or a day could be like an hour—a new perspective for him.

Rehearsing a trip

Next, George realized that the trip consisted of much more than just a plane flight. In fact, if flying were the only travel he did, he would not even get to the airport.

There was the car trip to the airport, perhaps a cab or subway ride to another part of the city, or trains, boats, and buses. In his business career, he had had to take many different forms of travel. Airplanes were only one of numerous vehicles he used.

He began rehearsing his mental journeys by imagining himself packing his suitcase. He would put in it all those things he would need. Packing his mental suitcase became another cue for him. He could pack his relaxation and comfort, which were symbolized by his toothbrush and two favorite shirts.

Next, George tried to identify what it was about flying that made him most uncomfortable. He worked on this with self-hypnosis for several sessions. It was not immediately apparent what the source of his anxiety was.

After several rehearsed trips, George realized that he was afraid of giving up control over the situation. When he flew, his "fate," it seemed, was not in his hands.

But he also knew that when he traveled on a train or a bus or a taxi, he was not in control. When he looked at flying in relation to those other forms of travel and to other times in his life when he was forced to give up some control, flying began to seem a low-risk situation. The stock market, interest rates, consumer trends, and many other business conditions and factors were also out of his control. Yet he survived, quite well, in spite of that fact.

After another week of rehearsing how he would feel relaxed and change his anxiety and tension into comfort and calm, George was ready for a real test flight.

He selected a short distance, only 100 miles and back, for his trip. He got on the plane, opened up a book—another cue he had given himself for relaxation—and closed his eyes for a moment to picture his mental clock moving slowly.

When the plane landed, he realized he had flown for nearly 20 minutes with virtually no tension or anxiety. His hands were relaxed and holding the book, and his knuckles were a healthy flesh color—not gripped in a fearful white. He used each success as another posthypnotic cue to practice more with self-hypnosis. With each small success, it became easier to move on to the next flight.

Of course, it took more trance rehearsals and self-hypnotic cues, but after several months, George was able to fly from coast to coast without beads of sweat on his forehead. In fact, he stated that flying for him was now just another way to travel.

IS IT IMPORTANT TO KNOW THE CAUSE OF A FEAR?

The need to understand the root cause of a fear is not very significant in desensitizing the reaction. The amount of insight gained is often not very helpful because most people are already conscious that their fear is not necessary. They do not have to be convinced that their fear of flying or of closed spaces is irrational or caused by some childhood trauma.

George, for example, may have wanted to find out why he didn't want to give up control. Eventually, he might do work on understanding the root cause of his fear. But the most important thing for him at the moment was undoing the fear symptom.

Most likely you have already over-analyzed your fear logically and rationally. You may feel your fear is stupid. To try to understand more about the need to put aside the fear is like trying to fill a lake that is already full. It merely spills over, making the banks around the lake muddy. Chances are that most people's lake of awareness about their fears is already full and the banks are already muddy.

Phobias can be quite debilitating and understanding their sources will not necessarily mean that the fears will suddenly go away. It is much more effective to work directly on overcoming the symptoms of the fear. Then, if you want to delve into the reason the fear began, do so.

However, if you feel that the source of your fear reaction is important to unraveling your symptoms, then do try to gain some insight into it. You can do this with self-hypnosis, too, using the self-exploring techniques from Chapter 16, or try using this next approach.

One person's need to know

Marsha suffered from stomach pains and severe anxiety much of her adult life. At age 42, she also had strong fears and anxieties of any "new" situation. It didn't matter if "new" was at work, with people, or places she would need to drive to. This fear blocked her potential and basically stunted her growth emotionally and mentally.

Her fears gripped her so that Marsha was often afraid to go to certain new places or to try new experiences. Her warmth as a person did not help her control the anxiety, but it did help her interpersonally with others.

Marsha used self-hypnosis to discover why she was so unhappy in some levels of her life, while quite happy in others. Specifically, she learned to relax first, then go into her fears and pains in her stomach, one step at a time. She estimated that there would be 10 layers or levels of fear and pain for her to discover. The number of levels was something she felt she would need. You may find that six or 16, or 18 are the best number of layers for your situation.

Recognize how this sets up an incremental goal. You are allowing yourself to achieve knowledge in as many steps as are needed by your unconscious mind. If you first decide 10 layers are right, you can always extend the number if you haven't yet succeeded in reaching your goal.

Marsha's self-hypnosis would be directed to some of her symptoms, such as the stomach distress, and her awareness would "go into" that area of her body experience and ask a fundamental question: "What am I feeling, what do I remember about this feeling? What can I do for you (stomach)?"

She spent about ten minutes each day and also kept a journal to express any residual feelings, observations, thoughts, or memories. Marsha found it helpful to review her journal prior to some of her self-hypnosis sessions to help her focus on her goal.

As she went through 10 layers of peeling away, she discovered old memories of abandonment from childhood, how her mother would leave her alone at times, how she felt uncertain whether her mother would return for her or not. She also remembered how angry she became at those times. The anger would turn her stomach and disrupt her appetite, but never get expressed openly.

In this case, Marsha briefly sought the help of a qualified therapist to help her resolve her anger and feelings of abandonment, even as she continued to use self-hypnosis to desensitize her present anxiety over new situations and events. Soon, she understood the roots of her anxious responses and had mastered the unwanted feelings by acknowledging them, accepting her own feelings and expressing them in her trance and in her journal.

DEALING WITH LESS SEVERE FEARS

Many individuals are upset or uneasy at the thought of going to a social gathering where there will be many people whom they do not know. This is not a phobia, just an unsettling fear of new people and situations.

Many of us don't like being put on the spot, having to make a speech, or in other ways dealing with unfamiliar situations. This fear is closely linked with a lack of self-confidence.

There is a way to use self-hypnosis to overcome these relatively mild fears. Begin by developing your self-hypnosis for relaxation and physical changes.

After you are comfortable with entering a trance, develop images of the settings and activities in which you feel strong and confident. You may think of your work or a hobby. Perhaps you are good at sewing, gardening, playing tennis or golf. It does not have to be something big or complicated—anything you do well is fine. You do not have to be exceptionally good at it, either, just good enough to enjoy doing it.

Suppose that you are a good cook. You can use that as a basis for changing your fear of meeting new people, or other fears for that matter.

While in self-hypnosis, imagine cooking certain favorite dishes that you've learned to prepare well. You might imagine how you go about preparing one of those specialties. Perhaps you can also imagine how you would compensate for a minor ingredient you're missing. Visualize the food, the colors. Imagine the smells, the flavors, the sounds of the preparation and cooking.

Then, picture yourself cooking a new recipe. Imagine how you feel about learning to cook something different. Imagine how good you feel after you finish it and your family tries it and you all enjoy the different tastes and textures. Remember the last time your cooked a delicious new treat that turned out better than you expected.

As you go through these images, give yourself cues that meeting new people is like trying new recipes or new ways of cooking a favorite meal.

Discovering new people, interesting people, some more interesting than you have ever met before, can be just like trying a new recipe that is tastier than a previous one. You can give yourself positive suggestions that a party or a reception you're going to will be like cooking a new dish that can be exciting and delicious to try.

Load your suggestions with posthypnotic cues that will signal a response of relaxation and calm. Perhaps opening a door is like opening the oven door; all the ingredients are together and you can now sit back and comfortably enjoy the party.

You might give yourself the cue that music you hear will remind you of the blend of sounds you know can be soothing and relaxing. Maybe the taste of food or hors d'oeuvres at the party can remind you of how much fun and enjoyment you can have in trying out a new experience, just like a new taste treat.

Find several cues that will convey the same response. Try to develop many ways which can remind you of how relaxed and how comfortable you can be. Make as many actions and situations that you can think of into positive cues for you to respond to.

Rehearse these in your self-hypnosis for several days *before* the event, if you can. The responses you have programmed may not all occur the first time you try this technique. It is a building sort of experience.

Each time you go through this process you will be eroding a bit more of the fear you have developed over the years. Remember how long you have had this behavior; it will take some time to undo it. But it is possible to change your perceptions and your reactions to situations that once were intimidating to you. Disentangling is a result of going to the knots and untying, breathing through, and understanding.

Before you even realize it, others you know will notice how much more comfortable and relaxed you can be. Keep practicing the techniques for several weeks or months. You will begin to recognize small changes at first. These will become bigger and bigger until you will find you no longer need to work on this goal.

REFERENCES

Bakal, P.A. Hypnotherapy for flight phobia. *American Journal of Clinical Hypnosis*, Vol. 23, 1981.

Cohen, S.B. Phobia of bovine sounds. *American Journal of Clinical Hypnosis*, Vol. 23, 1981.

Deiker, T.E. & Pollock, D.H. Integration of hypnotic and systematic desensitization techniques in the treatment of phobias. *American Journal of Clinical Hypnosis*, Vol. 17, 1975.

Ellis, A. Anxiety about anxiety: The use of hypnosis with Rational-Emotive Therapy. In *Case Studies in Hypnotherapy*. New York: Guilford Press, 1986.

Gray, J.A. *The Psychology of Fear*. New York: McGraw-Hill, 1971.

Gustavson, J.L. & Wright, D.G. Hypnotherapy for a phobia of slugs. *American Journal of Clinical Hypnosis*, Vol. 23, 1981.

Hartland, J. *Medical and Dental Hypnosis*. Baltimore: Williams & Wilkins Company, 1971.

Kroger, W.S. *Clinical and Experimental Hypnosis*, Philadelphia: J.B. Lippincott Company, 1977.

Landers, S. Phobias: A stepchild garners new respect. *APA Monitor*, (Mar), 1990.

Seagrave, A. & Covington, F. *Free From Fears*. New York: Simon and Schuster, 1987.

Spiegel, D., Frischholz, E.J., Maruffi, B. & Spiegel, H. Hypnotic responsivity and the treatment of a flying phobia. *American Journal of Clinical Hypnosis*, Vol. 23, 1981.

Waxman, D. & Hartland, J. *Medical and Dental Hypnosis*, 3rd ed. London: Bailliere Tindall, 1989.

Weitzenhoffer, A.M. Explorations in hypnotic time distortions. *Journal of Nervous and Mental Disease*, Vol. 138, 1964.

Wright, M.E. *Clinical Practice of Hypnotherapy*. New York: Guilford, 1987.

Zilbergeld, B. & Lazarus, A.A. *Mind Power: Getting What You Want Through Mental Training*. Boston: Little, Brown and Co., 1987

14
How To Relax Your Jaw and Stop Teeth Grinding

Do you grind your teeth or clench your jaw in your sleep or even during daytime? The symptoms can be tenderness or soreness in the jaw muscles and pain can radiate up above and behind the jaw, so it may seem to be an earache or headache. The pain can be so severe that chewing your food may be nearly impossible.

There may be an underlying organic or medical cause for the pain. Always have a physician or dentist diagnose any such pain or discomfort; remember that pain is first an alarm to get your attention. Such conditions are often called TMJ (temporomandibular joint) pain or bruxism. Bruxism is muscular clenching of your jaw or teeth grinding.

Chronic teeth grinding, either during sleep or even while awake, can actually wear away the enamel and create dental problems. Chronic bruxing, or teeth clenching, either during sleep or daytime, can cause muscle fatigue and soreness in the masseter, the major jaw muscle on each side of the face. In some cases, such clenching can eventually cause problems with the TMJ "ball and socket" which creates the hinge for your jaw.

Also, some people are sensitive to the mercury amalgams used in some tooth fillings. Neuropsychiatrist and behavioral neurologist, Sydney Walker (1987), an expert in this field warns, "Severe teeth grinding can cause mercury toxicity. A number of people have a sensitivity to even minute amounts of mercury. Symptoms from mercury sensitivity are related to the central nervous system and can include, muscle aches, pains, chronic fatigue and can be resolved by stopping the source of mercury ingestion, teeth grinding, if that's the cause."

If you hear a clicking or popping sound when you chew or bite down, consult a dentist and ensure that you receive proper treatment. In some cases splints or bite plates may be helpful to prevent further damage or to maintain proper jaw alignment. Your doctor or dentist may tell you that stress, tension, or anxiety are causing you to grind or clench. You may not realize that tension and stress have built up.

Possibly, you are able to manage the tension during your waking hours. At night, when your conscious controls over your jaw muscles are not operating, the stress can tighten those areas. After a few days or nights, the muscles begin to ache from the continued tightening.

Physicians may prescribe tranquilizers or muscle relaxants. These can have a short-term benefit, but if your stress or anxiety levels are not managed, the problem will often recur. Valium, Xanax and other tranquilizers, taken for too long, can become habit-forming. Other side effects can develop from their over-use and dependence. A more natural way to manage your stress is with self-hypnosis.

Using self-hypnosis for stress management can effectively defuse the symptoms of stress. Also, you can develop specific posthypnotic cues that will prevent jaw clenching or grinding at night.

WILL SELF-HYPNOSIS ELIMINATE THE SOURCE OF THE STRESS?

Most stress is created by the way you interpret an event or situation rather than by the situation itself. As is discussed more fully in Chapter 12, *how* you think about or perceive a situation is the greatest factor in how stressful it will be for you.

Therefore, you can use self-hypnosis to change how you think about and perceive a situation. In this way, you can use self-hypnosis to find and deal with the source of your stress. If you know, for instance, that pressure arises from your job, you can use the techniques in Chapter 12 on managing stress to change your way of reacting to those stressful situations.

Perhaps there are financial worries that are generating tension and pressure in you. With posthypnotic suggestions, you can change your perceptions of events and situations that might cause the stress. You cannot make your money problems disappear overnight, but you can use self-hypnosis to keep yourself from dwelling on those concerns. A good deal of the time, things that people worry about never happen. Unnecessary or excessive worry will not solve any problems—it only creates new ones.

HYPNOTIC STRATEGIES FOR JAW PAIN

Harold Golan (1975, 1989), a noted clinician in Boston, has written several valuable contributions on the subject of hypnosis and teeth grinding and clenching. One of his strategies to deal with the immediate pain is to use the "glove anesthesia" technique. With this approach you create numbness or anesthesia in one hand (see Chapter 18 on pain control), hence the term glove. You might imagine placing your hand in a bucket of ice water, for example, and imagine feeling your hand become cool, cold, and numb. Next you transfer this numbness in your hand to the soreness in your jaw, ears, neck, or anywhere the pain is felt.

Gradually, imagine the coldness or numbness or other feelings flowing into your cheek and muscles in your mouth, cooling the pain, soothing your jaw.

SELF-HYPNOSIS TO PREVENT CLENCHING OR GRINDING

Additionally, to deal with the clenching or grinding, Golan has his patients, while in a hypnotic trance, repeat to themselves suggestions like: *"Nothing is important enough in life for me to eat myself up, I can be awakened momentarily at night by the abnormal touching of my teeth or clenching of my jaw, I can smile, realize that my unconscious mind is protecting me, then I can turn over and go right back to sleep, letting go of the tension in my mouth as I become more aware of it."*

You will want to program yourself to relax at bedtime, just as you can relax while in trance. Morning practice with self-hypnosis is best to give yourself suggestions for effects to take place at night. Morning practice gives your unconscious mind all day to absorb your messages.

Another suggestion can be the following: *"When I close my eyes at night to sleep, I may notice that with a couple of deep, satisfying breaths, my body can relax. That relaxation can be just as deep, just as comfortable as now, while I'm in self-hypnosis. I may also find that my mouth and jaw muscles can be particularly relaxed. I can see, right now, how relaxed and loose those muscles can be.*

"I can move my mouth around to loosen it, much as I can move a stiff arm around to relax and loosen the muscles there. As I ease into a comfortable position with my body, I know that my jaw can also relax and ease into a comfortable position."

You are setting the nighttime stage for relief of the stress symptoms you have been experiencing.

Milton Erickson used hypnosis with his patients who suffered from bruxism and he also used the technique of having the patient awaken when clenching or grinding began. He transferred clenching from the patient's mouth to a hand. Here is a self-hypnosis suggestion based on Erickson's approach:

"It is a very nice thing to have a good grip of the hand, and some people are so lazy about exercising. I may find myself getting a grip on myself at night . . . or anytime my unconscious becomes aware of my teeth touching with nothing to chew on. I can get a better grip at those times by clenching my fist like I do around a racquet, a bat, a broom, a golf club, or anything I can grasp. It will help my fingers and hand to open and close and gain strength in my hands."

DEVELOPING POSTHYPNOTIC CUES

One approach that can be very helpful is to become aware of your sleep environment and notice any recurring sounds that you can use as posthypnotic cues.

Find material from your own sleep setting to use. Here are some examples:

Perhaps you have an electric blanket that has a thermostat. All night long that device will make a tiny click as it regulates the warmth of your covers. That can be a cue for you to release and regulate your tension and muscular stress.

A ticking clock can provide an audio cue and so can the whir of an electric one. The sounds of traffic passing or other background noises can be used as ongoing signals to remind your unconscious mind to keep your jaw relaxed through the night.

You can unwind like a clock, or have the tension flow away from you like the traffic. Use your imagination to find your personal cues and develop post-hypnotic suggestions, for example:

"While I am asleep, I may hear the sounds of my refrigerator turning on and off through the night. Those sounds can be a signal to me, while I sleep. Just as the refrigerator has an electrical switch that allows current to pass or stop, my own unconscious mind is a switch that can turn on my awareness. In this way, throughout the night I can alternately be aware of the tension and turn it off when it builds up. Just as the refrigerator keeps a nigthtime guard over its contents, I can keep a guard over the relaxation and comfort of my mouth and jaw muscles."

Remember to keep your suggestions flexible. Allow for the possibility that some of your tension may dissipate immediately and some of it may take time. Notice that your suggestions are phrased positively; try to prevent "Nos" and "Nots" from slipping into your suggestion language.

Your suggestions should be as *detailed* as you can make them. Use your own expressions to describe how relaxed, how loose your jaw can feel. Also, use your imagery to visualize the symbols of relaxation and the cues you suggest to yourself.

Be persistent. You may not feel a change the first night or the second, but soon you will. Some people notice relief immediately, others only after a week or more.

Be patient with yourself. Set reasonable goals. Once you begin feeling some relief, add to and continue with your suggestions. Make the cues a lasting influence on your sleep and on muscle tension in your jaw. The remedy you have developed can be with you for the rest of your life.

REFERENCES

Bell, W.E. *Clinical Management of Temporomandibular Disorders.* Chicago: Year Book Medical Publishers, 1982.

Cherasia, M. & Parks, L. Suggestions for use of behavioral measures in treating bruxism. *Psychological Reports*, Vol. 58, 1986.

Clarke, J.H. & Reynolds, P.J. Suggestive hypnotherapy for nocturnal bruxism: A pilot study. *American Journal of Clinical Hypnosis*, Vol. 33, No. 4, April, 1991.

Erickson, M.H. Life reframing in hypnosis. In *Hypnotic Realities* (Eds. Rossi, E. & Ryan, M.), New York: Irvington Publishers, 1985.

Finklestein, S. Hypnosis and dentistry. In *Clinical Hypnosis: A Multidisciplinary Approach* (Eds. Wester & Smith). Philadelphia: J.B. Lippincott Company, 1977.

Golan, H.P. Temporomandibular joint disease treated with hypnosis. *American Journal of Clinical Hypnosis*, Vol. 31(4), 1989.

Golan, H.P. Further case reports from the Boston City Hospital. *American Journal of Clinical Hypnosis*, Vol. 18, 1975.

Kroger, W.S. *Clinical and Experimental Hypnosis*. Philadelphia: J.B. Lippincott Company, 1977.

Walker, S. The central nervous system effects of mercury, chromium, lead and bismuth. S. Walker (Chair), "Electrolytes and trace metals affecting brain dysfunction and behavior." Symposium by Southern California Neuropsychiatric Institute. Sept., 1987.

15

Your Power To Stop Smoking

It is an encouraging fact that fewer people in America are starting smoking and more smokers are quitting. The discouraging news is that more women than ever before are smoking and the serious health consequences associated with cigarettes are now befalling women in nearly the same ratios as men have been affected. The issue of passive smoke means that more people are impacted than previously recognized.

It has been found that most people quit smoking in stages or steps. For some people quitting is simply a matter of resolve, for others it takes many attempts and often outside help.

There are generally three types of serious smokers:

1. The first group acknowledges the hazards of smoking, yet continues *because* of the danger. These smokers mistake their disregard for the risks of smoking for bravado. They derive a distorted sense of excitement from smoking in spite of the admitted danger. They resist treatment. These people may pay lip service to quitting, but only in a casual way.
2. The second group has faced the facts of smoking, and because of their respect for their bodies and in the interests of their health, they stop poisoning themselves. This group often stops smoking on their own accord and without any outside treatment.
3. The third group is made up of smokers who want to quit, but need something besides harsh words from their doctors or other scare tactics. These smokers have a high motivation and recognize their need and desire to stop smoking. They are looking for a method to direct and convert their desire to quit into action.

This third group will benefit greatly from self-hypnosis. If you are in this last group, then you can stop smoking.

It is helpful for you to understand very clearly the degree of your smoking habit before you try to quit. The following brief questionnaire will be a starting point for you to end smoking. Answer each question openly and honestly and use a separate sheet of paper.

SMOKING QUESTIONNAIRE

1. When did you start smoking cigarettes?

2. At what age (approximately) did you first smoke?

3. How many cigarettes do you presently smoke per day?

4. What time of day do you smoke most heavily?

5. When do you smoke your first cigarette?

6. When do you enjoy a cigarette most?

7. How many times have you tried to stop in the past?

8. For how long were your other attempts successful?

9. Why did you resume smoking?

10. What are the three main reasons for your wanting to stop smoking?

11. What is the one main reason you are currently smoking?

12. Would you be unable to stop smoking right now for any reason?

13. On what date would you like to stop smoking?

14. Name other people who will appreciate or benefit from your nonsmoking.

15. List three fears you may have of continued smoking.

16. What fear might you have of quitting smoking?

USING THE QUESTIONNAIRE FOR DEVELOPING SUGGESTIONS

Review your answers to the questions. There are no right or wrong answers, of course. However, did you answer all the questions openly and honestly? Did you explore your fears of smoking and quitting smoking?

Your answers can provide the material from which you can personalize your suggestions to stop smoking.

For instance, the times you enjoy a cigarette most can be developed into a posthypnotic cue to help you practice your breathing or to take a walk and avoid smoking in those situations.

The date on which you wish to quit smoking can be given in your self-hypnosis suggestions as a target date. We have found that the best way to quit smoking with self-hypnosis is to set a date and time and quit completely on that date. Weaning oneself away can work for some people, but that is not the way this self-hypnosis method works best.

A common reason for smoking is to relax. Nicotine does seem to have a sedative effect at first. This is partially due to the carbon monoxide depleting oxygen in your system and causing lethargy, not true relaxation.

Suppose one of your reasons for smoking is to calm yourself from work. What is relaxing about smoking a cigarette with dozens of irritating chemicals that cause disease and cause you to cough? There are better, healthier ways to accomplish this.

Your conscious mind agrees. Now, you have to convince your unconsicous mind, your deeper self, perhaps the adolescent part of you.

It can be very helpful to recall that earliest memories of when you were deciding to smoke. Make that early decision conscious again and redecide. Maybe redecide what it is that makes an adult: Is cigarette smoking adult? Perhaps reconsider the consequences of your smoking as a possible rebellion against the wishes of parents or others who might have been smokers themselves, or are there better ways to rebel? If you talk to yourself in self-hypnosis you will not notice the availability of new ideas and perspectives that turn you into your own teacher.

HEALTH CONSEQUENCES OF SMOKING

When you answered question 10 about the main reasons for wanting to stop smoking, did you list any health reasons? Of course, cancer is a one big risk we hear a great deal about. Emphysema and other breathing disorders are also common results of long-term smoking.

Are you also aware of the circulatory problems, heart disease, sudden cardiac arrest, and other consequences of smoking? There are compounds in the chemicals inhaled from burning cigarettes that enter the blood and accelerate the formation of arterial deposits associated with hardening of the arteries. The chemical nicotine acts as a stimulant on the heart muscle while carbon monoxide deprives that muscle of needed oxygen.

When you realize that chemicals such as benzene, sulfurs, nitrites, ammonia, hydrogen cyanide, vinyl chloride, formaldehyde, cadmium, nitrosamines, volatile alcohols, and urethane, among dozens of other hazardous compounds, are taken into your lungs and then into your blood system, you can see that smoking is a systemic process: that is, smoking can affect virtually every system in your body.

So, it is not just your respiratory system that is affected, it is your digestive system (ulcers, and gastrointestinal problems are frequently associated with smoking). Your circulatory system (arteries, heart, circulation itself) is also affected and smokers often have cold hands and feet for this reason.

While this chapter is not intended to provide a comprehensive listing of the negative effects of smoking, you can get detailed information from the American Lung Association or the American Cancer Association in your area. There are many health factors that are affected by smoking. That's the bad news.

The good news is that most negative health consequences of smoking stop and many problems reverse themselves when you stop smoking. It has been found that even the lungs of smokers of several decades duration begin to rejuvenate themselves upon stopping. After between five and seven years of no smoking, a former smoker's lungs can return to a level of healthiness appropriate for one's age at the time.

What this means is that it is never too late to stop smoking. And, certainly, if you are smoking, there is no better time than the present to quit.

THE SELF-HYPNOSIS METHOD FOR STOPPING SMOKING

First, you can recognize that most people began smoking before the age of 20. The studies done by the Surgeon General's office indicate that over 90 percent of smokers began prior to age 20 and 60 percent began prior to age 16. Clearly this is an adolescent onset habit.

This can be useful information to you. Think about the circumstances under which you began. Was there peer pressure? Did you believe that smoking made you appear more mature, more adult? Did your parent or parents (perhaps smokers themselves) tell you not to smoke?

Adolescence is a time of decision-making based on limited information and you may want to use self-hypnosis to remember and review your original decision to smoke. Given what you know now, would you have made a different decision then? Perhaps you can redecide that early decision now.

Making conscious the decision to smoke or not allows you to more easily redecide and enlist the cooperation of your unconscious mind through self-hypnosis. You may wish to use the committee meeting strategy in Chapter 21 for discovering the parts of you that may want to smoke. Know those parts of you and give them a voice. This will release the pressure in your unconscious.

Second, list or at least consider what health concerns you may have about smoking. Do you just cough a little? Has your physician recommended you quit smoking for health reasons? Are you easily tired, with less physical stamina than you remember? The negative effects of smoking are cumulative and subtle and you may not even be aware of all of them. Dulled taste, dental and gum problems, even stomach upsets are caused or made worse by smoking, yet seldom do smokers associate these comparatively minor problems with their smoking habit. Acknowledge the feelings, all of them, and write then down. Be honest with your whole self.

Third, focus on your own reasons for stopping. You may have quit or tried to quit many times in the past. That's perfectly normal. Most people quit in stages, as we stated earlier, so your earlier successes or partial successes, or even attempts can help prepare you for stopping smoking now. Be as simple in stating your reasons as you like, yet be specific and clear.

Structuring self-hypnosis suggestions

Try to structure your suggestions to be positive. Use as few negative words such as "No," "Not," or "Never" as you can.

Use direct negative suggestions, such as, "I will not smoke," only if you feel you will respond well to them. Likewise, suggestions of aversion are seldom effective. Suggestions such as, "The taste of cigarettes will be like sewer water," can be used if you think you will find them effective. Try them and learn what works best.

Recent studies have found less success with negative and aversion suggestions. More success comes from *positive* suggestions that incorporate your reasons for stopping and your fears of continuing smoking. Taking care of yourself is the priority.

There are a number of suggestion areas you can develop. Use material from your own life to create these suggestions. Also develop posthypnotic cues to reinforce them outside of your trance. The areas to focus on are:

1. *Relax without a cigarette.* You can justify a short break at work, at play, or any time and substitute deep breathing, closed-eyes imagery, rubbing your neck, stretching, or any other cues for relaxation.

2. *Communication and social situations are better without smoking.* Cigarettes can interfere with listening and sharing. Others can be distracted by your smoking. Use your imagery to see yourself being listened to intently, without a cigarette.

3. *Keep your hands and mouth busy* with other activities instead of smoking. Chewing gum, chewable vitamin C, sugarless candy, mints, throat lozenges, celery or carrot sticks, even toothpicks are preferable to smoking. Doodling, crossword puzzles, fist clenching, and some forms of handicrafts are better ways to occupy your hands. These can also be used as cues to reinforce your nonsmoking behavior.

4. *Exercise whenever possible.* After a meal, on a break, or during leisure time, take a short walk. Any type of exercise is healthy and is certainly more beneficial than smoking. You can develop suggestions that reinforce any activity. Smoking makes exercise more difficult; conversely, exercise can make smoking less necessary. Again, exercise can be used as a cue to reinforce your nonsmoking.

5. *Tobacco smell is repugnant.* It clings to clothes, furniture, ashtrays, and other people. Use the smell of other people smoking to remind you of the unpleasantness of smelly clothing, furniture, and carpeting and of the fire hazard of cigarettes. Your *sense of smell* can be a powerful help in creating posthypnotic cues.

6. *Health and longer life* are two important products of nonsmoking. Here is an opportunity to use your imagery. Visualize a hospital setting some-

time in the future with you lying in bed. Your doctor tells you there isn't much he can do for you now. You should have taken his advice years ago and quit smoking. Other visualizations can reinforce your image of yourself as a nonsmoker enjoying physical activities in your old age and sharing a hearty laugh with your doctor (including the inside of you).

Rituals

Smoking is a habit that you may have repeated 10, 20, or more times each day for many years. The process of smoking has become a ritual. You must first become aware of a ritual before you can change it. At your next cigarette, notice your own ritual: how you think about it, how you reach for a cigarette, withdraw it from a pack, how you light it, how you draw the first breath of smoke, how you return the pack to its place and the lighter or matches, too. Notice each individual step of the ritual of smoking.

For most people it takes between 15 and 25 seconds to get through this initial ritual of lighting a cigarette. The process of actually smoking the cigarette can vary from one to five minutes or more.

For a large number of smokers, a cigarette represents a ritualized form of mental or physical break from routine. So you have ritualized this momentary break almost every time you light up. Your unconscious mind has become accustomed to this brief diversion, this momentary relief or break from routine.

It is very important that you not take this moment of relief or break away without a replacement such as breathing deeply, walking, or other healthy break.

NLP uses the term "pattern interrupt" to describe the breaking up of your ritual in order to change your habit. For example, after the urge to smoke but before you would light up . . . take two deep breaths and say, "No thank you, I'm already okay." You interrupt the old pattern.

Just a breath away

It is very interesting that you can replace the process of smoking a cigarette with an experience that is so similar to smoking that your unconscious mind will feel contented. That process is taking in a deep, comfortable breath, holding it for few seconds, then slowly releasing the exhaled breath through your mouth. Try it right now.

You will immediately notice that the breathing experience is very much like taking a first, long drag off a cigarette—without the smoke. In fact, that may be a very satisfying and reinforcing component of the process. Taking in a deep and satisfying breath of air is a very natural process that we all do at certain times instinctively. Even babies sigh.

Here is the suggestion strategy:

"Whenever I feel stressed or tense, or even if I were to have a craving for a cigarette, what will really relax me and satisfy me is a deep and comfortable breath of fresh air. Even now as I think these words . . . I can breathe in. . . . . slowly. . . . and hold my breath for a few seconds. . . . . . then as I exhale I can let go of tension, let go of cravings, let go of old patterns as I initiate new ones."

It is this breathing that becomes a posthypnotic cue to relax and let go of a craving, or stress, or concern. Reinforce this suggestion repeatedly in your daily self-hypnosis sessions. It is best if you plan two or three brief daily self-hypnosis trance sessions as you become a former smoker, an ex-smoker, now a nonsmoker. The trance sessions can be very brief, three to six minutes.

Repeat a version of your breathing suggestion and then imagine the next part of your new ritual. Select some replacement item for your mouth. Chewing gum works very well for many people; mints and candy (sugarless if you are counting calories) or celery stalks can work well also as an oral replacement for the cigarette. Remember, we want to replace something if we are taking something away. That way, the unconscious mind is not seeking to fill a void created by removing habitual patterns of behaviors.

Replacement rituals

As you breathe deeply and give yourself the suggestions that you can enjoy such a deep breath, you also can begin imagining how you will slowly draw out a stick of gum or reach for a carrot stick (or whatever you have selected).

We have found that individuals have an easier time with this replacement ritual when they envision how many steps are involved in cigarette smoking and then find a replacement that is as similar as possible. For example, it might be better if you were to select a more complicated packaging for your replacement item.

Imagine a large package of gum, with individually wrapped pieces. You pull out the package from your pocket or purse . . . you draw out a single piece, you unwrap it . . . you place the gum into your mouth . . . you may fold or crumple the wrapper . . . you will then put back the large package to its place in your pocket, purse, or drawer.

Individually wrapped candies work better than ones you easily tap out of a container. Mints or throat lozenges that are wrapped and stored in tin containers work well. Carrots or celery stalks, sliced and chopped to about the size of a cigarette and stored in plastic baggies, may work well for you. Even flavored toothpicks, individually wrapped and carried in some small container, can be a creative item. You may wish to create your own replacement item or items for different circumstances.

This part of your suggestion could be something like this: *"As I breathe deeply and comfortably, I can imagine how I will withdraw my package of gum (or other replacement item) . . . unwrap it, put it into my mouth and savor the flavor . . . in fact, I can almost taste how good it will feel as I slowly replace the package . . . slowly fold the wrapper in my own way. Taking several deep and satisfying breaths and chewing slowly and knowing my hands and mouth and fingers have all participated in helping me remain an ex-smoker, a non-smoker, for health . . . for life."*

You might want to include burning your cigarettes in a fire to ritualize an end and a new beginning. Then review it in your self-hypnosis. Onno van der Hart (1983) in his classic book on rituals in psychotherapy quotes Fritz Perls, the brilliant teacher of Gestalt therapy, who said that if there were no rituals at all at an important occasion—no toast, no handshake, no ceremony of any kind—the event would seem meaningless and flat.

Other rituals

Another ritual that many smokers have developed is a cigarette after a meal. Here again, it is best to have a replacement ritual for a while to help transition from old to new habits.

A good replacement ritual for the mealtime smoke is to get up from the table and go wash your hands whenever possible at the end of every meal you should be able to wash your hands most places. Some people use brushing their teeth.

The act of excusing yourself from the table to go to the washroom interrupts the old ritual of smoking and establishes a new one in its place. Here is the suggestion strategy which you can personalize with your own circumstances (substitute teeth brushing, hair combing, or other activity, if you wish):

"Whenever I conclude a meal, I know that I can remind myself of my decision to remain an ex-smoker, a former smoker, with a specific cue. I can excuse myself from the table . . . or drape my napkin across my place to inform myself that I am finished, or I can simply push my plate aside . . . get up and go to the bathroom and wash my hands. As I wash my hands, or brush my teeth . . . and I can imagine myself doing that right now, I know that I am also washing away an old habit . . . washing away the unhealthiness, and instilling a new habit . . . instilling a new and healthy decision to remain a nonsmoker. I can imagine now how I will look at myself in the mirror and congratulate myself on my continuing decision to remain an ex-smoker, for health, for life, for good."

Then, when the appropriate time comes, consciously get up from the table and go and wash your hands. Each time you fulfill this ritual, it will become a stronger and more effective posthypnotic cue. Now recognize that you are doing this activity only at the reasonable and appropriate time of meal conclusion. You will not be washing your hands or brushing your teeth at other times, nor excessively. This is a very natural and reasonable replacement for an after-meal event.

When you look at yourself in the mirror, when you actually complete the process, you can smile at yourself and acknowledge that you have reaffirmed your positive decision again at that moment. Feel the gratification that comes with sticking with a good choice.

Another suggestion you might give yourself is: *"As I visualize myself finishing a satisfying meal, I know that the healthfulness and vitality of that meal will be enhanced if I get up and take a short brisk walk. Habits such as smoking after a meal can lead to cancer, chest pains, and a shorter life span. Taking a walk after a meal is healthy and can lead to a longer life and better breathing. I am starting and continuing . . . now and later."*

Reinforcing your reasons for stopping smoking

Perhaps a reason you gave for quitting smoking was to set a better example for your children. Or to not cloud your children's lungs with your smoke in the house, car, or other places where you are together with them.

Your suggestions could be: *"Just as I explain to my children about issues such as honesty, fairness, and personal safety, I know that my example in these matters is the best teacher. I can best teach my children respect for their bodies and concern for their own health by quitting smoking. My example of letting go of cigarettes will be the most sincere form of teaching and will benefit them also by keeping their air clean and free of smoke."*

After putting yourself in a trance, you might also emphasize these points, which are emphasized by Spiegel (1970, 1978), in your suggestions to yourself:

1. *For my body, smoking is a poison. I am made up of many components and the most important is my body. Smoking is a poison for my body.*
2. *I cannot live without my body. It is an irreplaceable physical spacesuit through which I experience life.*
3. *To the extent that I want to live and experience life, I owe my body respect and protection. I am my body's keeper. I understand the fragile, precious nature of it and see myself as my body's protector. Just as I acknowledge my commitment to respect and protect my body, I know that I have the power to have smoked my last cigarette.*

Another technique for developing cues is to place an ashtray with several cigarette butts on your night stand. Give yourself suggestions that when the smell becomes so obnoxious that you can no longer stand it, you can remove it from your bedroom. As you remove it, you will also be removing from yourself the desire to smoke.

Just as you may not be able to remove all the desire all at once, you will only move the ashtray into the hall—or somewhere just outside your bedroom door. In this way, you progressively remove the stinking ashtray. Along with the ashtray, you suggest that your smoking behaviors and your interest in and desire to smoke are leaving too.

Imagine you are a nonsmoker

Rehearse your role as a *nonsmoker.* Using imagery, see yourself in situations where you are not smoking—perhaps at a party where others are smoking, but you no longer need to light up; perhaps at work, when there is boredom or pressure and you might have smoked a cigarette before.

Another kind of image you might use is that of a road—the road you are traveling in life. Ahead of you is a fork in the road. To the right is a bright, clean, safe, straight path that goes off into the distance, farther than you can see.

The left branch is a dark, dirty, unsafe, dead-end path. Of course this represents the smoker's road. Which road you take is your choice!

Another way for you to give yourself positive suggestions for being a nonsmoker is positive reasoning. Rather than giving yourself negative reasons for not smoking, approach your goal from the healthy, positive aspect.

You can also suggest the fact that increased oxygen intake from deep breathing will neutralize the withdrawal symptoms of quitting cigarettes. Also, your increased oxygen supply will increase your stamina, sexual ability, and brain activity.

When you are developing posthypnotic cues, remember that you will need to *repeat* your suggestions in many successive trance sessions. You may notice an effect immediately or it may take several sessions before the suggestions begin to take effect.

Also, develop *several cues* for the same goal. If you are trying to reduce the desire for a cigarette, you might suggest that every time you smell cigarette smoke you will be reminded of the health damage to your lungs. Or you might suggest that, like the environment, you will need a fresh start . . . new rules . . . new skills to survive.

Self-hypnosis as an aid to quitting smoking is most effective when your motivation to stop is high. Self-hypnosis is not magical and there are no mystical cures involved. You must truly want to quit smoking and you must work regularly toward that goal.

Work in this case means practicing self-hypnosis often, perhaps two or three times per day in the beginning. Practice particularly in the morning, which is the best time to program and plan your day.

The self-hypnosis program

1. Complete the questionnaire, in writing. Study your habit. Become aware of why, where, and when you smoke.

2. Set realistic goals for yourself. Decide the date you want to be a nonsmoker and give yourself enough time to let your suggestions have an effect— perhaps a day, or three weeks, or a month.

3. Practice your self-hypnosis regularly at least twice a day in the beginning. Give yourself suggestions to relax and to exercise more. Also, develop suggestions to achieve and reinforce your short- and long-term goals for not smoking. Include many posthypnotic cues for specific actions or circumstances that will encourage smoking less or avoiding smoking.

4. Use result and process imagery to mentally rehearse your role as a nonsmoker. Do this sort of visualization in your self-hypnosis at least once a day. It is even better to take the time to use imagery in each of your trance sessions.

5. You may want to prepare a taped script for your suggestions and cues. Chapter 11 will help guide you in preparing a tape.

6. Review your work at intervals— at one week, two weeks, and a month. See if your suggestions are working or if they need to be changed and improved. Be patient, however; suggestions may need several weeks to show an effect.

7. Keep an accurate chart of your progress. Keep a copy of it out in plain sight, perhaps on your refrigerator door, bedroom mirror, or a message board.

	Monday	Tuesday	Wednesday	Thursday	Friday	Saturday	Sunday
Number of cigarettes							
Activity & feelings before smoking							
Activity & feelings after smoking							
Amount of time spent relaxing today							

YOUR STOP SMOKING CHART

You may stop smoking with your first trance session or you may begin giving yourself suggestions and continue to smoke for several weeks, then suddenly losing the taste or desire even before your target stop date has arrived. Accept your own pace.

Even when you have stopped smoking for several months, you must still reinforce your success and your posthypnotic cues.

You can't let up just because you have passed the first hurdle. If you have been smoking for more than a few years, the habit will be so ingrained that you will need to keep reinforcing your new behavior for six or eight months, perhaps longer. Taking care of your body and your whole self has delicious results for you.

REFERENCES

Field, P.B. Smoking and hypnosis: A systematic clinical approach. *International Journal of Clinical & Experimental Hypnosis*, Vol. 18, 1970.

Hall, J.A., & Crasilneck, H.B. Development of a hypnotic technique for treating chronic cigarette smoking. *International Journal of Clinical & Experimental Hypnosis*, Vol. 18, 1979.

Hartland, J. *Medical and Dental Hypnosis*, Baltimore: Williams & Wilkins Company, 1971.

Hyman, G.J. Stanley, R.O., Burrows, G.D., & Horne, D.J. Treatment effectiveness of hypnosis and behaviour therapy. In: smoking cessation: A methodological refinement. *Addictive Behaviors*, Vol. 11, 1986.

Kroger, W.S. *Clinical and Experimental Hypnosis*. Philadelphia: J.B. Lippincott Company, 1977.

Rabkin, S.W., Boyko, E., Shane, F., & Kaufert, J. A randomized trial comparing smoking cessation programs utilizing behavior modification, health education or hypnosis. *Addictive Behaviors*, Vol. 9, 1984.

Sanders, S. Mutual group hypnosis and smoking. *American Journal of Clinical Hypnosis*, (Oct), 1977.

Spiegel, H. Single-treatment method to stop smoking using ancillary self-hypnosis. *International Journal of Clinical & Experimental Hypnosis*, Vol. 18, 1970

Spiegel, H. & Spiegel, D. *Trance and Treatment*. New York: American Psychiatric Press, Inc., 1978.

Straatmeyer, A.J. Hypnotic aversive and positive imagery in the cessation of smoking and the maintenance of nonsmoking behavior. *Journal of Mental Imagery*, Vol. 8(2), 1985.

Tuomelehto, J., (et al.). Long-term effects of cessation of smoking on body weight, blood pressure and serum cholesterol in the middle-aged population with high blood pressure. *Addictive Behaviors*, Vol. 11, 1986.

van der Hart, O. *Rituals in Psychotherapy*. New York: Irvington Publishers, Inc., 1983

Von Dedenroth, T.E.A. The use of hypnosis in 1000 cases of tobaccomanics. *American Journal of Clinical Hypnosis*, Vol. 10 (Jan), 1968.

Watkins, H.H. Hypnosis and smoking: a five session approach. *International Journal of Clinical & Experimental Hypnosis*, Vol. 24, 1975.

16
Self-Exploration—Be Your Own Counselor

Looking inward to your past experiences, and interpreting your behavior, words, and feelings can give you new insights and a fuller understanding of yourself. This may be one of the most valuable goals you can pursue with self-hypnosis.

In the process of self-exploring, you may find the need to let go of certain emotions or feelings. This releasing of emotions is called *catharsis*. It may be an emotional tension that you were previously unaware of. Perhaps you may have been aware of a particular feeling, but not of its depth or magnitude.

Getting in touch with sadness, anger, frustration, or resentment is common when people begin to look carefully within themselves. Catharsis can be a very healthy, releasing experience. If you feel too strong a reaction from your feelings or if they are difficult for you to control, that may be a signal to you that you need a professional consultation. You can call your local chapter of the American Society of Clinical Hypnosis in Des Plaines, Illinois, or the American Psychological Association for a referral in your area.

There are dozens of possible ways to express and to let go of repressed and newly surfaced emotions. You may use whatever way is most natural and comfortable for you.

Sometimes there is some discomfort that is experienced in order to become more comfortable afterward. That can be part of the process. Often, a change will produce some temporary uneasiness or sorrow or regret in moving toward a new experience of calm.

Occasionally, people will find that crying is a way to release newly discovered, pent-up emotions. This might happen even while you are in a trance. This is fine. Crying is one way to release tensions and leave them behind you at the end of the trance session.

Let go of an emotion or feeling after allowing it to surface by visualizing the emotion as a piece of baggage placed on an outgoing airline flight, or a departing train, or a truck. Acknowledge or experience the feeling and then put it into the past.

It may be that the release happens later—outside of self-hypnosis. That is fine, too. You may even give yourself suggestions to that effect.

Here are several ways for self-exploration of past emotions, events, or traumas:

1. Perhaps you can set aside one night—when you can be alone—to deal with feelings you've been holding inside. Maybe pick a day when you can take a nice long walk and talk to yourself. Talk about the emotions, the feelings, and you might re-experience some of them right then.

2. You may wish to mentally create a special room in your imagery. Hammond (1990) uses what he calls the Master Control Room techniques with certain clients. You can use a variation of this concept for your self-hypnosis work by imagining a control room, a place in your mind or brain where you mentally regulate, sense, and select awareness , action, and feelings. Create such a room where you can mentally go to do your self-exploratory trance work.

3. You may give yourself suggestions—while still in trance—that when you take your walk, each step will be a cue for taking a positive step towards change. Allow your anger, resentment, disappointment, sadness, or whatever you are feeling to come to the surface. If your emotions involve the actions of someone else, you may imagine expressing directly to that person what you are feeling.

4. Perhaps talking with a friend as a sounding board is a way you have dealt with feelings in the past. Maybe you haven't used this method recently. Try using that technique again.

5. Writing in a journal is another way you can give some resolution to your emotional release.

6. A very effective method is to *write letters* to those people responsible for or involved in the emotion. Start the letter: Dear Mother, Dear Son, or whomever. In the letter you can express the feelings that need to be released. Tell your parent, child, sister, spouse, ex-lover, boss, or whomever exactly what you felt but couldn't express at the time. Perhaps read the letter again after a few days. After writing the letter, you may simply throw it away or burn it. In that act, you can also get rid of the guilt, anger, worry, or other emotion you kept from feeling before. Whether you mail the letter or not, a heavy load can be lifted. You may even want to try writing your letter while in self-hypnosis.

It is the *action* that comes from insights and self-exploring that creates a change in your life. Like taking a deep, satisfying breath, the change is toward more balance, toward centering yourself.

Accept yourself and your past, even if you are in pain, suffering, sad, or lonely. Be willing and ready to move on, to change from this point forward. Rather than denying your present reality, work on why you might want to deny it. Find understanding of the present.

That acceptance allows you to change. So long as you are fighting a part of yourself, you are inhibiting change. In fact, the very act of accepting yourself signifies the beginning of change.

Be as sensitive and understanding of the parts of you that you seek to change as you would be of a friend or family member who needed comforting and help. Give yourself that same gentleness and TLC (Tender Loving Care).

Start making small changes first. When you look at the past, you may realize that you did not develop your present behavior overnight. Give yourself reasonable goals and enough time to achieve them.

The time you are spending doing this work in self-hypnosis is like an investment. With each trance session, you are making deposits toward your future. The more you deposit, the greater the payoff. You can't lose when you're investing in yourself.

Using self-exploration techniques, you can develop the perspective to resolve difficulties, undo mental interference, and remove internal obstacles to self-change.

WHY DOES SELF-EXPLORATION WITH SELF-HYPNOSIS LEAD TO CHANGE?

As you have discovered from the earlier chapters, self-hypnosis opens the doorway to your unconscious mind. Your unconscious knows you best. Seeking answers and information from your "reference librarian," your inner self, is the most direct way to draw information from the vast storehouse of your experiences, memories, impressions, feelings, and thoughts.

The conscious mind is part of our rational and logical self. It is a great gift as well as a big limitation. Our conscious mind prevents us from being more imaginative and gaining many different views of a situation.

Your conscious mind tends to filter, influence, and prejudge material. That influence is the reason two people who view the same scene may report different "facts" about it. They "see" it through different colored glasses, so to speak.

The varying hues are caused by the conscious mind interpreting the information based on wants, needs, prejudices, past experiences—good and bad— and many other emotional factors.

As children, we were much more in touch with our unconscious mind, that part of us that is associated with intuition and feelings. It is a more imaginative part of ourselves. As adults we may be *more* unhappy because we spend more of our lives in conscious thought. When you access your unconscious you have a much clearer notion of what is happening inside you.

Buried in your unconscious mind is often a *more* accurate record of events, conversations, and memories than your conscious mind holds. They were stored with fewer influences superimposed by your biased, conscious mind.

Using self-hypnosis and self-exploration, you can better glimpse your inner self. You can, without judgments, examine your behavior in interactions, your feelings in specific situations. You can review more objectively how you reacted in situations at work, in family, and in social interchanges. Inner exploring while you are in a trance can afford you a perspective on yourself and your actions that is unclouded by the smokescreen of conscious thought.

You can also accept yourself as you are presently—right now. From that acceptance you can move on and make any desired changes in yourself.

THE METHOD

The following is an outline of the steps you can take in exploring your inner self with trance techniques.

Before entering self-hypnosis

First, set your goals—in writing—that you want to achieve. For example: "I want to better understand why I am short-tempered with my father," or, "What am I doing and feeling that is causing my spouse to accuse me of insensitivity to his/her feelings?" The goal should be specific and open to all possibilities.

Accept yourself where you are right now. Don't pretend with yourself. Be open to correcting an imbalance in your life or body—*you* want to change. This is important. This is a way to ensure that you are disengaging your conscious mind from the self-exploration process, that conscious part of you that resists change. Encouraging your own openness may lead you to find options that can help you break down resistances to change.

Establish a priority for this work you are doing on self-understanding and self-change. Make the work important to you. Take it seriously enough to plan a schedule for practicing—once a day, twice a day, or whatever you can devote. You decide how often and how long you will practice. Plan that time and be attentive to your desire to make changes in your life.

It is important to work with material gained from your self-hypnosis—you will need to incorporate it in your life. Simply gaining insight into your problems is only the first step. You must work with that knowledge in an *active* way in order to create a *change* in yourself.

Increasing your awareness will nearly always happen when using trance for contemplation. But awareness alone may sometimes be insufficient. You may need to give yourself active suggestions for positive changes.

Following are some steps and examples of how to proceed in using self-hypnosis to gain insight and implement change.

While you are in self-hypnosis

1. After you are relaxed and have developed a comfortable trance, go over the past few days, weeks, or back a year ago—whatever time frame is rel-

evant to your problem or goal. Examine your interactions with people at that time. How did you feel about your situation? How do you think others felt about your actions and words?

2. Answer yourself *honestly* about your feelings relating to your problem. Talk to yourself in this state—aloud or internally. Go over an entire day, if necessary, from getting up in the morning through your work, play, and social engagements, and even try to remember your sleep. Was it fitful, restless? What did you dream? How did you feel?

3. Trust yourself in trance to know what is important and what is not. Remember, you know yourself best. Let your unconscious be your guide. If your mind wanders, let it. Possibly, where your mind drifts to is also relevant to your feelings. Examine those mental side trips.

4. You can make remembering your trance thoughts easier if you associate them with a color or a number. For instance, pale yellow may remind you of something from long ago. You might associate blue with a sense of strength you once felt. Imagery and visualization of these reviews can help make them more vivid and easily remembered. You will also be able to understand them better the more detailed they are.

5. You might give yourself a posthypnotic cue to remember certain elements of your review and particular insights. You could use a simple cue such as: "*When I awaken from this trance, I may be able to close my eyes and again see the words and pictures I want to record. I may feel my back-bone become stronger and my posture improve. That can be a signal that I can be more confident in my ability to make positive changes. I can change just as a caterpillar can change into a butterfly.*"

6. Rehearse situations that relate to your problem. Imagine the many ways you might react differently. Visualize others' reactions to you. Try out the many positive and negative actions you could take. Work out the tensions and anxieties of failure. Improve the ways you can react in your best interests. Use your imagery to create symbols or metaphors of the improvements you wish to make. A muddy pond turning clear can symbolize the clearing of a specific problem in your life. A bird changing from dull feathers to brightly colored ones can represent your more outgoing nature that is emerging.

7. Most important, while you are still in a trance, imagine what you can do to change or improve yourself. Imagine how you can alter your reactions to situations based on insight gained. You might imagine opening a door to new ways of reacting and closing a door to old patterns you wish to leave behind.

8. Write down, after your trance, what you have learned from the session. Even memories, thoughts, or feelings seemingly unrelated to your goal might have new relevance.

9. In separate trance sessions, you can work on making changes based on the insights or observations you gathered from previous self-hypnosis

practice. You can have many choices; self-hypnosis helps you become aware of them.

10. It may take several sessions or days of practice before you actually gain some new perspective on your problem or goal. Self-exploration is not an automatic quick-fix. Awareness sometimes comes rapidly, but other times it develops only after continued effort.

11. You may find it best to slow the work on a goal if after a week or so you seem to be getting little change and understanding. Move on to a new problem or some other goal. Most of your goals will be related in some ways. Often a solution or insight will pop up days or weeks later in self-hypnosis or while you are involved in a related situation.

12. Don't try to force an answer if progress seems slow. Perhaps the scope of your goal or question is too broad. If you are not having success with gaining some awareness of your problem, go back and reevaluate your written goal. If you suspect it may be too big to solve in one package, rewrite it to be more specific.

A SAMPLE PROBLEM

Here is an example of how self-exploring might yield an insight and how that new awareness can be used for positive change.

Sue tried to understand why her boss keeps heaping more and more work on her for reasons that are not clear. Her goal—to better understand this situation in her work life and as a result, reduce stress.

After entering a comfortable, relaxed trance-state, Sue recreated those days immediately preceding the times when her supervisor asked her to do extra work or gave her unreasonable deadlines.

She mulled these events over for some time. She focused on some specific dialogue the two of them shared. There were some peculiar circumstances that surrounded those days. It took more than one trance session to accomplish, but with time, like watering a seedling in her garden, she nourished her own growth; like the seedling, she took some time to grow.

Sue discovered that one time she had said to her boss, jokingly, that her job was easy. She innocently commented that she was bored another time and made some other comments she did not mean to be taken seriously. That was her form of humor.

That observation led Sue to explore how she may have said things in other situations when she was joking, but her comments were taken seriously. Sometimes she was trying to be witty or to express some personal frustration and was misunderstood. Other times she had become tense or anxious and made a joke to cover up her nervousness.

Work on a change and rehearsals in self-hypnosis

Those were valuable insights for Sue. She was being taken more seriously in her remarks than she wished to be. Fine. Next, her insight needed to be converted into an action to bring about change.

While still in self-hypnosis, Sue suggested to herself that in order to prevent the problem in the future, she will stop and think for a moment before she jokes, particularly when she is nervous or tense. She will ask herself, "Is this something which, if misinterpreted, can lead to a negative feeling or reaction?"

When doing this for yourself, you may wish to write down or know in your mind, afterwards, that you want to do some rehearsal in your next self-hypnosis. It may be helpful to mentally picture situations where the problem might occur in the future.

By actually going through rehearsals in this way, you can anticipate situations and respond with more effective and positive behavior. This sort of run-through is very valuable in restructuring your actions and preparing for an actual situation to test out your new behavior.

In her trance scenes, Sue recreated the situation many times. She would deliberately mess up one time so that she could work out any anxieties about failure. She made the most absurd comments she could think of. She joked in the most ridiculous way possible. She imagined the worst.

She visualized for herself the response she would get. Sue allowed herself to feel the anxiety, tension, or humiliation. Then she let it go. She would laugh it out to loosen herself up. This was a practice session; she was striving to understand her feelings and then to release them and move on.

This way of rehearsing defuses the pressure, anxiety, and fear from future settings. It allows you to practice your new way of behaving in contrast with your old way. You can try out several variations while in self-hypnosis. Trust your unconscious to help you select the best new behaviors.

This sort of practice might take several sessions, perhaps many. The rehearsal process may lead to new insights, as well. This new awareness may lead to still other changes.

Remain open and accepting of yourself. Keep yourself open to change, also. Your self-hypnotic trance will help you to keep your ego and defense mechanisms from preventing you from accepting the insights. But you must be motivated to change your behavior. In fact, motivation itself is a goal you can enhance using these same techniques.

ARE THESE REAL CHANGES OR JUST ACTING?

The changes you will be making are not robot-like or artificial. They are genuine changes in your behavior. You are finding the best approaches to situations for *you*. Though new behaviors often feel uncomfortable at first, the positive benefits outweigh the initial temporary discomfort of change.

This same process goes on continually throughout our lives. For example, you adjust your behavior when working in a new place with different responsibilities. You are just speeding up the time it takes to make these adjustments. The conscious mind often resists making changes though you are capable of much more.

You may decide you want to learn different communication skills in a variety of settings. Dating, marriage, having children would all cause you to alter your behavior, either deliberately or unconsciously. These changes can be even more positive than you might expect.

The changes you are making through self-hypnosis are sincere changes in your personality. They are improvements you have elected to make based on the insights you have gained.

Just as you can improve your skills in other areas—athletics, academic, or social areas—you can make fundamental changes in your way of dealing with any situation. These are not superficial behaviors that are designed to fool someone. They are real changes you are making to help yourself.

Be proud of yourself for being able to make these changes. Feel good that you are capable of becoming the best person you possibly can be. You've always carried around this capacity to change. Self-hypnosis is a way for you to direct yourself, but it is *you* making the changes in your life.

GIVING YOURSELF SUGGESTIONS FOR CHANGE

When you have decided what alterations you would like to make, give yourself suggestions to reinforce those positive changes. Here is an example of the way you can make suggestions for turning your insights into action.

Begin by developing a comfortable and relaxed trance-state. The suggestions to follow, like all those in this book, are merely one set of possibilities. The best suggestions and symbols for change will be those you formulate based on your own experiences, preferences, and wording.

"As I am comfortable in self-hypnosis, I can count backward from five to one. As I reach the number one, I may also know that I can reach the most relaxed state I desire. I can be more relaxed, comfortable, and focused on my goals. I can count from 5 to 0, two or three times and go deeper each time."

This is a way to enhance your trance-state. With this sort of suggestion or any counting or deepening technique, you strengthen your trance. But even in a light level of self-hypnosis you can make significant changes and develop posthypnotic cues.

"I am the number one person working on my goals. I may repeat the number one, three times. Each time I say the number one, I may find I can become more and more clear about my goal."

Suggestions such as these prepare your unconscious mind to receive some new positive thoughts. Continuing the example of Sue, above:

"I may be able to see that several times in the past week, I have said something to someone that was interpreted differently than I intended. I recognize that those situations have resulted in some anxiety and worry for me."

This is restating the problem. You are putting the suggestions that will follow, into perspective with the problem and your goal. Further, you may want to review at this point the entire process which led you to the insight. The value of doing that is that it reinforces your motivation for change.

Motivation to change is a crucial element in achieving success with self-hypnosis. Do everything you can to raise your desire for positive changes. Once your motivation is at a high level, strive to keep it there.

"I can see that in those situations (describe them in detail), I was more nervous than I needed to be. I said some things trying to make humorous or joking comments to cover up my nervousness and put myself at ease. Some of the things I said may have been misunderstood or taken in the wrong way. They may have been less appropriate than they could have been.

"As I'm feeling more relaxed and more open, it is more clear to me now that I can be more relaxed in those situations. I can be as relaxed in those problem situations as I am right now.

"From this moment on, before I arrive at work or any situation that is important to me (be specific about the nature of the situation), I can practice self-hypnosis and I can rehearse the conditions I will be involved in. In these experiences, I can be far more effective, more at ease, more confident than before."

These suggestions set the stage for changes you wish to make. You have elevated your motivation. You have reinforced the notion that mental rehearsal will help create the desired changes. Now the rehearsal can enhance your abilities to deal with the situation more effectively.

"As I rehearse work settings in my mind, I can picture going there. Perhaps to relieve myself of any fears or worries I can imagine tripping over a cord, kicking the desk, stumbling for words, and saying silly things. I can even be amused by what I am doing. This will help me get rid of any tension and anxiety so I may work more freely on my positive changes. Now that I've imagined all the possible errors I might make, I can be more open to the positive possibilities."

Here again, you are visualizing absurd behavior so that you become desensitized to it. This is a good way to leave behind the tension and fear of making a mistake, desensitizing yourself to it.

"The way I want to change is to feel more calm, more relaxed—as I am right now—when I enter work (detail the setting of wherever you are experiencing the problem). I can enter the room, sit down, take several deep, satisfying breaths, and experience many of the cues I can give myself to feel more relaxed, more in control, and more effective."

Next come the more specific suggestions you develop for yourself, the posthypnotic cues you will use to prompt the response you desire. You might use colors, specific actions, objects, or anything that will remind your unconscious mind of the changes you seek. Chapter 5 on posthypnotic suggestions and cues will show you how to develop effective cues.

The following are some basic approaches that you can personalize by using your own examples.

THE PICTURE TECHNIQUE

Suppose you are are seeking more insight into your ability to relate to your spouse, lover, friends, family, or coworkers.

Imagine yourself in a photograph. Visualize a picture of yourself that someone has taken. There is a *positive* print of it and a *negative*. There are positive and negative aspects of all of us.

While you are in a relaxed state of self-hypnosis, examine for a few moments the negative part of yourself. See the ways that this negative part undermines you, cuts you off from others, or turns other people off. Observe the negative aspects of the ways you interact with others, the ways you communicate— socially, sexually, verbally, and nonverbally.

Imagine vividly your negative behaviors and perhaps recognize why you act negatively. Look closely at the part of you that keeps you down, keeps you weighted, and prevents you from doing all the things you might like to do. Examine the parts that feel inadequate, that lack confidence. Try to understand more about these aspects of yourself.

Self-exploration of your negative side while in trance should not be dwelled upon. Allowing yourself to indulge in an orgy of criticism or guilt defeats the purpose of the exercise, which is to understand yourself better. (*Set aside any self-criticism or guilt; you are only exploring and observing*).

Be conversational in your trance. Use flexible, open language that is your own. For instance, you may say something like: "*I can imagine myself when I get angry at my brother. The negative side of me wants to pick things up and throw them. I feel like yelling at the top of my lungs. I may say things that are really not true, because I want to hurt him. I can see myself become stubborn and refuse to see the truth, even when I may be wrong.*"

Further suggestions might be: "*As I look and I see negative aspects of myself, I can pay close attention to these elements. I can understand these actions better. I can even separate them out from the positive parts of me. I can imagine just the negative aspects of me getting into a relationship, at work, or experiencing sexuality.*"

As you develop this imagery further, you may sense where some of your negativity comes from. Perhaps from your parents. Maybe from childhood experiences. You can be more clear with yourself in this trance state.

This process may take several sessions. Take your time and develop the imagery of your negative side as clearly as you can *(without getting down on yourself)*. The process is somewhat like trying to rub oil off a window to see more clearly. At first the grease merely slides around. With more effort you can thin out the obscurity and see the causes for your negative, self-defeating actions.

Once you feel you have explored your negative side, you can imagine the positive photograph of you again. You might see the negative alongside it in stark contrast. Spend as much time or more exploring your positive side and the changes you can make, as you did exploring your negative side.

You can suggest to yourself: *"The dark parts of me can easily begin to* change *into* light *shades of* the *positive, just as a negative can be developed into a positive photograph. With my new understanding from this experience of self-exploration, I can turn most negative parts of myself more toward the positive. I can make positive changes in my life through awareness, thought, and acceptance."*

GROWTH ON THE FARM

After entering self-hypnosis, imagine yourself like a large acreage of farmland. Parts of the land have been separated for the best crops. But one section has many weeds and seems to be the least productive.

Your mental monologue could run along these lines: *"I recognize I want to get rid of some of these weeds. It may take some work to pull the weeds and clear this area. I certainly want as much of my farmland to be clear and productive as possible. So I'm going to find ways to get into that negative, weedy area of myself to understand these unproductive parts of me and clear them away.*

"As I understand each negative part of myself, it is like pulling out another weed. Some weeds are choking and stifling, like some of my negative actions can be. Other weeds, like other parts of me, can block the sun, the energy, and keep things from growing beneath. I can eliminate some of the more obscuring, more restricting vegetation. The more I understand about myself the more I can clear my field.

"I also understand the need for balance in my life. I know that I may want to pull out the weeds that I can reach—the negative parts that are the most interfering. But I also know that to have balance I can accept leaving some of the weeds. It is not necessary to remove all of them to have a more fruitful and bountiful harvest."

DRAWING YOURSELF IN COLORS

From a level of calm, relaxed trance, imagine getting a box of crayons, colored pens, or some paints. Pick out the colors you think best illustrate how you feel right now. Mentally draw yourself.

Perhaps part of you feels pink and another part blue. It doesn't matter what colors you choose, maybe different shades of green, yellow, red, or purple.

After you have drawn yourself in colors, go into those colors and see what shade is your favorite. Then explore which shade is your least favorite and those that represent the least helpful aspects of you.

Look closer at that shade that signifies the darker, more negative side of you. Perhaps you can see what is in you that is most closely related to that unpleasant color. Take some time to examine that part carefully. Turn it around and upside down in your imagery.

Maybe it is a darker shade of blue that is the negative part and a light, powder blue that represents the more positive, confident, creative side. Using your imagery, perhaps you can discover what it might take to make those darker shades become lighter. Ask yourself that question.

Maybe more light and better understanding will turn the dark areas lighter. Perhaps your picture needs more light—more exposure to certain people, certain places. So you may want to give yourself suggestions to go somewhere new or to meet new kinds of people.

Using the symbols of color to signify change, you can explore the negative and positive aspects of yourself to establish the palette and canvas for awareness and for suggestions for change.

THE HAPPIEST YOU

While in self-hypnosis, create an image of yourself as the happiest person you can be. Then ask yourself, "*How old am I as I see myself as this happiest me?*"

Are you five years old? Perhaps 20, 40 or 65 years old? Whatever age you are in your image, combine that image in your mind with the person you are right now. Create an ability to see yourself more clearly then and now. And if both ages are the same, develop a clearer image of who you are right now.

Go again to that age when you feel you are most happy. Ask that part of you—perhaps a younger you, maybe an older, wiser you—what is the best way to answer the question or achieve the goal you have for this self-exploration. Accept yourself as you are now, and look forward to positive changes through this work.

You know the old adage that two heads are better than one. Perhaps your own two heads, your conscious and unconscious, can work together toward achieving your goal.

IMPROVING SELF-ESTEEM

There are some people who want to improve or develop self-esteem. As Michael Yapko describes in his book *Trancework* (1990), discovering you are more capable and effective than you thought is one way of improving your self-concept of worth and value.

For example, while in trance explore where you seek approval—work, family, friends, social acquaintances. Look for how you have survived disapproval in the past. How do you deal with approval and praise? Do you discount it and say, "Yes, but . . ." or do you accept praise and compliments with a simple, "Thank you"?

In trance you can absorb the positive comments, take them in and feel their glow, fan those embers of self-approval. Right now, are you giving yourself credit for learning (at whatever level you have progressed so far) new skills? Remember that the work and reading you are doing *right now* is making you more capable and effective than you may have thought.

THREE SIDES OF THE COIN

This is a variation on the Happiest You Technique. Separate out three different parts of your personality: the parenting part, which supervises you and takes care of you; the student part, which wonders and questions and learns about life; and the wise self, which manages, compromises, and helps you balance and find resolutions. You might imagine them as three sides of a triangle, or perhaps as surfaces of a coin, with the outer rim being the third side. Be creative in the image you choose; imagine these three levels of yourself in any way that is easiest for you.

While you are in self-hypnosis, you are able to be more focused and directed. The time you are in trance is undistracted and allows you to pay close attention to the benefits from your unconscious mind. The benefits are in your ability to separate these different perspectives of yourself, to examine them, and to actively work on yourself.

The parent side of you might be telling you what you should do. You can explore that aspect of yourself, both the positive parts and the negative, limiting parts. Your parenting aspect is like your conscience and embodies patterns of behavior you have learned or developed.

Then you can turn to the student in you that wants to learn. That side of you may also have lots of needs and expectations. There may be uncertainty and weaknesses there. You may discover some childish, unpredictable, self-defeating behavior there. Examine that side of you closely, also.

Finally, you can *consult* with your wise self. That is the element in you that creates balance, that is the leader. From this perspective—after having looked at yourself from the other two vantage points—you can gain some insights about changing your total self.

Experiment with this technique. Perhaps set aside at least one trance session for each part of your triangle, coin, or other shape. Take notes immediately afterward to record your feelings, observations, and ideas for change. The process is like taking field trips to areas within you. Review your notes before each new exploration.

SELF-EXPLORATION FOR PHYSICAL PROBLEMS

Many physical problems such as skin conditions, ulcers, colitis, obesity, and high blood pressure often have a psychological basis. Part of the cause may be emotional—tension, stress, held-in emotions like anger or guilt can result in physical symptoms. You are looking for a way to change those causative factors that are manageable.

Recognize that some of your problem may be physical—bacteria, viruses, chemicals, or other irritations may cause skin problems. For any physical illness or imbalance, you should first consult with a physician and receive medical attention.

In addition to such medical treatment, you may wish to do some self-exploring to uncover possible psychological causes for a troublesome physical problem.

For example, your skin is an organ closely associated with your nervous system and is often one of the first areas of your body to become disturbed due to emotional factors. (See Chapter 19 for more about skin problems.)

We will use skin problems to illustrate how you can use self-hypnosis to explore for psychological causes of physical problems. However, the same methods can be applied to many other physical conditions as well.

You can begin—while in a relaxed, comfortable trance—by focusing on the area of your body that is affected. Feel that part a bit more than you are feeling the other areas of yourself. Pay attention to how it feels, how it has felt in the past. Imagine how much more comfortable it can be in the future.

Bring some change to that area. Imagine that it is tingling as if a medicating cream were being applied. Visualize it cooling, as if cold water or a cool breeze were flowing over that area.

Remind yourself and suggest to yourself: "*My skin is my body's largest organ, and may be the first to react to my emotions. When I am embarrassed, my face will blush. When I am angry, my skin will flush. If I become frightened, my skin will turn cool and damp.*"

Your skin is sensitive to temperature and to pressure. It protects your inner organs from injury.

Begin to imagine the parallels that your skin has to particular experiences in your life. If it is your feet that are primarily affected, explore the connections between your feet and the problems they have. For example, explore the reason you may have warts predominantly on your soles or why one foot should be more affected than the other.

Ask yourself a variety of questions, and answer them as best you can. Pay attention to your responses. Do this in a conversational way. Talk to yourself while in self-hypnosis as you might talk to a friend or counselor. Be your own counselor. Mentally, visually, and verbally explore the various aspects of your condition. What you are looking for are connections and associations, something to click in your unconscious mind to which you can make positive changes. Something that says, "Hey, I never noticed that before."

Suppose you have a skin problem with your hands. You might suggest: "*My hands are able to feel the cold of things that I touch. They can sense the heat of a fire. I am able to get a handle on many kinds of sensations with my hands. I can use my hands to grip things.*" Perhaps you might make a fist at this point, as if you were grasping something.

If it is another part of you that has a problem, perhaps you might get "ahead" of the problem or look "back" on something.

Perhaps notice the way you gesture or the way you scratch yourself when you're nervous or frustrated. The trance state is one of heightened awareness. Turn that awareness toward whatever area is affected.

While in self-hypnosis, you might visualize looking into a crystal-clear lake. Try to see your reflection in it. Perhaps a memory, a person, a place, or an event may come to mind. Possibly your own reflection of your parents, coworkers, or a spouse can provide some insight. Whatever springs to mind, review and remember any possible associations you have had regarding a memory and your skin problem.

Your unconscious mind is perfectly willing to communicate with your conscious self if you keep the lines open. Keeping those lines open is one benefit of self-hypnosis.

This is an evolving process. You may or may not find insights the first time or two that you practice this technique. You need to make a commitment for a routine of practice. It may take a week of daily practice before you have any insight into your problem.

Experiment. Look for even small hints of a new perspective, a small sliver of new understanding can sprout into a tree if you nurture it. In the process of your personal exploration and evolution, you can be as excited as you were as a child exploring a cloudy pond full of life. Be patient with your work. You are acting as your own therapist and therefore, you have decided how you would like to be treated. Now treat yourself that way.

You are using the techniques of self-hypnosis to get a better understanding of yourself. If you are feeling very depressed or even self-destructive, seek professional help. This chapter is not intended to substitute for professional help if needed.

THE POWER OF RITUALS

Onno van der Hart's book *Rituals in Psychotherapy* (1983) offers an excellent example of the use of rituals in self-exploration to release or resolve stuck points, such as grief. An example is a young woman who had developed anorexic patterns. She had eaten very little since the death of her younger brother in a tragic auto accident. The family was quiet about the loss of the son and did not encourage nor allow emotional expression of the grief for over two years.

Eventually, the father did decide it was time to dispose of the son's clothing. This brought the emotions up to the surface and it was discussed what to do with the clothing. The suggestion was to bury the clothes in the yard. They dug a hole in the garden area. The anorexic sister participated in the digging and in the placing of the clothing in the hole.

The family planted a tree on top of the clothing. Soon afterward, the sister began to eat again. She also began to talk about her brother again.

If there is some sort of loss you feel a desire to resolve, creating a ritual for yourself to release the thought, feeling, items, or other symbols of your grief can be very helpful.

CREATING YOUR OWN IMAGES AND SYMBOLS FOR SELF-EXPLORING

The process of looking honestly and openly inside yourself is best done using symbols and images that come from your own experiences. One way to find those symbols is to answer this question:

Where can I best see my own reflection?

Have you seen yourself in a mirror? What kind? Perhaps it was a round mirror, or a full length one on a door, or a bathroom mirror, or mirror tiles on a wall.

Maybe you remember a time when you saw yourself reflected in a window or in a clear, still lake. Maybe you remember your reflection in a dish or on a shiny metal surface. You've seen it in so many different places. What comes to mind for you? Was it at your home, in a store, at the beach, in your car?

Use whatever way of seeing yourself that you can remember or imagine clearly. Mentally, direct your self-hypnosis trance to take you to that place. Describe the place to yourself. Put yourself there and experience what it feels like to be there. From your reflection in that place, you can better define who you are, who you have been, and who *you* want to be.

It is personal relevance that makes self-hypnosis effective. You give yourself the power to make changes from within. The metaphors you use for your suggestions don't have to be perfect. Bend and mold them to your own uses. Your unconscious mind knows what your intent is. That part of you is only waiting for the opportunity to speak up and help you make positive changes.

Many other chapters in this book refer you back to this chapter. With the skills you've learned here, you can better understand the psychological conflicts and anxieties that may be behind such problems as asthma, poor sleep, self-doubts, fears, or dilemmas. While in self-hypnosis, you can be more open, understanding, and objective with yourself.

SUMMARY

1. Begin by writing your problem or goal for inner exploring with self-hypnosis, as specifically as you can.
2. Do some reviewing of the circumstances and situations surrounding your problem or goal. Use the trance state to be open to your present situation and to be open to changing it. Make a commitment to working on the changes you seek.
3. While in self-hypnosis, rehearse the settings and situations that involve your problem or goal. Use imagery and visualization to mentally rehearse past and future situations. Imagine both positive and negative events. Desensitize yourself to possible failures or embarrassments. Accept yourself as you are right now. Begin your work from this point onward.
4. Write down, during or after your self-hypnosis, any feelings, thoughts, insights, or suggestion ideas you have observed or developed during your trance.
5. Give yourself plenty of posthypnotic suggestions and cues that will prompt the changes you desire. Develop the cues that will reinforce your changes and your motivation for achieving your goal.

REFERENCES

Crasilneck, H.B., & Hall, J. A. *Clinical Hypnosis: Principles and Applications.* New York: Grune & Stratton, Inc., 1985.

Hammond, D.C. *Handbook of Hypnotic Suggestions and Metaphors.* New York: W. W. Norton and American Society of Clinical Hypnosis, 1990.

Hartland, J. *Medical and Dental Hypnosis.* Baltimore: Williams & Wilkins Company, 1971.

Jobsis-Murray, J. Hypnosis with severely disturbed patients. In *Clinical Hypnosis: A Multidisciplinary Approach* (Eds. Wester & Smith). Philadelphia, J.B. Lippincott Company, 1984).

Kroger, W.S. *Clinical and Experimental Hypnosis.* Philadelphia: J.B. Lippincott Company, 1977.

Van der Hart, O. *Rituals in Psychotherapy.* New York: Irvington Publishers, 1983.

Yapko, M.D. *Trancework: An Introduction to the Practice of Clinical Hypnosis,* 2nd ed. New York: Brunner/Mazel, Inc., 1990.

17

Relief for Allergies and Asthma

It is likely that you either have an allergy or asthma condition or know someone who does. There are more than 35 million allergy sufferers in America.

Within this large group of people is a wide range of allergic responses and degrees of suffering. Allergic reactions can vary from a runny nose to a breakout of hives. For asthma sufferers, symptoms include breathing difficulty and chest tightness, which can be scary and, in some cases, life-threatening.

Allergy and asthma sufferers can be sensitive to anything from animals to zinnias. And because there is so much diversity among allergic individuals, there can be no standard, cookbook formula for using self-hypnosis to gain relief.

If you have not already gotten a medical evaluation of your condition, do that first. You need to know as much as you can about your allergy or asthma condition.

If you suffer from an allergy or from asthma and have to avoid particular substances or certain animals, you can find relief with self-hypnosis. Begin by using self-hypnosis to relax your body and reduce some of the anxiety related to worry or concern about your allergy or asthma symptoms.

Next, you may want to do some of the self-exploration suggested in Chapter 16, to explore your memories for emotional connections to your asthma or allergic responses.

Milton Erickson often focused on helping people discover new ways to look at old problems as a change technique. He would offer allergy and asthma sufferers the opportunity to write down their questions or reactions to their body's stress or psychological woes.

While experiencing hypnosis and writing down their points of view, people are often surprised to discover clues to help them solve an old riddle and find what may spell relief for them.

DEVELOPING A JOURNAL

Make some notes and observations about the history of your problem. Is your allergy seasonal? Is it linked to any action or situation that makes it more or less severe? When did it first appear? How has it changed with the passing years? Are there times when you don't seem to be allergic to whatever triggers your attacks? How and when was your reaction the worst/least? Ask yourself as many questions as you can about your allergy or asthma and write them down. Often, writing can be a way to get a feeling or thought out of your body by putting it onto the paper.

Make a record of your observations and recollections. If your memory can't provide some of the answers, ask your family and other people who have known you for a long time. You might be surprised to find that they noticed things you overlooked.

The purpose of a journal is to help you open yourself up through understanding and acceptance of your present conditions. Of course, the next step is to change by using self-hypnosis suggestion strategies.

Detailed knowledge of your allergy will help you design more effective suggestions for its relief.

THE WAY ASTHMA DIFFERS FROM ALLERGIES

There are many similarities between asthma and allergies. The differences, though, are worth noting.

In an asthma attack, breathing is affected. There can be a constricting of the throat or bronchial passages that in severe reactions can be life-threatening. Allergic people tend to be simply annoyed by a limited problem. Asthma can be much more serious and debilitating.

Many studies such as that done by the noted physicians T.M. French and F. Alexander (1941) indicate that the asthma sufferer may have an emotional basis for his or her problem. Often the asthma sufferer requires psychological exploration to discover why the asthmatic condition may have arisen in the first place or what emotional connections may help trigger a reaction.

In many cases, repressed feelings may add to asthma symptoms. Emotions such as anger, sadness, or fear, if not openly expressed, may produce an "all choked up" feeling. A physical expression of that emotional blockage can be a "choked up" asthmatic reaction.

Often, suggestions in self-hypnosis can help release blocked feelings. Your suggestions can help you to develop better communications with yourself, family, and friends. You may need to outwardly express your emotions, rather than holding them inside.

If you are suffering from asthma, it may be necessary for you to release the sadness or grief you have been carrying over some loss. Perhaps, as a child you were unable to finish some emotional response to a crisis you faced. Holding in—repressing—that emotion from your childhood may have helped develop an asthmatic vulnerability.

As with allergies, you may be able to get relief from asthma by treating only the symptoms. Try that first, if you wish. But with asthma you may do better to work on both the cause and the symptoms at the same time.

If the cause of your asthma is psychologically based on repressed feelings that started the asthma, relief can follow. If you have reason to believe that the repressed memory of an event or situation is at the root of your asthma and is buried too deeply in your unconscious mind for self-hypnosis to uncover it, you may want to try clinical hypnotherapy and age regression with a professional therapist to unlock your memories.

Many times, though, self-hypnosis and strong motivation on your part will provide sufficient comfort and symptom relief.

BEST TIME OF DAY TO USE SELF-HYPNOSIS FOR RELIEF

What is the best time of day to use self-hypnosis for symptom relief? Practicing each day in the morning allows you to program control into your day and to prevent attacks. Morning practice can also clear away problems from yesterday and give you a fresh start on each new day.

In the evening, practice again to reinforce your day's successes and to work on suggestions for the next day. In the beginning, this sort of progressive, building cycle of self-hypnosis will yield the best and quickest results.

Remember that your most effective approach to allergy and asthma reactions is prevention. Work on sensing the signal or precursor to an attack so as to stop the attack before it begins. Posthypnotic cues can be used to prevent a full-scale reaction before it takes over.

DEALING WITH AN ACUTE ATTACK

Dealing with an acute attack of asthma or a serious allergy reaction is more difficult. Anxiety, fear, and tension make such attacks more severe. To deal with them, you should first relax as much as possible. This may be hard to do with an asthma attack. But posthypnotic cues for relaxation can help reduce your anxiety and tension. Give yourself specific cues for dealing with situations you know often trigger an attack. Following are some examples.

Suggestions and posthypnotic cues for symptom relief

Find experiences in your life that symbolize the feelings you would prefer to have when your symptoms are removed. If you have asthma, think of images and experiences related to the openness of your lungs and throat and create cues with those symbols. For example: *"I can feel more open now, just as open as* the tunnel I drove through on my vacation." Or, if you fly quite a bit: "I recall the openness of the canyons or plains I flew over, and the vast winds of cool air that make up the sky flowing over the wings, and I can feel that openness now".

If you work indoors, a suggestion might be: "I can recall the opening of a door into a large uncongested room and visualize the curtains expanding from a breeze that blows through an open window, which can remind me of how I can feel less congested, more open, like a breeze flowing throw me."

If you are a plumber or a gardener by profession, hobby, or necessity, you might relate to the expanding of a large pipe or hose. Or you can envision the wide opening of a bucket or pail.

Any of these images could be images of your chest or throat expanding and opening—and they are images that you control. Give yourself suggestions that whenever you visualize these symbols, you can respond positively as you did while in a trance-state.

If you have an allergy, feel itchy eyes turning to dry eyes, just as plants can go from moist to dry or as the wet springtime turns to dry summer.

You may want to spend 10 to 15 minutes with your posthypnotic suggestion work. Suggest and imagine that whenever you think of your images, you can elicit the desired response. While in your trance, rehearse how this change in response might take place in your everyday life. Recreate situations mentally and react to them while you are programming yourself to change.

You might also use more direct cues and suggestions based on the work of psychologist Don Gibbons (1990), suggestions such as: "When I feel an attack approaching, I can take a deep breath and clench my fist. I can sense the changes inside of me (describe the changes you feel). I will open my clenched fist at the same time I open my lungs and throat, even more."

These direct cues can also desensitize you to your allergy and allow you to feel more opened up. Just as your car can draw in air as you rev the engine, so can your lungs draw in a comfortable, easy breath.

A PROGRAM FOR DEALING WITH ALLERGIES AND ASTHMA

It is important to begin with a clear awareness of the parts of your body that are affected by the allergy or asthma. Something that will help you do this is the diagram of your body on this page. Take colored pens or markers and shade the areas that are aggravated by your condition.

Use colors, if you can, that represent the sort of irritation or unpleasantness you feel. See the area of your body where you break out as a color; perhaps red or orange represents skin irritation to you. Maybe yellow is how you visualize eye irritation. Blue might signify the choking or breathing difficulty of asthma in your lungs or throat. Pink could be a runny nose.

Develop visual symbols of your allergy or asthma by coloring the affected parts of yourself with one color and the non-affected parts with different colors.

What colors you choose should come from your imagination. It is important for you to get a mental picture of your body and the areas affected. Mentally "see" where your discomfort is. And if you can't "see" a color to associate with your discomfort, just pick one. The first color to pop into your head will work just fine.

Visualize colors blending into other colors, the bad colors from your body diagram turning to good colors. Visualize tightness turning into looseness.

Imagine also a taste or smell or sound that you can associate with your allergy. By changing your unconscious view of an allergy- or asthma-triggering stimulus you help remove the allergic response. Associate a nonallergic image with an allergic substance or stimulus. This will help to desensitize you to the allergic trigger.

For example: "*Often when I'm around cats, I react with watery, itchy eyes. I may find that I can have a different reaction in the future. Whenever I smell a cat, I may find that I can be reminded of the smell of a coat I once had (some specific smell which you can remember). Of course I was not allergic to my coat, so I may find I'm also not as allergic to a smell that reminds me of my coat.*" With repeated suggestion, this becomes a posthypnotic cue and, along with other cues, can change your reaction.

You could add suggestions that involve your visual perception of cats, also. Such a suggestion might be: "*Whenever I see a cat in a closed area with me, I will notice that there is a great variety in the markings of different cats. In fact, seldom are two exactly the same. I may notice that my reactions to cats can change and be varied also. I may find that my reactions can change and become less noticeable as I take more notice of the variety in cats.*"

This approach creates choices and your mind may talk to your body in self-hypnosis, so that you can relax and let your experience improve. Rehearsing your imagery in self-hypnosis can begin to alter your experience. Also, a little more control can build your confidence and provide a base for more improvements, which you will enjoy.

YOUR SELF-HYPNOSIS PRACTICE

Your self-hypnosis practice can take this form:

1. First, relax and calm yourself. Control your breathing. Use any of the techniques described earlier in the book to develop a self-hypnotic trance.
2. Let your mind become like radar for your body. Create a greater awareness of your body. You may want to progressively relax each body part. Examine areas that are always free from allergy or asthma. Then examine parts that are affected. Contrast the two. Compare them. Become more aware of the changes that take place when you have an attack.

Detect even small changes that take place when you are beginning to have an attack. Simulate or visualize in your mind the feeling or signal of an attack coming on. Examine the imagined feelings of an attack beginning, then feel it recede. Capturing the aura of, or prelude to, an attack is a self-hypnosis technique also used by some epileptics to help prevent seizures. Use your imagination to control the aura and move it away from you.

Practice this in your trance. Feeling these precursors, auras, or signals of an attack and then pushing them away is a way to learn control. Do this exercise for several minutes.

3. Use imagery and suggestions for changing your perception of the substances or situations that trigger your attacks. Alter the way you react to these triggers.

For instance, you can change your perception of long haired cats to short haired. *"I can see how easy it is for a long haired cat to have a haircut."* Maybe you can even imagine giving that haircut.

While in self-hypnosis, you might visualize a particular offensive flower and then see it change—just as the seasons can change—into a different plant. It may turn into a different flower or it may transform into pieces of tissue paper. Change it into anything that frees you from an allergic response. Practice with new perceptions, color more than texture, calming more than tensing, and relaxing more than ever.

You might change strawberries in your suggestions and imagery into carrots. Imagine rabbits eating the strawberries. Suggest that you too could eat those kinds of carrots that look like strawberries. Spend about 10 minutes working on these kinds of suggestions and imagery in each practice session.

NOTE: If you suffer from several different triggering substances, you may want to do the above process for each. However, do them one at a time. Achieve some success in desensitizing yourself from one substance before proceeding to the next.

4. Next work on preventing allergic reactions to substances by creating post-hypnotic cues to use should you encounter such substances. This is another angle on treating the symptom. Part of this work can help you to be aware of when you should elect to leave the site of an allergic substance. You are developing a skill to enhance your success. Practice daily.
5. Finally, summarize the suggestions you have made to yourself. Reinforce the desire for changes. Recap the posthypnotic cues.

Then, give yourself cues for reentering a trance more easily, more quickly. This should be a part of every self-hypnosis session.

End your session with suggestions for either going to sleep, or feeling alert and well. Once you have finished this final step, *go directly to some other activity.* Your suggestions will be more effective if you don't try to analyze them. Self-hypnosis involves an unconscious process—leave it that way and enjoy the results.

HOW LONG WILL IT TAKE TO SEE RESULTS?

You can work on both self-exploration and symptom relief in the same trance sessions. Work for 10 minutes or so on self-exploring to understand the cause of your symptoms. Then spend 10 or 15 minutes giving yourself suggestions for changing your perceptions of the triggering situations or feelings. During this second part of your trance you can also give yourself posthypnotic cues for dealing with the allergic response.

You may notice feeling more calm and feeling more control over your attacks in the first few weeks of daily practice. You may see a 10 percent improvement. Remember to set reasonable goals for yourself. A long suffered problem often takes time to correct.

Work toward getting 20 percent relief in the first month or two. A 50 percent improvement in about six months could be expected. But remember, your progress will depend on your motivation to practice, the severity of your problem, and the nature of the cause. You will have an individual level of success.

If after a month you see no progress, your problem may require more work on uncovering its emotional root. Anytime that you feel a change in suggestions is needed, don't hesitate to try a different set of metaphors or different cues. You will need to experiment.

Be patient with yourself

Be encouraged. You possibly have suffered with your allergy or asthma for a long time. You are now investing in long-term relief. The longer you have suffered, the more ingrained your pattern of sensitivity may have become. It takes time to erase this pattern—but it is not indelible.

Accept your own pace. Look for a percentage of relief as an intermediate goal. Chapter 9 on motivation and goals will aid you in setting reasonable goals and expectations.

Take a playful approach to developing your metaphors and images for change. Rather than looking at your practice time as a treatment you have to endure and force-feeding yourself suggestions, take a lighter, more imaginative view of it. Self-hypnosis can and should be a relaxing, enjoyable, enriching experience you look forward to. Keep that in mind as you prepare for your practice sessions.

SELF-HYPNOSIS FOR CHILDREN WITH ALLERGIES AND ASTHMA

If your child suffers from allergy or asthma attacks, you can teach some self-hypnosis methods to your child so that he or she can gain some control over the problem.

Children have a remarkable ability to use self-hypnosis already. They go in and out of trance very easily.

When children are engrossed in a TV show or at play, you may notice how absorbed they can be. They are often in a trance-state. A child may go in and out of a trance-state many times in a single day. Mostly, these trances are undirected; they have no goal.

Psychologists Gary Elkins and Bryan Carter (1990) have described a technique of flexible suggestion strategies for use with children between six and 13 years old. We have adapted their technique for use specifically with asthma or allergy symptoms. Use the idea of play or a game to introduce suggestions to your little boy or girl. *"Would you like to play a new game called 'Imagine This'? Let's sit together, close our eyes, and see if you can imagine this."*

Children will create their own trance. You simply help them with direction toward the goal of allergy or asthma relief. It's not necessary, at first, for them to make a connection between their "game" and their problem. Here is an example.

Scott had allergies and asthma from ages six to 10. No one seemed to understand why he had them or what to do. He received medical attention and injections, he avoided lots of things and substances that might provoke an attack, and he struggled through most of the time.

When he was 10 years old, Scott learned self-hypnosis to relax and he often used the image of going down a staircase with 20 steps. When he imagined reaching the bottom step, he would be in 'Nintendo-land' where every game lived and almost anything was possible. Once there, he created a game that he played as if it were happening inside his body.

By designing a maze with passageways, Scott focused on the concept of new paths, new openings, new passages. After several weeks of practice with this imagery in self-hypnosis, he was more relaxed and feeling better, and his allergic and asthmatic attacks had not reappeared. Previously, the longest time he had gone without an attack of any sort was one week.

Continuing the self-hypnosis practice helped Scott reduce nearly 80 percent of his symptoms, in frequency, and he also reduced the intensity of the attacks.

When you begin to teach your child self-hypnosis for allergies or asthma, choose a time when he or she is in a somewhat quiet or relaxed mood—perhaps in the evening, before going to bed. You will know best when the youngster is open for this sort of play.

You will need to do a little bit of homework. Select several characters that your child is used to seeing in cartoons, "Sesame Street," or perhaps from a favorite movie. Pick good guys whom your child can relate to, as well as some corresponding bad guys.

Have your youngster close his or her eyes and imagine a favorite "good guy." If the child chooses the roadrunner bird, for instance, then ask the child to imagine the roadrunner's opponent, the coyote.

Ask the child to picture the two characters together. The coyote is bothering the roadrunner, being a nuisance, getting in the way. Explain how the roadrunner is able, through his own efforts, to find a way to control that pesky coyote.

Suggest to your child that the way the roadrunner controls the coyote is by building a shelter that keeps him from coming in. Let your youngster imagine creating a shelter and encourage him or her to describe it to you.

Then you may suggest that the coyote, or whoever the villain is, tries to huff and puff and blow the shelter down, but without success. The roadrunner is so much more clever that he's able to outsmart and control the coyote with the shelter he has built.

This process implants a positive image that allows a child to feel that he or she can control the villain—the allergy or asthma. You can develop similar analogies with other types of allergy symptoms. The villain might try to bury the shelter with peanuts, or cats, or whatever the allergy is connected to.

Be creative, and listen to your child's ideas. Incorporate images or experiences that your boy or girl might suggest. You know where you want the action of the imagination to ultimately go. Direct the child's mental pictures toward that goal; in these scenes, the hero always wins!

After the good guy triumphs, suggest that the hero take a long walk in a meadow. You could say, for instance, that the roadrunner felt so good about his victory over the coyote that he went for a *good* long walk, maybe a walk through the desert or the forest. Ask your child where the roadrunner might take this walk. Let your little one fill in the blanks of how, where, and what. You give the essential directions.

Walking is very good for the cardiovascular system. It involves deeper breathing and is very healthy for an asthmatic condition. You are helping your child develop a posthypnotic cue to encourage more walking, better breathing, more comfort, and more control over the villain. All of these translate into more control over the allergy or asthma.

In another session, you might use another set of good and bad characters and develop a similar scenario. Blend the characters into scenes that give the hero a sense of control. The control will be developing in the hands of the real director/writer of the script—your child.

Let your youngster provide most of the color and the details, so it will become his or her little movie. If your child's story strays from the direction you know the scene should go, *suggest* or *imply* the proper course. Don't command, scold, or force a change. If the story drifts a bit, that's fine. Suggest a twist that will bring it back on track again.

Children easily identify with the heroes in the stories they create. If your child has given the roadrunner power and control over the villain, then the child, too, has a bit of power and control over his or her own villains, the allergy or asthma. That power can expand your child's comfort.

REFERENCES

Aronoff, G.M., Aronoff, S. & Peck, L.W. Hypnotherapy in the treatment of bronchial asthma. *Annals of Allergy*, Vol. 34, 1975.

Chong, T.M. Treatment of asthma by hypnotherapy. *Medical Journal of Malaya*, Vol. 18, 1965.

Collison, D.R. Hypnotherapy in the management of asthma. *American Journal of Clinical Hypnosis*, Vol. 11, 1968.

Dennis, M. & Phillippus, M.J. Hypnotic and non-hypnotic suggestion and skin response in atopic patients. *American Journal of Clinical Hypnosis*, Vol. 7, 1965.

Edwards, G. Hypnotic treatment of asthma. *British Medical Journal*, Vol. 2, 1960.

Elkins, G.R., & Carter, B.D. A science fiction-based imagery technique. In *Handbook of Hypnotic Suggestions and Metaphors*. New York: W.W. Norton & Company and American Society of Clinical Hypnosis, 1990.

French, T.M. & Alexander, F. Psychogenic factors in bronchial asthma. *Journal of Psychosomatic Medicine*, Vol. 4, 1941.

Gibbons, D.E. Suggestions with asthma. In *Handbook of Hypnotic Suggestions and Metaphors*. New York: W. W. Norton & Company and American Society of Clinical Hypnosis, 1990.

Grant, R.T., Bruce-Pearson, R.S. & Comeau, W.J. Observations on urticaria provoked by emotions, by exercise and by warming the body. *Clinical Science*, Vol. 2, 1936.

Haley, J. (Ed.) *Advanced Techniques of Hypnosis and Therapy: Selected papers of Milton H. Erickson, M.D.* New York: Grune & Stratton, 1967.

Hanley, F.W. Individualized hypnotherapy of asthma. *American Journal of Clinical Hypnosis*, Vol. 16, 1974.

Knapp, P.H. & Nemetz, S.J. Sources of tension in bronchial asthma. *Journal of Psychosomatic Medicine*, Vol. 19, 1957.

Kroger, W.S. *Clinical and Experimental Hypnosis*. Philadelphia: J.B. Lippincott Company, 1977

Maher-Loughnan, G.P. Hypnosis and auto-hypnosis for the treatment of bronchial asthma. *International Journal of Clinical & Experimental Hypnosis*, Vol. 18, 1970.

Murphy, A.I. (et al.) Hypnotic susceptibility and its relationship to outcome in the behavioral treatment of asthma. *Psychological Reports*, Vol. 65(2), 1989.

Schneer, N.I., *The Asthmatic Child: Psychosomatic Approach to Problems and Treatment*. New York: Harper & Row, 1963.

Sutton, P.H. A trial of group hypnosis and auto-hypnosis in asthmatic children. *British Journal of Clinical Hypnosis*, Vol. 1, 1969.

18
Pain Control Strategies

Pain is like a burglar alarm. It alerts us to an immediate problem. "Take care," it shouts.

Acute pain is a signal of tissue damage, and we respond by seeking the cause of our pain. It is extremely important to obtain a good medical evaluation and proper treatment of any injury or disease we suffer. But after we have gone to the doctor, learned the cause of the problem, and begun proper treatment, we no longer have use for the pain. What can we do with pain which, like the burglar alarm that can't be disconnected, continues to irritate us?

The sources of many types of pain may be chronic and ongoing. Migraine headaches, back pain, arthritis, and gout are among the chronic pains that people suffer. Certain cancers, and even many treatments for them, can produce unnecessary pain. Dental pain, postoperative surgical pain, or discomfort from illness can be unneeded pain.

You can control any type of non-useful pain while leaving your alarm system intact. It is very important in the field of pain control not to try eliminating all pain, but to be selective. With self-hypnosis you can learn to control unwanted, unnecessary pain, but still experience any new sensation that is alerting you to a new problem or a change in the existing one.

Whenever pain outlives its usefulness, it is time for it to be squelched. No drug, no apparatus, no electrical connections are necessary with self-hypnosis. Yet it is so powerful that major surgeries have been done with self-hypnosis as the only anesthetic.

Victor Rausch, the dentist mentioned in an earlier chapter, used self-hypnosis to undergo removal of his gall bladder—a major abdominal surgery—with no other anesthesia or analgesic. (Anesthesia is an agent that makes you completely unconscious—you feel no sensations at all. An analgesic is a substance that eliminates or reduces pain in a particular area where it is injected or applied; but it does not render you unconscious.) Rausch's (1980) report of his experience gives us a unique perspective on the use of self-hypnosis for major surgery:

"At the precise moment the incision was made, several things happened simultaneously," Rausch said. "I felt a flowing sensation throughout my entire body . . . I was suddenly much more aware of my surroundings . . . My eyes were open and the operating team said I had no visible tensing of the muscles, no change in my breathing, no flinching of my eyes and no change in facial expression."

The operation took one hour and 15 minutes. Rausch recalled chatting with the nurse and the anesthetist (who had little to do but to monitor Rausch's vital signs) and he even told jokes he'd recently heard. He talked with the operating surgeon, who at one point asked Rausch not to control his bleeding, so that he wouldn't miss cauterizing any "bleeders" that might cause complications later.

When the final sutures were in place, Rausch walked, with help, back to his room. He felt no pain whatsoever and little discomfort.

Ten days after the surgery, Victor Rausch was back in his office, busy, fully functioning and feeling well.

Of course, Rausch was an exceptional person. He had years of experience with hypnosis and self-hypnosis in his dental practice, in teaching, and in experimental settings. Nevertheless, the profound levels of pain prevention and relief he experienced are available to all of us.

You may be seeking much less dramatic results. But relief from migraines, back pains, arthritis pain, and pain from other illnesses and injuries can certainly be dramatic for a person who is suffering.

HOW LONG WILL IT TAKE TO GET RELIEF WITH SELF-HYPNOSIS?

Some pain, even of long duration and deep intensity, will be positively changed with one's first self-hypnosis work. More commonly, relief occurs in the first few sessions. In other cases, it may take several practice sessions before results are noticed.

The relief you experience may or may not come at once. Some people notice that their pain subsides immediately. Others feel results hours after their self-hypnosis session.

If you have had chronic pain for many years, it will take longer to build the comfort level you may be seeking.

Dr. Milton Erickson, a renowned innovator in the use of hypnotic therapies, was once called on to help a terminally ill man. The patient, Joe, was dying of cancer and had been suffering tremendous pain for quite some time.

All other methods of pain control had been tried, and only large dosages of narcotic painkillers had any effect on the man's suffering. Joe did not believe in hypnosis and said as much to Erickson in their first encounter. Joe was, therefore, extremely skeptical of Erickson's ability to help him learn to reduce his pain in the few months he had left. But he was willing to let the doctor try. Erickson knew that the patient's lack of belief in hypnosis had little to do with benefiting from it. While talking about the patient's career as a tomato farmer, Erickson gently and indirectly wove suggestions for pain relief into the conversation.

By the end of two hours of pleasant talk, Joe had developed a light stage of self-hypnosis, directed by Erickson. He found that his pain had already decreased a bit. Suggestions had been given for more relief as time passed. By their next meeting, a week later, Joe was eager to tell Erickson that his pain was noticeably less, he couldn't explain why.

After a few more weeks of treatment, the man was able to finally get a good night's sleep, his first in nearly a year of suffering. Though his doctors had given him only a few more months to live—his cancer was extremely advanced—he survived for over seven. This extra time may have been due, in part, to the comfort he found from his pain relief.

ISSUES IN GETTING RELIEF WITH SELF-HYPNOSIS

Four things determine one's ability to obtain pain relief with self-hypnosis: 1. your success in developing a self-hypnotic trance; 2. your motivation to get pain relief; 3. proper handling of your fears of letting go of the pain; and 4. understanding that you have control over your pain.

We will examine each of these factors:

1. *Success with self-hypnosis techniques* is a matter of practice. You will need to experiment with various approaches, suggestions, and kinds of imagery. Chapter 11 will help you find your best way to experience success with self-hypnosis. At first, practice with relaxation as a goal.

   Relaxation in many cases will relieve a considerable amount of pain. Muscle tension often puts pressure on nerves; this aggravates discomfort. Easing your tension is the first goal. Then you can begin dealing directly with the pain.

2. *Motivation for pain relief* means freeing yourself from the need to keep pain in your life. It may seem unbelievable that you might "need" to keep pain. But often there are advantages as-well-as disadvantages to pain problems. If pain results in your avoiding work, gaining sympathy, obtaining workmen's compensation, or getting out of responsibilities you do not like, these benefits can defeat your motivation to feel better. They may be unconscious reasons—reasons of which you may not be aware—for keeping the pain. Read the strategies in Chapter 16 to help you develop ways of increasing your awareness of unconscious processes, patterns, or feelings that can help you with this issue.

   Look honestly at the pain in your life and why you might be holding on to it. This is only necessary, of course, if you find that you are having difficulty getting results at pain relief.

3. *You may fear letting go of your pain.* Because we know that pain can be a signal of something wrong inside us, we may fear shutting it off.

   Realize that self-hypnosis, unlike drugs, reduces only *unnecessary* hurting. With self-hypnosis, you leave intact your "alarm systems." Should further injury, disease, degeneration, or some other problem occur, you will be alerted. This selectivity makes self-hypnosis especially beneficial as a pain treatment. You may want to explore Chapter 13 to assist you in dealing with anxieties and fears.

4. *You can control your pain.* Pain is not an external sensation. We create the feeling of pain in our brains. It serves our survival needs and we have the ultimate control over it.

HOW LONG WILL PAIN RELIEF LAST?

Your motivation plays a big role in the answer to this question. As we have noted, in the short term there can be many side benefits to pain. Only you can determine to what extent these may be offset by the benefits of pain relief— freedom from suffering, resumption of a pre-pain lifestyle, and self-reliance.

Other factors in your life can increase the longevity of the relief. These include exercise, good nutrition, normal social interchange with people. An expansion of activities that will reinforce the benefits of pain reduction—work, play, and sex—is also necessary.

How long the relief you will obtain lasts varies for many reasons and may also vary with the kind of pain you have. At first, relief may last only a short time, but with each session you can expect your comfort to last longer. Follow-up studies have shown successes lasting over 17 years. Of course, we can expect a wide range of differences in individual success rates.

The length of time one has been suffering and the amount of time spent with self-hypnosis are important variables in this process. As more time is spent in the comfort of self-hypnosis, the longer the intervals of relief will be.

Generally, a person can learn to control pain for as long as he or she desires and works to control it. Control may require self-hypnosis *every day*, perhaps twice each day. Or one may need self-hypnosis for pain only once or twice a week. This is a highly individual matter.

Unlike with drugs, there is no tolerance level with self-hypnosis. The benefits build and get stronger with practice. More likely, as time passes and experience with self-hypnosis grows, the intervals of relief will increase, too.

THE INSIDE TRACK ON PAIN CONTROL

Why do we look to ourselves last to stop pain? It is within our own body and mind that the greatest power of pain relief can be found.

Because most other pain treatments are administered from the outside, you may not believe you can control your pain from the inside. We have been conditioned from our earliest years to believe that someone else makes our pain go away. First our parents would kiss our hurt and make it go away. Then the doctor would give us something for it. We've been taught by advertising to believe that only some medicine will fix us. But most of us have noticed that we can be distracted from feeling a pain sensation.

The exact mechanism through which hypnosis works is unknown. But it's not necessary to know the exact mechanism of hypnotic pain relief in order to take advantage of it.

Have you ever had an injury or pain in one part of your body, then forgotten it when you injured another part? Suppose you stub your toe while you are suffering a headache. The headache will be "forgotten" while you pay attention to your more recently hurt toe.

This kind of experience shows the power of distraction. You can be so aware of a new pain that your awareness shifts from the old one, even though you aren't aware that you have cancelled out the first pain. No medicine, no doctor, no electrical apparatus is needed for this result.

Loud music at the dentist's office and the "slap and stab" method a nurse may have used to give you an injection are other examples of how distraction can reduce or eliminate the pain experience. The effect of distraction is only one example of pain relief that comes from within you.

THE GATE CONTROL THEORY OF PAIN

There is still a great deal to be learned about pain mechanisms. We do know that nerve cells transmit the messages and if a nerve is cut or chemically blocked, generally, pain messages cannot be sent to the brain. If that happens, no sensations at all can be felt.

The actual interpretation of sensations, including those we experience as pain, is made in the brain. One of the most widely accepted descriptions of how pain works was formulated by Drs. Ronald Melzack and Patrick D. Wall (1965). It is called the "gate control theory."

According to this theory, when we stimulate our nerve cells through disease, injury, or other disturbance, the message is "telegraphed" to the brain. Along the way, first at the spinal cord, then in different parts of the brain, it is interpreted.

At one point the message may be translated in terms of a reflex. Touching a hot stove burner causes the hand to pull back even before the sensation of burning is registered. This is as if a prerecorded response were being engaged.

Perhaps, in another part of the brain, the nature of the pain is decoded. We perceive whether it is a shooting pain or a dull ache, whether or not it moves—in general, what it is like.

In perhaps a different place in the brain, a part of the message is translated into discomfort, unpleasantness, or the urgent feelings of wanting the pain to stop.

HOW SELF-HYPNOSIS PAIN RELIEF WORKS

The different "interpreting regions" for pain may be separated. That is what may happen in hypnosis.

As Drs. Melzack and Wall (1965) describe the effects of hypnosis on pain, "It changes the way you feel pain. You can turn off the region that feels the awfulness, the unpleasantness, yet you can still sense and describe the pain—where it is and what it is, without feeling the discomfort from it."

There can be several ways to accomplish this separation of the sensation from feelings of discomfort and unpleasantness. Distraction and imagery are two of them. These techniques will be explained later in this chapter.

Can pain be only in your head, a mental experience only?

Pain is interpreted in your head, but the source of the stimulus can be anywhere in your body, including your head. Sometimes a pain is experienced when there seems to be no cause in the body. This is often called psychogenic pain—meaning it originates in the mind. The mind may be using the pain sensation as a means of communicating a psychological problem or disharmony.

The philosopher Descartes held the notion of duality or separateness of the body and mind. Conventional medicine, which treats only the body with painkilling drugs, perpetuates that concept. They often only treat the symptoms, not the cause.

However, there is growing evidence that the mind and body are interwoven so deeply that it is impossible to make that separation any longer. Even pain which originates in the mind clearly affects the body.

A kind of pain that demonstrates this blending of mind and body is "phantom limb pain." Phantom limb pain is experienced by people who have had an amputation, but still feel often excruciating sensations in the missing limb. It was once supposed that the damaged nerve endings in the stump were the cause of this pain, but this theory is not consistent with the evidence.

Another theory is that people try to maintain an intact "body image" even after losing a limb. This body image starts in infancy and builds with succeeding years. People who have lost an arm or leg very early in life or through birth defect do not have phantom pain. Also, adults who have a very low self-image, such as skid row outcasts, seldom develop phantom pains.

These observations, in addition to those of the hypnotic phenomenon, support the concept that the experience of pain, or its absence, is both psychological and physical. The fact that people can have pain without organic cause suggests that the brain can initiate the message of pain sensations as well as receive and interpret them.

Such pain sensations can be just as "real," just as intense, as if the stimulus came from a current injury.

WHAT ABOUT DRUGS FOR PAIN?

There are a myriad of drugs and compounds for reducing or eliminating pain. Many, like Darvon and Vicodin, are available only by prescription. Nearly all of these are habit-forming and have a wide array of negative side effects.

Darvon was introduced in 1957 and promoted as potent painkiller without the potential for addiction. In the eyes of many researchers, however, it is addicting. In 1976 the Justice Department ruled it a narcotic. Deaths have been attributed to it, and at present Darvon is a restricted drug. This was a drug once thought to be a safe, potent painkiller with virtually no side effects. All the other narcotic drugs such as codeine, Demerol, and Percodan, are extremely addictive. Also, they carry a host of side effects that can be as damaging as the pain they are meant to stop.

As many chronic pain sufferers can attest, even the most powerful painkillers can lose their effectiveness after a time and their dosage must be increased. After a point, the side effects of the increased dosage become a new problem.

There are no long-term benefits from chronic pain, but there are no drugs that will give safe, long-term relief. It is ironic and valuable to know that the mind/body is responsible for creating chronic pain and it may be only the mind/body that can provide ultimate long-term relief.

There is another reason you may not want to chemically cut yourself off from all feeling. Milton Erickson (Barber & Adrian, 1982) states, "In painful disease, sedatives, analgesics and narcotics are employed that may deprive the patient of the privilege of knowing that he is alive and of enjoying the pleasures that are available; they also deprive others of adequate contact with an alert person. Hence, medication should be administered only in the quantities that meet the physical requirements, without obstructing or defeating those psychological needs vital to the total life situation."

ARE CERTAIN TYPES OF PAIN UNAFFECTED BY SELF-HYPNOSIS?

Hypnotic analgesia can work for any and all types of pain. The nature of all pain seems to be similar, as explained earlier in this chapter by the "gate control theory." Self-hypnosis can intervene in the discomfort and unpleasantness of all pain. It will still allow you to perceive the feelings of the injured or ill part of your body. And if a new problem occurs, you will be able to feel it, also.

Can anybody use self-hypnosis for pain?

Everybody who learns self-hypnosis can use it for pain relief. Just as pain and suffering vary from person to person, so will the quality of pain relief vary.

Are there different kinds of pain?

There are, of course, different kinds of pain in the sense of burning, stabbing, shooting, throbbing, dull aching pain, and so on. Those are "diagnostic" perceptions that tell us something about the nature, location, intensity, and extent of the injury or illness.

Another important idea is that there are different components of pain: sensory pain, suffering, and mental anguish.

1. *Sensory pain* is the way we feel the hurting. It is the sensation of a deep piercing pain, or burning on the skin or a dull ache over a wide area.
2. *Suffering* is the feeling of unpleasantness, discomfort, or wanting the pain to stop at any cost. It is this component that self-hypnosis works on most to minimize or eliminate this component.
3. *Mental anguish* includes the feelings of sadness, hopelessness, depression, and frustration that can accompany chronic pain. It becomes more intense as time wears on. Self-hypnosis is an effective tool in dealing with this component, too.

How can self-hypnosis help the mental anguish of pain?

People who have experienced pain for a length of time may be feeling as though their suffering will be with them forever. They may have given up hope of ever feeling "well" again. Even though the reason for their pain may not be a threat to their life any longer, the pain is a constant reminder of their problem. If the illness or injury still poses a threat, then the pain is another burden for the mind.

Chronic pain sufferers have usually been to doctors, taken medication, perhaps sought less conventional therapies—acupuncture, biofeedback. They despair at losing important parts of their lifestyle to pain—sports, social functions, dancing, sexual mobility or enjoyment. Their whole life or a great part of it is consumed by their awareness of pain.

The anguish of pain often leads to secondary problems such as depression, drug or alcohol abuse, family or marital problems, joblessness, and low self-esteem. Hope can diminish and frustration can dull any effort to break this vicious chain of bondage.

Self-hypnosis can help a person face his or her present situation. If you have a pain problem, self-hypnosis can allow you to acknowledge the problems that you have, and to look at yourself with inward clarity. It can help you realize that you are your main resource. Using the techniques provided later in this chapter, you can examine your pain, your suffering, your expectations, and your capacity for change.

By knowing that there is something *you* can do to help yourself, you can regain hope and take action. By examining what your pain has done to you and those around you, you can begin to unravel the bonds of depression and despair.

With self-hypnosis, you can reduce your suffering from pain and reprogram your mental attitude for the future. You can also reduce the anxiety or fear of the pain returning.

The process takes time. The longer the pain has been endured, the more work it will usually take. But because your motivation to succeed may be high, finding a way out of the maze of anguish may happen more quickly.

CAN YOU GET RID OF ALL YOUR PAIN?

In pain relief with self-hypnosis, some amount of discomfort is usually allowed to remain. This is especially true in cases of long-term chronic suffering. It is best to think in terms of achieving a substantial percentage of relief.

Imagine your suffering on a scale of 1 to 10 with 10 being the most pain imaginable. If your pain is presently at 7, you might first try reducing it to a 6 or a 5. That could seem more comfortable. Should you succeed in reducing it to a 3 or a 2, that would be even better.

Some people can eliminate their pain completely. That is wonderful. But if you can reduce your pain by 90 percent, you would surely feel successful and enjoy a new degree of freedom in your life.

WHAT TIMES OF DAY ARE BEST FOR SELF-HYPNOSIS?

You will get the most benefit from self-hypnosis for pain by practicing in the morning. By doing your practice first thing in the morning, you put aside any accumulation of pain from your night's sleep and can "program" your day to come.

Milton Erickson personally suffered a great deal of physical pain. Those of us who studied with him at his office in Arizona could see two different people in him.

In the very early morning, Erickson might be seen in his wheelchair, drawn, eyes dull, slumped over, his face and voice contorted with suffering. An hour later he would be eating breakfast, cheery, eyes twinkling, alert and in lively conversation.

His metamorphosis came from the 45 minutes to an hour he spent in hypnosis each morning.

When Erickson was 17, he suffered paralysis from polio. At first he could move only his eyes. He taught himself upper body movement by finding memories for how he moved before his illness. He would mentally rehearse a movement for hours just to get a muscle to twitch.

Though confined to a wheelchair the rest of his life, he began each day rehearsing how well he could feel during the entire day ahead. Even in his 70s, he was able to shed the yoke of pain each morning to teach, travel, lecture, and treat patients.

Your morning session of self-hypnosis is the most important one. However, you may need to practice several other times a day, also.

You will need to experiment to find the best schedule for your situation. Three times a day may be a good way to start. As your posthypnotic cues become more effective and their effects last longer, fewer sessions may be necessary.

WHAT IF YOU ARE IN TOO MUCH PAIN TO DO SELF-HYPNOSIS?

There are two basic ways to deal with this problem.

First, try to find a time when the pain has subsided a bit, perhaps after a period of relaxation or while in a form of physical therapy. Maybe while you're in a whirlpool, or while in some type of heat therapy, or under cold packs, you may find a bit of relief from the pain. Use that time to practice self-hypnosis techniques.

Once you become familiar with self-hypnosis, you will find it easier each time. The posthypnotic cues you give yourself will help you to lessen some of the pain later. Additionally, they will help you to reenter a trance.

Normally, relaxation is the initial goal of self-hypnosis practice. It is usually the vehicle to entering a trance. But with chronic or acute pain, relaxation may be impossible.

Using pain as a focus

The second technique is focusing your attention and concentration, which is of the chief ingredients of all hypnotic methods. If you are unable to find a moment's respite from your pain, use the discomfort itself as a point of concentration. It is the most prominent sensation in you and will make concentrating on it easy.

This approach may seem absurd or opposite to your interests, but if pain is interrupting all else, then focusing on it is the most dirresct approach to changing the intensity of it.

Examine your pain thoroughly. Describe it to yourself. Is it a burning sensation? Is it like a hot poker in your back? Does it feel as if hot oil is spreading over your shoulder? Does your head throb with the pulsing of your heart? Is it like needles stabbing your foot?

Mentally picture what the pain looks like. Perhaps it is a large coin, a vivid color, or a pool of water. See the coin or color or pool of water get smaller as your pain recedes, even slightly. Keep your mind concentrating on just the pain. You may want to try three or four different images of your pain to find one that is easiest to work with.

Incorporate deep, regular breathing with your imaging. Take slow, deep, satisfying breaths. Continue to focus on the pain and imagine a tiny portion of your pain escaping with each escaping breath. The image of a coin, pool of water, or whatever image you have chosen could begin to shrink. Or if you are imagining a color it might begin to fade to a different shade.

As you inhale, call back the pain that left. Continue this cycle. Visualize the pain as you first described it. As you continue this process, see and feel the pain becoming less each time you exhale. See more of it leaving each time. Then see it all coming back as you inhale.

You may wonder, "Why is it important to call the pain back? Isn't my goal to get rid of it?"

True. That is your ultimate goal. But what you need to learn first is to control the pain. That means being able to call it back whenever you desire. Control means having the ability even to recall the pain if you choose. This may be a difficult process to understand, but the value of having the control to retrieve pain is that you can learn to remove it that much better.

This sort of control is obtained through body awareness. That is the reason for clearly describing your pain and visualizing it. Imagine it as an object or perceive the temperature of your pain. Give it dimension, shape, texture, and even taste. The more vividly you can imagine it, the more control you will ultimately have over it.

Learning this will take some time and practice. It may not all happen in your first session. Be patient and continue practicing until you notice some small variation in the intensity of your pain as you exhale.

Once you have varied the pain just a little, you know that you have demonstrated control. If you can do it that tiny amount, you can learn to do it more. With practice, the control can increase. You will have used your own pain and your breathing to create a self-hypnotic trance. You will have begun to control the perception of your pain.

Acceptance of your situation can refocus you

Pain is an indispensable protective system—an alarm system—to notify you of an injury or disease. It is for guiding a doctor to a correct diagnosis and treatment for your problem.

When this has been done, pain is no longer necessary. You can keep the sensations in reserve, in case of a new development, but you can let go of the discomfort and unpleasantness.

If you are in pain, if you have suffered an injury or an illness which has been diagnosed and treated or is being treated, yet the pain continues—these are facts you cannot escape. You must acknowledge them.

You cannot easily deceive your unconscious mind. You must begin your self-hypnosis by facing your present situation. From here, you can make progress. Accept yourself where you are now. Give yourself permission to be where you are presently, whether you are ill, injured, or whatever.

TIME REGRESSION FOR PAIN RELIEF

You have not always been in pain. Before the accident, before the illness, you had experiences that were free from this pain. Perhaps there have been moments since your injury or illness when you felt some period of comfort, some time of relief.

Find a sitting or lying position that gives you the most comfort possible. Take several deep, satisfying breaths. If doing that is uncomfortable, breathe in the most comfortable manner you can.

Start by remembering the situation of your injury or illness. Suppose that you injured your back while lifting. Lifting can be a form of counterbalancing, a system of leverage, perhaps. Use the symbols of your injury as a beginning point for time regression. Find the images and words that symbolize the circumstances of the injury, visual and verbal associations that can represent a similar situation.

For example: *"Just as lifting a heavy object can cause strain or damage, it can also be like lifting another heavy load—pain. The balance and smooth movements of a seesaw can lift enormous weights with the proper counterbalance."*

You create a more favorable image of the situation surrounding your injury. This will allow you to remember the accident without the tension and pain returning. This is important in achieving long-term relief. Regress yourself to your memory before the pain. Create a better association of those memories with the present and with the accident. This will help free your unconscious mind from the discomfort and aggravation of pain.

"The lifting of many objects can be accomplished by adjusting the point of balance forward or back to accommodate the differences in weight. Just as when I was a child and able to sit on a seesaw and lift a playmate on the other side, I can lift the pain I feel."

Search for any comfortable, pleasant experience you have had. Know that you can create a new comfortable feeling, now. Perhaps imagine sitting on the seesaw, with pain on the other side; you can lift the pain. Visualize raising it just as you can lift it off your back.

Find several ways of expressing this notion of comfort and pleasantness before the injury. Perhaps you can relate it to what your were wearing at the time of your pre-pain memory. *"The blue shirt I wore reminds me of the ocean, cool and relaxing."*

Maybe you can find a memory of a specific place that always felt good. Use your imagery and suggestions together—for instance: *"I can put my pain up on the top of the mountain I climbed last year. When I climb down, I can leave my pain up on the mountain top."*

If there is a particular position that you feel comfortable in, use that as a point of reference. For example: *"I can remember lying comfortably on my back in front of the TV, a bowl of popcorn balanced on my stomach. I can practically smell the butter and the salt, now."*

You may find many rich memories of positions and situations that felt good, with relaxing, comfortable sensations. Recall those and allow your mind to visualize and create those pictures as vividly as possible.

Keep a constant flow of imagery and mental suggestions focused on the goal of recreating those past memories of comfort.

Perhaps you can incorporate some instances of lifting that did not cause pain. Recall examples of lifting that resulted in benefits and pleasure.

"I can see in my mind that first time I lifted my newborn baby from its crib. What pleasure and pride I felt." Expand a pleasant memory like this, in your own words. Find other examples from your own past that can be associated with your injury situation or illness.

"I can remember the feelings of satisfaction I felt when I raised the flag in the Boy Scout ceremony." Or, *"What a tremendous feeling of pride and excitement I can remember, when I picked up my bride and carried her over the threshold on our honeymoon."*

Perhaps you once changed a flat tire and lifted it into place so that you could continue your journey. You can also lift yourself above the pain to continue the rest of your life's journey.

Your objective with this technique is to create a new association with the injury or illness. From a memory of a terrible or painful experience, you create a memory associated with progress and growth.

While in self-hypnosis, recall some feelings of comfort from the past. This will help to reprogram your body and mind to accept feelings of freedom from pain. Practice positive mental rehearsals based on pleasant past experiences.

Health-related pain can be dealt with in a similar manner. For example, suppose your pain is from arthritis in your foot.

Remember the times before the onset of arthritis, when your feet were free from pain—the hikes you may have taken, the short trips to the kitchen to get a late night snack. Recall how good it felt to get up in the morning and stand in the shower, with the warm, soothing water flowing over you, or how good your feet felt when you put them up on the coffee table after coming home from work.

Do this recalling while in a self-hypnotic trance if you can. Describe each scene in as rich detail as you can. Recall the colors, the smells, the sounds that were around you. Make the memory as clear as possible.

From within your self-hypnosis you could suggest to yourself: *"I can remember how well my feet glided effortlessly that night of dancing. I felt like I was floating on air. The taste of champagne, the sounds of the New Year's crowd, the streamers and banners across the room. I can recall that feeling now, as if it were just happening. My feet, even now, feel more comfortable, like I was resting them on air.*

"I may find that as I remember that wonderful time, my feet will feel numb or maybe cool, perhaps more light than numb. I may notice that whenever I think of dancing, my feet get this same numbness or coolness. I may find that the comfort in my feet lasts for a short time or perhaps it will last longer than I thought possible."

Be aware of even a small change in the amount of pain you feel. Encourage and expand that small feeling with more suggestions, such as: *"I notice that a slight tingling feeling has begun in my right foot. It is a nice feeling. I may find that just as a drop of blue dye in a pail of water spreads out, this cool numbness can also spread. It can be like walking down a hill, with each step easily gliding into the next. Momentum can take the walking into a trot, like the numbness in my toes can go into my foot."*

That slight numbness may be all you achieve in the first few practice sessions. That is fine. Keep practicing and each time it will get easier, though it may happen that one session may not be as productive as another.

There are always going to be variations in the quality of your self-hypnosis practice sessions. That is natural and to be expected. Do the best you can. You are striving for long-term benefits as well as short-term. Keep practicing, and notice the benefits from week-to-week as well as day-to-day.

HEADACHE, STOMACHACHE, AND OTHER ACUTE PAIN

Unlike chronic pain, which may be constant and of long duration, acute pain comes on quickly and leaves in a relatively short time as well. However, it may be recurring, as with migraines or other headaches.

These types of suffering are best prepared for ahead of time. Preventative self-hypnosis is the most effective. Practice self-hypnosis when you are feeling well—free of pain. Get rid of tensions and give yourself plenty of posthypnotic cues for dealing with stress and tension.

Clenching your fist as if you are getting a grip on the tension and pressure that can cause pain, then letting it go as you exhale, can be one good posthypnotic cue. Or you might shrug your shoulders and gather up all the muscular stress and strain there as you deeply inhale. Then, as you exhale fully, you can let your shoulders slump and let the tension slide off of you.

These are two cues you can develop. Find several more for yourself. The cues can be any action you can take or even an image you form in your mind at the time you wish the desired response to occur.

You can review Chapter 12 on stress management to get some other ideas for cues. By creating these posthypnotic cues, you will develop a response that can take place whenever you perform the action, even outside of the trance.

These same cues can then be used to stem a headache or arthritic pain before it gets too severe. Stopping these pains before they get going is your best approach. When you first begin to notice the pain starting, relax yourself with one of your cues and develop a pain-free level of comfort.

Warming your headache away

Another self-hypnosis technique for quieting some kinds of headaches is to suggest that your arms are getting warm. Keep suggesting warmth in your arms and then even in your legs or perhaps your hands and fingertips.

The reason this works is that by directing the blood flow into your extremities—which is what creates a warm feeling—you are lessening the blood pressure in your head. That may be a contributing cause of some recurring migraines and vascular headaches. Experiment and see if this will help your headache.

Expanding relief

When a pain such as a headache has already begun and it's too late for prevention, then acknowledge the pain. Know that you will eventually feel better. Then focus on a part of your body that feels well.

Maybe it will be your legs that feel comfortable, your arms, or only your pinkie finger. Find one or more areas that feel good.

The strategy is to be aware of the discomfort, but also to be aware of the parts of you that are well. Compare the two. Know that just as one part can feel very tender and hurting, the other can feel the opposite sensations of comfort. Contrast one with the other. Your purpose is to find a blend with which you can *dilute* the pain. Find a way to spread the wellness of one area of your body to the part that hurts. As the good feeling spreads, encourage this transfer of relief throughout your entire body.

Maybe one side of your head hurts like a bell being rung, but the other side feels all right. Perhaps it can be like visualizing the colors red and purple and seeing the differences between them. You can give yourself suggestions comparing the two. Create other symbols that contrast the two feelings. Then blend them together like the colors can blend.

For example: *"One side of my head feels like a red bell, pounding with each beat of my heart. But my big toe feels cool, well, and pleasant. My toe feels like a purple plum, cool, soft and comfortable.*

"I can see the contrast of the colors and the contrast in the feelings of these two areas of my body. I can even imagine the purple plum as it might strike the red bell. The softness of my toe would make a soft sound as it hit the bell. Perhaps the purple of the toe might rub off on the redness of the bell. I can feel how the softness and gentle wellness of my purple toe might blend with the redness of the bell and make it ring more quietly. I may even feel my head throb less, as I imagine the red turning to purple."

This strategy of combining the pain with the wellness may take some minutes to accomplish. Perhaps spend three or four minutes examining each of the two contrasts—the pain and the comfort. Make several associations, like those of color (red/purple) and shape and sound (bell/plum).

Don't be discouraged if this technique takes some time to master. Each subsequent time it can be more effective, and require less time to get results.

Distraction strategy

Distraction is used for the relief of pain by your dentist when he has you listen to music through a headset while he is drilling. Distraction relieves pain when you forget about your headache as you drive past an accident scene or forget the pain in your shoulder when you stub your toe. With self-hypnosis, you can master the art of distraction.

Select a part of your body that feels fine. Concentrate on it intensely. As you develop your self-hypnosis trance, focus your attention on the well areas, the parts of your body that are comfortable.

You may want to begin this technique with progressive relaxation, starting with your toes and working through each body part. Pay particular attention to the areas that feel good. Examine how good they feel.

If you are having too much pain to concentrate for long, practice for two or three minutes at a time; come out of your trance, then go back into it for several minutes and out again.

While you are out of the trance, acknowledge the pain you are experiencing. When you are *in* the trance, concentrate on the parts of you that are feeling well.

Think of the two or three minutes of self-hypnotic concentration as brief visits *away* from pain and visits *to* wellness. Even if you are not sure you are actually in a trance, focus your attention on well parts of your body.

Give yourself suggestions for small amounts of relief. For instance: *"As I focus on my hand and notice how comfortable it feels, how calm the fingers are, I may notice a slight tingling, coolness, or warmth in the tips of my fingers.*

This small feeling may last only a few seconds, yet it may last for a minute or longer.

"I can remain focused on any well-feeling part of my body for perhaps a few seconds or maybe a minute, perhaps even longer than I thought possible."

In this way you can suspend your pain by distracting your attention to another part of your body. Use visualization and imagery, too. Visualize your feet in a cool tub of water, when your pain is in your shoulder.

You may be surprised to find that the feelings of comfort you suggest and visualize will yield comfort to the suffering part of your body. Let the distraction displace the pain.

Time distortion

A middle-aged woman suffering from cancer was in a tremendous amount of pain. She was taking as much pain medication as was possible. It still did not suppress all of her suffering.

Because she was too ill to go about daily activities, she found the time she spent between painkilling medication was unbearable.

She was first hypnotized by a clinical hypnotherapist and then taught to use self-hypnosis. Using the methods she was taught, she stretched her comfortable, relief time beyond the effects of her medication. She also compressed the unbearable time in her mind to just a few minutes of pain instead of hours.

Time distortion can be a valuable technique for many people, particularly for those who may be suffering too much pain to function normally. Have you ever noticed how quickly a good movie seems to be over or how you lose track of time when you are visiting with a good friend? These are examples of ordinary time distortion. With self-hypnosis, you can turn this ordinary capacity into an effective strategy for expanding the time when you can feel comfort.

When using any technique discussed in this chapter, you will find moments when your pain is diminished or absent. It is during these times that you can most easily use time distortion.

You may be in a trance and notice that through distraction or imagery you have achieved some level of comfort. While in self-hypnosis, focus on that moment of comfort. Imagine it to be part of a long-running movie, a visit from a good friend, or an absorbing, enjoyable hobby activity. Visualize whatever image will convey the idea of stretching time.

Perhaps you would enjoy experiencing your comfort as a long, slow balloon ride. Or maybe as writing a long letter, eating a 10-course meal, or looking through an old picture album; any such experience can be used for stretching time. Here are some examples of how you can do this. But remember, use your own imagination to create more material for your trance.

You are starting from a point of comfort and are encouraging that experience to expand.

You might visualize and talk yourself through a description of each scene of a favorite movie: *"This comfortable feeling is like watching* Gone With The Wind. *It may be a fascinating to see how long this feeling will last. It may be a pleasurable feeling to watch each scene unfold and the story develop . . ."*

Another approach could be: *"I may find that time is like a rubber band that can stretch and pull a long way. My feeling of peaceful comfort can expand and stretch in the same way . . ."* You might imagine giant rubber bands, small ones, inner tubes, perhaps chewing gum being pulled and stretched. See yourself in comfortable settings and see the time in those settings stretching and expanding like a balloon being filled with air.

Here is another example of how to expand your image to stretch your periods of comfort: *"I can imagine taking a long trip and passing through many towns. Each town has a gas station where I can stop to rest. I can feel the comfort and relaxation of that first station right now.*

"Perhaps this comfort and level of relief will last until I travel to the next station. As I pull out of the driveway, I can look up the street and almost see the lights of the next town and the next station.

"I may find that the road to that town is shorter than I might think. I may be surprised or curious, or perhaps more amazed than curious, to find that I still feel comfortable and soothed as I come up to that next station. I can visualize the station now, getting closer and closer . . ." The trip can take as long as you like. And you can begin to fill the space between stations with descriptions of what you might see along the way.

Through this sort of suspension and expansion of time, you may find that your conscious mind loses track of the minutes. Perhaps even hours of time may go by at this level of relief. In this way you can lengthen the span of your relief and the intervals of pain will get shorter.

You will need to experiment with this technique and the others to find which works best for your situation. It may be that several work well or that you can combine them.

Before practicing, find several examples of metaphors and images to use during you session. Allow your creative mind to expand on each of your images once you are in self-hypnosis.

Many of the examples of metaphors and images presented in other chapters can be adapted for use in pain relief. It is most important for you to find examples that are similar to your own memories. Adapt or modify the samples in this book to fit your own experience.

REFERENCES

Barber, J. & Adrian, C. (Eds.) *Psychological Approaches to the Management of Pain.* New York: Brunner/Mazel, 1982.

Benson, H. *The Mind/Body Effect.* New York: Simon and Schuster, 1979.

Edelson, J. & Fitzpatrick, J.L. A comparison of cognitive-behavioral and hypnotic treatment of chronic pain. *Journal of Clinical Psychology,* Vol. 45(2), (Mar), 1989.

Elton, P., Burrows, G.D. & Stanley, G.V. Hypnosis and chronic pain. *Australian Journal of Clinical & Experimental Hypnosis,* Vol. 8,(Nov), 1980.

Erickson, M. The Interspersal hypnotic technique. In J. Barber & C. Adrian (Eds.), *Psychological Approaches to the Management of Pain.* New York: Brunner/Mazel, 1982.

Feverstein, M. & Skjei, E. *Mastering Pain.* New York: Bantam Books, 1979.

Freese, A.S. *Headaches: The Kind and Cures.* New York: Doubleday & Company, 1973.

Hilgard, E.R. & Hilgard, J.R. *Hypnosis in the Relief of Pain.* Los Altos, California: Wm. Kaufmann, 1975.

Hughes, R. & Brewin, R. *The Tranquilizing of America.* New York: Harcourt, Brace, Jovanovich, 1979.

Levinthal, C.E. The effects of indirect hypnosis, direct hypnosis, and progressive relaxation on the primary and secondary psychological symptoms of chronic headache. *Dissertation Abstracts International,* Vol. 49(7-B), (Jan), 1989.

Melzack, R. & Wall, P.D. Pain mechanisms: a new theory. *SCIENCE,* Vol. 150, 1965.

Patterson, D.R., Questad, K.A. & DeLateur, B.J. Hypnotherapy as an adjunct to narcotic analgesia for the treatment of pain for burn debridement. *American Journal of Clinical Hypnosis,* Vol. 31(3), (Jan), 1989.

Rausch, V. Cholecystectomy with self-hypnosis. *American Journal of Clinical Hypnosis,* Vol. 22 (Jan), 1980.

Sacerdote, P. Techniques of hypnotic intervention with pain patients. In J. Barber & C. Adrian (Eds.), *Psychological Approaches to the Management of Pain.* New York: Brunner/Mazel, 1982.

Sachs, L.B., Feuerstein, M. & Vitale, J.H. Hypnotic self-regulation of chronic pain. *American Journal of Clinical Hypnosis,* Vol.20, (Oct), 1977.

Spinhoven, P. & Linssen, A.C. Education and self-hypnosis in the management of low back pain; A component analysis. *British Journal of Clinical Psychology,* (May), 1989.

Wain, H.J. Pain control through use of hypnosis. *American Journal of Clinical Hypnosis,* Vol. 23,(Jul), 1980.

19
Skin Improvements— Warts, Herpes, Eczema and Psoriasis

Your skin is the largest and most visible organ of your body. It reacts to stimuli from inside you and out. Goose bumps appear when we chill or become frightened. We flush when we have exercised or become angry.

The epidermis (outer skin) is durable yet sensitive, tough enough to walk on all day yet vulnerable to internal stresses. Our skin is the container for our bodies and a barrier to outside invaders.

It is much easier to understand skin problems when you realize that both the skin and the nervous system spring from a common ancestry in the embryo stage of human development.

While many skin problems have clearly physiological causes, it should also not be surprising that our skin can be the first place a call for help is issued from our nervous system or our psyche. A rash, hives, itching and pimples can be the first signal that something inside is out of balance. That "something" may be physical, psychological, or both.

Not every itch, pimple, and rash is an internal cry. Poison ivy, fleas, mosquitos, or clogged pores, among other things, can be responsible, too. Have a physician check any skin problem to see if there is an organic irritation.

Many skin disorders are caused by outside irritants, bacteria and viruses and are *aggravated* by internal conditions. Warts, psoriasis, eczema, herpes, and pruritus (itching) all are affected by emotional factors and stress.

It is not easy to catalog skin disorders as being caused by either psychological or organic conditions. As we have discussed in other chapters, there is no clear separation between mind and body—the two systems are interwoven. Disease and illness can be brought on or allowed to develop because of a lowering of our immune system.

We might just scratch, put on some calamine lotion or cold compresses, and soon our symptoms will go away. But go away where?

If our skin conditions are caused by emotional problems, the stress, conflict, or repressed feelings that we have ignored will find another body part to aggravate. Usually, what we repress becomes stronger until it finds a way to be expressed, ventilated, or break out. Perhaps the stomach will be next—ulcers? Maybe the circulatory system—high blood pressure?

We would be smart to pay attention and turn an ear inward. Is an unexplained rash or itching a voice from within, a call from the assistance operator inside us? We need to be sensitive to events, feelings, and situations in our lives that may need finishing—anger expressed, stress released, or anxiety calmed.

Anxiety is often related to skin problems. Self-hypnosis is an excellent prescription for the desired improvements as well as for an understanding of the cause.

Charles Mutter, M.D. (1986) writes that hypnotic applications have been used throughout the history of medicine. Self-hypnosis can often achieve improvements in far less time than traditional approaches. It offers a direct route to the unconscious source of irritation and effects healing through uncovering and resolving traumatic material quickly.

With skin disorders, people often get more anxious because they feel their body is out of control or because the problem may be so easily seen by others.

Hypnosis operates very closely with the autonomic nervous systems which controls involuntary body functions such as heart rate, blood pressure, blood flow, temperature regulation, metabolism, respiration, and many blood chemistry processes that influence the immune system. Self-hypnosis can be effective in gaining relief from many skin conditions because it can be used to positively affect these autonomic functions.

WARTS

It is a hearty virus that causes warts to grow. The fact that a person is in contact with the virus, however, does not mean that warts will develop. It has been observed that emotional distress can aggravate warts and cause them to spread.

Such was the case with Billy who was 16 years old and had dozens of warts on his hands, fingers, and elbows. They were quite unsightly and caused him a lot of embarrassment. He refused to go to some social events because of the warts. Other times he wore Band-Aids to cover them.

Billy was normal and healthy in other regards. But he was at the dating age and was very self-conscious about his appearance. The warts were causing him anxiety.

His parents had tried every other treatment possible—chemicals, electrical cauterization, freezing, surgical removal. They had spent a great deal of money and the warts still grew back. Often the treatments were more uncomfortable than the warts.

After nearly two years of other treatments, Billy's physician referred him for hypnotherapy. It became clear in the first session that there were many problems in Billy's family. His father had left home and remarried a woman who did not accept Billy. Billy was living with his mother and sister and often had arguments with them.

That kind of "disruption" is much like an "eruption." What erupted for the young man was his skin, almost as if to say, "I can't handle it anymore, I'm really upset, but how do I express it?"

Though part of the reason for Billy's warts was psychological disruption, that was not the only cause. There may have been nutritional or circulatory deficiencies that contributed to the virulent activity of the wart virus.

Billy was taught self-hypnosis and instructed to use it to produce physical changes—heart rate changes, temperature increases and decreases in his hands and fingers, and heaviness and numbness in various body parts. This sort of practice gave him a sense of control over his own body.

It was pointed out to Billy that he did have some emotional turmoil in his life, but his treatments with self-hypnosis were directed toward his symptoms—the warts.

He was encouraged to eat good, balanced meals. These balanced meals were used as posthypnotic cues for him to regain balance and harmony in his skin.

In a few weeks he gained the skill and confidence in using self-hypnosis to experience some control over his body. Though his warts were still there, he could create warmth or coolness in his hands; he was also able to relax and to relieve much of the stress and tension that built up throughout the day.

This control gave him the feeling he could do something about his warts. Next, Billy began giving himself suggestions to deal directly with the growths.

The suggestions were aimed at decreasing the blood flow to the warts, just as he was increasing his control over other physical sensations. Making his hand cooler, it was pointed out, is a result of decreasing the blood circulation to it, something he had learned to do. He gave himself the repeated suggestion "*No blood to warts!*"

He also suggested that the warts were dissolving and getting smaller. For example: "*My warts are beginning to shrink like the fishing pond in summer. They're getting smaller and smaller each day.*" Billy imagined them shrinking, becoming flatter, and then disappearing.

Sometimes, he would imagine that his hands were under a magnifying glass or a microscope and that he could actually see the warts shrinking. Other times, he would visualize them washing away a little at a time, whenever he washed his hands. Washing his hands became a posthypnotic cue for his body to wash away the warts.

Within a few weeks, the warts on his right hand had nearly gone away. Many of the small ones had completely disappeared. After a month and a half, there were warts only on his left hand and these, too, were getting smaller. Within four months, all the growths were gone, except two small warts on his left hand.

Billy was told not to expect all his warts to go away. It is important not to try to eliminate all your warts. Try to get rid of 80 or 90 percent. This makes your goal more reachable. It also allows a few warts to remain if there is still some psychological reason for them.

If one assumes that the warts were a result of Billy's emotional upset, because Billy had not completely resolved the turmoil and disruption in his life, a few small, remaining warts might prevent some other symptom from developing in their place.

In this young man's case, the majority of his warts were gone and his embarrassment left with them. His physical control was an example for Billy to develop more emotional control relating to himself and his family. It took several more months of self-hypnosis to achieve some resolution that worked for him. He learned to focus his attention and be understanding while releasing his emotions and feeling more relief.

GENITAL WARTS

This variation of wart appears on the genital organs and anus of either men or women who have come in contact with the virus. The location of these warts can cause great anxiety in sufferers because of the embarrassment and feelings of guilt or shame. Psychotherapy or hypnotherapy can often help deal with these self-sabotaging feelings. Other people find emotional relief through support groups or other forms of reducing the isolation and misunderstanding that can distort one's perspective.

It can be helpful to know that hypnotic applications have been successful with genital warts as well with as those affecting other parts of the body. Clinician Diane Roberts Stoler (1990) has success using a guided imagery process that creates the metaphor of a garden fortifying one's immune system, with water having special properties to dissolve the warts and the images of ponds of positive emotional nurturance.

Dr. Dabney Ewin (1990) employs, with his patients suffering from genital warts, images of blood flowing to the warts to bring antibodies and white blood cells to fight the virus and heal the affected area.

Other clinicians use suggestion approaches that the warts will begin to feel dry, then they will turn brown and fall away, causing no more concerns, and that the focus can turn to other matters. Any of the suggestions strategies in this chapter can be utilized or personalized by you and can be effective with any type of wart.

Suggestion structures

It is not necessary for your imaging to be anatomically or physiologically exact in order to be effective. Regardless of whether Billy's suggestions were "No blood to warts" or "More blood to warts," it was the INTENTION of the suggestions that was most important.

Therefore, use whatever mental concept or notion of healing that *makes sense to you* to create positive change. If you are the sort of person who likes to read and research and know all you can about your condition, then it's fine to base your suggestion strategy on that knowledge.

However, if you would prefer developing suggestions from your own present concept of how the body works, those suggestions will work equally well for you. It is your desire and intention to experience relief that form the dynamics of the suggestions for physical change.

Hypnosis or placebo effect?

The hypnotic phenomenon is acknowledged by both the American and British medical associations and is taught in medical schools in both countries. Yet the mechanics of hypnosis are not completely understood and some scientists look with skepticism at treatments or cures that are unexplainable.

In the treatment of warts, it is not known whether the anti-wart response to hypnotic suggestions is due to increased immunity functions, more or less blood circulation, some unknown chemical action, or some other process. How the unconscious mind is able to prompt warts to disappear when conventional treatments fail is still not fully known.

Some scientists compare hypnosis to the placebo effect. Indeed, there are similarities.

The placebo effect, or the "effect of the empty pill," is the effect often observed when a patient is given an inert pill along with an explanation of what powerful effects it will have. If the patient believes the person administering the pill, often the described effects will come about.

New drugs are often tested in a "double blind" fashion. This means that neither the administrator of the drug nor the patient knows whether a pill is the test drug or an inert substance. Only the originators of the test, who never see or speak with the patients, know which is which. The object is to eliminate any expectations or placebo effect from the results.

A study in 1978 by Tasini and Hacket reported in the *American Journal of Clinical Hypnosis*, compared hypnosis with acid treatment on warts and compared those treatments with placebo and controls. The study showed the hypnosis group lost significantly more warts than the control groups.

It is thought by some people that placebos function in a way similar to hypnosis—that is, the unconscious mind directs and stimulates the sought after response or healing.

When a patient is made aware that he or she has been given a placebo pill, a non-effective substance, the patient usually soon stops benefiting from it.

Belief in the substance's curing properties seems to be the crucial element, regardless of the patient's motivation to get better or feel a response.

However, it is not necessary to believe in hypnosis for it to be effective. *The hypnotic effect can take place even with total disbelief of it.*

What is essential for hypnosis is *motivation* to gain success, to achieve control or relief or whatever the goal may be.

With a placebo, the unconscious mind is tricked into believing that the source of the change or effect is coming from the outside—the pill or injection. The unconscious then causes the expected response.

It has even been argued that all medication operates, at least to some degree, through the placebo effect. Drugs may produce some physical change that triggers the unconscious to make the final curing action.

But with hypnosis, you are responsible for creating the change. There is no deception. If the motivation to make the change is present and is stronger than any motivation to oppose the change, then the change can occur. Whether you choose to believe the change is due to hypnosis or not is beside the point.

There may be innumerable ways of tapping into the unconscious mind and using it as a resource to make positive changes from within.

From our earliest years we learn that doctors make us well. They give us medicine, which we must take to get better. It's no wonder that we grow up to find it implausible that we can often make *ourselves* well again. It's even less a wonder that some physicians find it hard to understand the same phenomenon.

But even scientists are unable to find explanations for many a drug's method of creating change. Simple aspirin, the "wonder analgesic"—its exact pain relieving action isn't known. Many effective medications listed in the *Physician's Desk Reference*, the bible of drugs, are described with the phrase "The exact chemical mechanism of action is not known." Such incomplete knowledge does not prevent us from starting the treatment or from getting benefits from these medications.

Until we completely understand the way in which the unconscious mind creates its effects on our bodies, and vice versa, we should keep our minds open to using those methods that do produce positive changes. Certainly, like using aspirin, you can use self-hypnosis.

HERPES

Cold sores and genital herpes are produced by herpes simplex viruses. There are dozens, perhaps hundreds of individual strains of these viruses.

Once the virus enters the body, whether on the lips or in the genital area, a lesion (sore) may appear within a few days. The virus usually runs its course in eight to 14 days.

As its cycle completes, some of the remaining virus migrates down the nerve sheath from the originally infected area. The virus resides within the nerve sheath, unreachable by the body's natural defense mechanisms. When conditions are favorable, the virus migrates back up along the nerve and causes another infection outbreak.

Presently, there is no cure for the virus once it obtains a foothold in the nerve sheath. There are antiviral drugs now that are effective for some sufferers in reducing the severity and frequency of recurrence of infections, as well as in reducing the contagiousness.

One of the most difficult aspects of a genital herpes virus outbreak (like genital warts) is the emotional turmoil it produces. "For most people, herpes is not terribly debilitating, but it can be a horrible psychological problem," comments Sam Knox, of the Herpes Resource Center (Freudberg, 1982).

In our society, we have been led to believe that nothing is really impossible—not for long, at least. There is always some cure. But for the herpes virus there still is no cure. Frustration prevails.

For sufferers, the notion of having this infection "forever" can be a helpless, hopeless feeling. It need not be so.

The outbreak of cold sores on people's lips never stirs the emotional trauma that genital blisters can create. In a presentation titled "Psychological Responses to Genital Herpes" (Freudberg, 1982), Dr. Elliot Luby cited a sequence of responses to the virus, observed by clinicians at herpes self-help centers.

1. First, shock and emotional numbing, similar to reactions to a serious or life-threatening illness or disease.
2. After the shock subsides, there is a frantic search for a cure or some sense of disease management.
3. There begins a sense of isolation, helplessness, and loneliness. The patient develops an awareness of peculiarities of the disease, while its incurability cracks through the initial denial. There is an inner questioning of the disease's impact on relationships, future companionship, and the possibility of having children (for women).
4. Anger can now become a dominant emotion. Directed at a person suspected of transmitting the disease, this rage can sometimes reach murderous dimensions. Or anger can be focused on the physician who is unable to provide a cure.
5. Fear can develop involving many areas of the patient's life—contagion, cancer possibilities, childbirth. When and how should potential lovers be told about the virus? What are the individual's responsibilities about the disease?
6. After a while, patients can feel contaminated, ugly, or undesirable. Fear, shame, and guilt can cause social isolation. Relationships can seem to require too much energy and become overly complicated.
7. Depression can deepen with each recurrence. Job performance can be affected. The "Why me?" phase can bring feelings of self-hatred, unwor-

thiness, and even thoughts of suicide. A feeling of entrapment and hopelessness often dominates the patient's life.

It is necessary for a person with the herpes virus to break this distressing, despairing cycle. To stay too long in the grip of hopelessness is like saying to the disease "OK, here I am. I'm not worth anything any more because I have this infection. I give up." That sort of attitude is crippling and is an excuse to avoid interpersonal relationships.

Not all patients, Dr. Luby reports, are affected in this dramatically negative way. Many patients adapt readily to their recurrent infection.

Hippocrates once said, "A wise person should consider that their health is the greatest of human blessings, and learn by his own thoughts to derive benefit from an illness." It seems that herpes patients who have learned this are most often older, are married, and have a good understanding of themselves as well as of their disease. They are open with their mates and have sexual relations only when they are not having an outbreak.

Indeed, some people report that while they are by no means glad they have the virus, they have used the situation to launch into self-exploration and reevaluation of personal and sexual relationships.

Many people have found that their personal worth and self-confidence need not be linked with an infection. You would not question your self-worth if you had become infected with measles or the flu. Why allow a virus smaller than a skin cell to rule an entire body that has the capacity to resist?

Self-hypnosis and herpes control

Whether you are suffering from an outbreak or are between infections, the emotional stress brought on by the presence of the virus can be severe.

Whenever you feel yourself thinking too much about the herpes virus or worrying about getting another infection, take some time to practice self-hypnosis for 10 to 15 minutes. Use some progressive relaxation to release tension in your body. Reinforce in your unconscious mind that you have the power and ability to prevent many different kinds of infections.

In 1981, Dr. R. Arone di Bertolino, of the University of Bologna, reported (Freudberg, 1982) using hypnosis to treat nine patients who had severe weekly or bimonthly genital herpes attacks. A year and a half after treatments, six of the patients had not had any outbreaks and the other three had had only one or two recurrences yearly.

More recently, Sol Gould and Doreen Tissler (1984), at the New Mexico Pain Clinic in Albuquerque, reported using hypnosis successfully to reduce the severity of outbreaks of herpes in several cases, reducing their recurrence and the general anxiety that accompanies genital herpes outbreaks. Their strategies were patterned after the visualization work done by Carl Simonton (1982) and his team working to enhance immunity in cancer patients. See Chapter 6 for more on the Simontons' work.

Cold viruses are in and around you constantly, yet you may only "catch cold" infrequently. You may be exposed to the flu, but you may not always come down with it. In the same way, your body can keep its defenses in good working condition and experience an outbreak of herpes virus infrequently.

A specific strategy called the Committee Meeting, in Chapter 21 on weight loss, is an excellent approach to use for emotional release. Such emotional awareness and letting go can help with how parts of your unconscious may feel about herpes or any skin condition.

The role of stress in triggering outbreaks

Many people who suffer from recurring infections find that emotional stress and tension can trigger an outbreak.

Stress, as we discussed in an earlier chapter, can reduce your immune system's strength. It is believed that the virus can somehow detect when your immune system is weak and that it then begins its migration toward a new outbreak.

Self-hypnosis can be an effective way to deal with stress and tension before they cause a new infection. Study Chapter 12 on stress management and develop several posthypnotic cues for dealing with day-to-day pressures. Keeping your stress levels in control may be the best way to control the herpes virus.

Here is an account by one young woman, Marie, of her method of using self-hypnosis to relieve tension and stress relating to her herpes virus:

"*I had a lot of tension over the past few days, but I hadn't done anything about it. So, when I awoke one morning, my heart was pounding and there was a tight knot in my stomach. I got into the shower and as I stood there with the warm water running down me, it occurred to me that this water could wash away my tension and the potential for another outbreak.*

"*I put myself into a light trance, standing with the water flowing on my back. I let the water carry away the tension. I imagined it going down the drain and I visualized it melting the stress off me. It took about 10 minutes. By that time the hot water had begun to run out and I felt completely relaxed for the first time in days, and no infection came. The feeling was so good, I can easily recall it. I use the same method now whenever I become tense or anxious—it really works.*"

Another way to use self-hypnosis to dissolve the tension and stress is expressed in this account by another sufferer, Paul:

"*During the first year after I got herpes, I would go into a tailspin every time I broke out with sores. I wouldn't even see my friends for a week or more. I was embarrassed and never told anyone about it. It was so depressing, sometimes I'd sit at home and cry, feeling sorry for myself.*

"Some time later I learned self-hypnosis from a therapist I was seeing. In my self-hypnosis, besides being able to get rid of all the tension and jangled nerves I was getting, I would go over all the other things in my life that were good.

"I'd remind myself that I can still be good at my job, my friends and family were still there. Other than a few weeks of this minor infection every couple of months, I was in good health. For me, it was a boost knowing that I had value to myself and other people, above and beyond the herpes. I concentrated on that in addition to regular suggestions to reduce my stress.

"My herpes doesn't come nearly as often anymore, maybe twice a year. And when it does, I don't get depressed and upset. I think there will come a time when I won't get any outbreaks at all."

Can self-hypnosis help against an active infection?

It is always better to try to prevent an outbreak, rather than to attempt to get one to go away. If you are having an infection, it can produce its own anxiety and tension.

First, deal with the stress and tension from the infection. Give yourself suggestions that remind you that the infection is temporary—it will end soon. "*Just as a cold or the flu ends after a time, so too will this infection end.*"

You may also use suggestions and imagery of the virus being overtaken and destroyed by your immune system. You might visualize your white blood cells as eagles that flock together to consume and eradicate the virus.

You may picture your body's defenses as an army that descends upon the herpes virus at the site of the lesions. The soldiers of your immune system can kill each virus and take no hostages.

Or you may visualize the virus being locked up by the body's defenses. The white blood cells and lymphocytes can round up the virus that are causing the infection. Maybe they store them in miniature capsules of stainless steel.

You may imagine the virus being carried away from you: perhaps visualize it flowing out of you along with stress and tension during a progressive relaxation exercise.

When she does have an outbreak, here is one method Marie uses to deal directly with the attack:

"The ocean has always had a strong pull on me. I decided to use it to 'pull out' my herpes. As I stood on the shore watching the birds and waves coming in and out, I closed my eyes and put myself in a trance.

"I imagine each wave coming on into my body and carrying away the viruses to a better place for them. I envision the viruses being glad to leave my body because it is less hospitable for them than the ocean. I visualize them leaving me with each outgoing wave."

Marie's outbreaks last only about a week when they do occur.

Self-hypnosis for stress reduction is valuable for preventing outbreaks of the virus. Using hypnotic visualizations and imagery for dealing with the symptoms of an attack also have demonstrated effects on shortening the duration of the infection.

If you feel you have been exposed to a herpes virus and want a strategy to use even if you have not had any outbreak, you may use an approach borrowed from a concept in the television program "Star Trek: The Next Generation."

Create your own version of a bio-filter device that can eliminate undesired bacteria and viruses from your body. It doesn't matter how you imagine the process. Your suggestions might expand on the following imagery.

"As I imagine my body, I can imagine a filtering system in and around my body. This filtering system will let pass through only what is important and necessary for me and my body to exist in a healthy state. This bio-filter can remove virus and bacteria that are nonessential."

More research and experimenting needs to be done with self-hypnosis to directly affect the body's ability to completely prevent the virus from causing infections. As the ancient Greek philosophers have said, "There is no illness of the body apart from the mind." Cures for the incurable may reside within us.

Keep healthy through your diet

Maintain good nutritional balance. You might consider experimenting with vitamins and supplements that bolster the immune system. Check with your physician to ensure that whatever vitamins or other supplements you take are compatible with your present health condition.

Vitamins A, B-1, B-6, C, and E, and the amino acids cysteine, ornithine, and pantothenic acid are among the nutrients that enhance the body's immune system.

ECZEMA AND PSORIASIS

The exact cause of these common, noncontagious skin disorders is not known. However, millions of people in the U.S. suffer from one or the other of these two similar problems.

Psoriasis is characterized by pink, scaly patches of skin along the hairline and thickened, yellowish fingernails, with pitting and notching. Sometimes, large areas of the body can be covered by scaly, sometimes silvery or pink plaques. But the elbows and knees are the most common sites of outbreak.

Eczema is also an inflammation of the skin. It appears as a red, scaly, sometimes blistery or weeping surface. Eczema begins as microscopic blisters which break open and ooze. The eruptions soon spread to other areas, mainly the neck, forehead, wrists, forearms, and bends of the knees.

Eczema is different from psoriasis in that eczema is a moist, bright red, itchy rash. Psoriasis is dry with pink or silvery scales. Psoriasis rarely appears on the face, while eczema can involve any area of the body.

While neither is a fatal disorder, they can be crippling, both physically and emotionally. There is no true cure for psoriasis. Both conditions have been observed to be aggravated or provoked by worry, stress, tension, and emotional problems. Oversensitivity, aggressiveness, and suppressed feelings of resentment and anger sometimes underlie the disorders.

Eczema and psoriasis can be arrested and brought under control with medication and stress management. Do you hold in hostility and anger, guilt or fear? As mentioned earlier in this chapter, your skin can be the first place where repressed feelings emerge.

Using self-hypnosis to manage stress and emotions

You may want to use self-hypnosis to explore your feelings and emotions. See if there is any unfinished emotional "business" that may be "under your skin." Chapter 16 on self-exploration in this book will help you do this.

Creating you own program of self-hypnosis and self-understanding may be a valuable adjunct to medical treatments for psoriasis or eczema. Develop posthypnotic cues that will allow you to relax and relieve stress before it triggers a skin eruption.

You may want to self-explore while in a trance. Look for any connections between the primary sites of your psoriasis or eczema outbreaks and some event or action that may have caused an emotional reaction. While you are in self-hypnosis, try to go back in your memory to the first time you remember the skin aggravation. Was there anything happening in your life at that time that may have caused you to be upset, aggravated, angry, or have some other strong emotion?

This is not an easy task. You probably have been suffering with your skin problem for quite some time. Practice these self-hypnosis techniques for several weeks before trying to analyze your desired success. Often people will try and try for weeks with no success at remembering any significant connection, before the thread of a memory begins to appear.

It may also be that there is no one incident or situation that prompted your condition. It may have been caused by an accumulation of stress, repressed emotions, or other factors. It is most important to deal with any present stress in your life. Eliminate as much excessive worry, tension, and pressure from your mind as you can.

Practice self-hypnosis in the morning, before you begin your day. Program yourself to be as relaxed as you possibly can be.

Self-hypnosis for the symptoms of itching and irritation

Just as self-hypnosis can alter the experience of pain, it can change the sensations of itching and irritation from psoriasis or eczema. First, learn to develop some basic physical changes in your body while in a trance: slow your heart rate; create numbness, coolness, lightness, or heaviness in your fingers, hands, around your mouth, in your feet, anywhere on your body. The first section of this book will teach you how to use self-hypnosis for these basic changes.

Practice daily with self-hypnosis techniques and focus on the areas of outbreak on your body. Visualize what the discomfort is like.

Describe the irritation to yourself in your own way. The better you can visualize what your discomfort feels like, the better you can redirect your perception of it.

Suppose you feel the irritation to be like needles prickling your skin. Visualize the tiny needles. See them turn to filaments of cool soothing water. Feel the needle-like water numbing your skin.

Itching may be like being tickled with feathers or scratchy like tiny needle pricks. Perhaps it feels like an insect crawling over your skin.

While you are in a trance, create imagery to be as vivid and as real to you as possible. Use your description of the itching or irritation to transform it into a more acceptable sensation.

Combine your description of the discomfort with the new feeling, like the metaphor of the needles and spears of cool water. You might transform a feeling of insects crawling lightly over your skin into snowflakes melting and cooling your irritated skin areas.

Be creative with your imagery

Chapter 6 on visualization and imagery will help you. Also, you can develop posthypnotic cues to deal with irritation and discomfort outside of your trance. For instance, you might give yourself suggestions such as: *"Whenever I feel the itching or irritation of the psoriasis (or eczema) and need to scratch it, I can take three deep breaths and remember how cool and refreshing it felt to imagine cold, icy water flowing over my skin."*

You can use any visual image of water as a trigger for this posthypnotic cue. Use something in your environment that is often present—a water fountain, a sprinkler, a stream, or even the faucet at home or work could act as a visual stimulant for a posthypnotic cue to feel relief.

The suggestion while in self-hypnosis might be: *"Whenever I feel the need to gain more comfort, more relief from the symptoms of the eczema or psoriasis, the water dispenser at work will remind me of the comfort I know I can dispense to myself."*

Find several symbols like the water fountain and faucet that you can use to recall the comfort and relief you felt while in your self-hypnosis trance. Even closing your eyes and visualizing the soothing sensation of the water, while taking several deep breaths, can act as a cue.

The same sorts of cues and associations can be developed for any soothing feeling you may find helpful to your condition. The relaxed warmth of the sun or the soothing feeling of a salt water bath can be a source of comfort.

Cues can be created for the sensations of relief you get from everyday occurrences. For example: *"I may find that whenever I turn on the heater of my car, the warm air blowing over me can remind me of the comfort and relief I felt from lying in the sun on a summer day."*

Chapter 5 on posthypnotic suggestions will provide further examples for developing effective cues. The techniques of dealing with the symptoms of your skin conditions need to be worked on and adapted to your specific problem.

Take the time to develop several different approaches to dealing with the symptoms as well as with stress reduction. Adapt suggestion strategies from the various skin conditions to use on your own situation. What you are investing in is a long-term method for gaining relief and remission of your skin disorder.

REFERENCES

Barber, T.X. Hypnotic suggestion and psychosomatic phenomenon: A new look from the standpoint of recent experimental studies. *American Journal of Clinical Hypnosis*, Vol. 21, (Jul.), 1978.

Benson, H. *The Mind/Body Effect*. New York: Simon & Schuster, 1979.

Benson, H. *The Relaxation Response*. New York: William Morrow, 1975.

Ewin, D.M. Suggestions with condyloma acuminatum (genital warts). In *Handbook of Hypnotic Suggestions and Metaphors*. (Ed. C. Hammond). New York: W.W. Norton & Company and American Society of Clinical Hypnosis, 1990.

Freedman, A.M., Kaplan, H.I. & Sadock, B.J. *Modern Synopsis of Psychiatry*. Baltimore: Williams and Wilkins Company, 1972.

Freudberg, F. *Herpes: A Complete Guide to Relief & Reassurance*. Philadelphia: Running Press, 1982.

Gould, S.S. & Tissler, D.M. The use of hypnosis in the treatment of herpes simplex II. *American Journal of Clinical Hypnosis*, Vol. 26(3) (Jan), 1984.

Grossbart, T.A. Bringing peace to embattled skin. *Psychology Today*, (Feb), 1982.

Hamilton, R. *The Herpes Book*. Los Angeles: J.P. Tarcher, 1982.

Hartland, J. *Medical and Dental Hypnosis*. Baltimore: Williams & Wilkins Company, 1971.

Mutter, C. The many applications of hypnosis. In *Hypnosis: Questions and Answers*, (Eds. Zilbergeld, Edelstein, & Araoz). New York: W.W. Norton & Company, 1986.

Sheehan, D.V. Influence of psychosocial factors on wart remission. *American Journal of Clinical Hypnosis*, Vol.20, (Jan), 1978.

Simonton, C. & S. *Getting Well Again*. New York: Bantam Books, 1982.

Stoler, D.R. Suggestions for vaginal warts. In *Handbook of Hypnotic Suggestions and Metaphors* (Ed. C. Hammond). New York: W.W. Norton & Company and American Society of Clinical Hypnosis, 1990.

Tasini, M.F. & Hacket, T.P. Hypnosis in the treatment of warts in immunodeficient children. *American Journal of Clinical Hypnosis*, Vol.20 (Jan), 1978.

Wicket, W.H., Jr. *Herpes: Cause and Control*. New York: Pinnacle Books, 1982.

Zacarian, S.A. *Your Skin*. Radnor, Pennsylvania: Chilton Book Company, 1978.

20
Increasing Your Self-Confidence and Problem Solving

Ann doubted her decisions almost every time she made one. A recurring theme for her was, "*I should have done/said* [otherwise] . . ." Whether the decision was about the color of a new blouse or the selection of a preschool for her child, Ann frequently experienced a lack of confidence in her decisions and in her ability to accomplish tasks set by herself or others.

If you have some feelings of self-doubt, or in some way lack self-confidence, you are not alone. Those feelings, like a dense fog, drift over nearly everyone of us to some degree at various times.

Most people find it much easier to put themselves down about various aspects of their life than to accept themselves as they are. Most of us heard many more "Nos" than "Yeses" and "Don'ts" than "Go aheads" as children. For many of us our most impressionable age was filled with other people telling us what to do and when to do it.

Those outer-directed types of standards can be difficult for children. As children we depend on others—parents, teachers, relatives—to help set the level of our self-image and our levels of competence. We look to them to tell us when we are doing well and whether our appearance is all right. It is no wonder that many people feel about themselves the same way their family acted and felt toward them.

We sometimes tend to have a child's view of perfection, also. Often we believe that we must be perfect in our body, our actions, our words, and our decisions in all of our day-to-day functions. Worst of all, we determine what this perfection is by asking or listening to someone else, or replaying the high expectations of the past.

But as we become adults, the need to find our levels of personal best or to determine our self-image should come more and more from within. We need to set aside the old scripts (behavior patterns) of looking to others for approval. If you are always trying to please someone else or be like someone else, you may want to do some work with Chapter 16, "Self-Exploration—Be Your Own Counselor." Try to understand why you still feel this need to please others instead of yourself.

NOBODY'S PERFECT

In generating self-confidence and making effective decisions, drop the notion of perfection and start using concepts like, *"my best. . . . my maximum performance. . . . the most I can be. . . . extending my limits. . . . or, develop my unconscious potential."*

Those are the sorts of phrases that you will want to use when giving yourself suggestions to improve your self-confidence and remove self-doubt. You will definitely benefit from being honest with yourself and will begin making improvements.

It is amazing how easily we can be swayed by negative comments about ourselves. Yet we quickly question and doubt the sincerity or accuracy of a compliment.

We may spend time dressing the best we can for a party or other social event and get several positive comments. Then one person will say something about how the colors seem unusual or the shoes look uncomfortable. Zap, we go into a tailspin for the evening. All the positiveness we felt dissolves in the face of one negative comment. Our self-confidence is shaken—at least for the rest of the night.

We can all do better when we have an *inner sense* of who we are. That knack of looking within can tell us how good we feel about ourselves—not based on the comments of someone else, but based on how we see ourselves.

This is quite different from conceit or an inflated ego. True self-confidence is an inner acceptance, understanding, and support of our true selves. It is a positive ability to interact with others. It is an acceptance of a best decision as the best possible at that moment and in that situation. Mistakes, errors, bad outcomes are opportunities for learning.

REJECTING REJECTION

A self-hypnosis technique, created from American Indian rituals, is to imagine yourself as having a protective and invisible shield. Use your imagery to develop this concept in any form you choose, so that all negative comments aimed at you are repelled back to the speaker, while positive comments can flow right through. You can absorb the positive statements into every cell of your being.

True self-confidence is at no one else's expense

Self-confidence has nothing to do with being better than someone else. It is feeling good and solid about yourself. It is understanding your strengths and abilities, and knowing that you have the capacity to change and improve many aspects of yourself, as you choose to do so.

Self-confidence is depending on yourself to establish how attractive, intelligent, capable, and accomplished you are. You can learn to measure yourself only against what feels right for you, not what is right for anyone else.

If you want to improve specific areas of your life, you can do that, too. Set goals for yourself that are attainable, but not so low they provide no challenge.

PROBLEM-SOLVING HYPNOSIS

Shall I accompany my lover to a new city and leave my family, friends, and work? Would it be best to have my aging mother live with us or in a retirement home? How can I best make my proposal stand out from that of my competitors?

By opening up your unconscious mind, you will expand the input and understanding from a deeper part of yourself. You can have a private consultation with your wise inner self and create your own "Think Tank." With self-hypnosis, you can develop a reservoir of good ideas from which you can choose the best options for the problem at hand.

You can benefit from all your experiences and from the knowledge you have gained. You can develop more and better alternatives for any problem or challenge by separating your thinking process from your emotions and feelings. This allows you to utilize both, in measured amounts.

CHOICES AND DECISION-MAKING

Your big goal in problem solving with self-hypnosis is to search for many options. Try to derive many possibilities, so that you can later select the best for you.

Quite often, in our day-to-day flurry of pressure, activity, and responsibilities, we are tense when we seek solutions and make decisions to solve our problems. Emotions and obligations bear upon us and we make decisions without considering all the possible choices.

Perhaps only later, after our decision is made, we realize that there was another way, a better plan, a more effective solution. We wish we had seen it before we committed ourselves to a course of action. Nearly everyone has had that feeling at one time or other. Remember to accept that your decisions in the past were the best you could make *at that time and in those situations.* Stop chipping away at yourself for the past; it's done, you have learned what needed learning, now you can affect the present moment. That is your best focus now.

Are you making a major life or career decision? Are you trying to solve daily problems in your work or personal life? Self-hypnosis can give you *clarity* to see more *alternatives* than might normally be apparent.

Instead of making self-hypnosis a pressure situation to find the *one* answer to your problem, use it first to remove pressure, stress, and anxiety, to reveal *many* possible answers. Your confidence in your decision-making will improve as you develop some very small successes.

PROBLEM-SOLVING METHODS

Begin by narrowing the focus of the situation. Get a clear idea of the result you seek to achieve—what exactly is the problem or challenge? Is it the best design? The best sales proposal? The best site for expansion? How to most effectively arrange the furniture? How to organize your own time most efficiently? Which college to attend? Or some other situation of greater or lesser importance?

Tony Robbins, author of *Unlimited Power* (1986), states that people make decisions from two possible motivations: their wish to avoid pain or their desire to gain pleasure. He has helped people be more effective selling and living. Perhaps you can sell some good ideas to yourself.

Your first goal is not to decide which of the selections you already have is best. It is to provide as many different options as possible. This is important. *You can't possibly make the best choice if you don't have all the possibilities to consider.*

First, enter a trance and feel comfortable, relaxed, and in reasonable control over your physical body. Allow your unconscious mind to take a guided trip. Begin exploring something other than the immediate problem.

Perhaps go for a mental swim in some body of warm, safe, relaxing water. Feel free to look at the interesting fish through your swim mask. Imagine comfortably touching the various new and different plants. Examine the variety of textures and objects on the bottom.

Maybe you would rather take a mental flight in your trance-state. Put on a pair of wings. Climb into a balloon. Slip behind the stick of a small airplane or fly unaided by mechanical devices. Float into the clouds and see the passing of life around, above, and beneath you from a *new view.*

Explore the clouds from within and then allow those moisture puffs to float away from you. Look down from a new perspective and see birds flying.

You might take a long walk in a forest, maybe a drive through the mountains, or launch yourself deep into a space journey.

What you are doing with this fantasy voyage is preparing yourself—in fact, *practicing to "see" things in a new and different way.* You will be using a remarkable feature of the self-hypnotic state—that of stripping away the old and limiting boundaries of your thinking process.

Those limitations are put up by your conscious mind. With this sort of practice, you are starting a creative flow from your unconscious mind. Like shoveling through the snow, once you get a small pathway going you can enlarge it and widen it to accommodate whatever you choose.

So it is with opening your unconscious mind. Allow yourself to examine new, different, and unexplored places. Enjoy your practice and success from these positive, changing experiences. You can then expand into exploring your problem or challenge.

There are no right or wrong ways of doing these exercises. Take your time or move quickly through these experiences; whatever pace you set, you can be confident and you will do fine.

Giving yourself suggestions

Use imagery, use verbal descriptions to yourself, use fantasy situations or real ones, use whatever feels most comfortable for you. Develop your flow for creative ideas and perspectives.

Intermingle suggestions to feel good and confident about what you are doing and to look forward to many new alternatives. The exact structure of your trance is less important with problem solving because you want to develop your own rhythm and flow. A pace or form that works well for one person may be inappropriate for another. Follow the guidance of your own comfort.

You may want to begin your trance with general suggestions of positive feelings toward what you are doing with self-hypnosis. As you go through your fantasy exploration, you might want to include some suggestions of how similar fantasy exploring is to the exploring you will do of your specific problem.

For instance, suggest: "*How easy it is to lift myself above the clouds of conventional solutions and see the many different varieties of options, like the variety of flowers in a field or the variety of trees in a forest. I can get the flow of my thoughts going in the direction of openness to new ideas and variations.*"

You can give yourself many suggestions with that theme. Use your own words and symbols, and repeat the suggested idea several times in each trance session.

SELF-HYPNOSIS AND SELF-CONFIDENCE

Here are some ways that self-hypnosis can help you increase your self-confidence:

1. Your desire to change should come mostly from within you. It should be little influenced by what others tell you. Self-exploring (see Chapter 16) can help you better understand and accept your own uniqueness.
2. Self-hypnosis will allow you to relax and learn to control many parts of yourself. This will let you recognize that you have always possessed the abilities and skills to make the changes in yourself you wish to make.
3. You can learn to be your stronger self and feel more comfortable. You can learn to make specific suggestions and develop posthypnotic cues to deal

with specific situations. In areas of work, social situations, family or personal relations, self-hypnosis can help you develop your inner strengths.

4. Once you have learned to be more self-confident, you will become a better listener. You will no longer need to duck or ignore other people's comments in fear. You will learn to understand that you can choose to accept or reject others' views of you. You will be able to separate your feelings about yourself from those of others.

Self-confidence in your physical appearance

There are some things about yourself which you can change only a bit. You can't make yourself taller or shorter, for instance. You may wish you were more muscular or that your eyes were a different color.

Remember that you can improve in most areas and need not compare yourself with others. If you feel good about your appearance—meaning that you are as attractive and well groomed as you can be—others will find your appearance pleasing, also. You may not look like a fashion model, but that's not necessary to lead a happy, rewarding life.

We all have qualities, strengths, and abilities that make us unique. Most of us have room to improve, also. The objective of self-hypnosis is to help you develop your own qualities and give you control over those areas of your life which you can change positively.

Methods for developing self-confidence

First, identify which area of your life spawns the most self-doubt, the least self-confidence. It might be in your work. Perhaps it is being around people of the opposite sex. Maybe being around your parents makes you feel the most uneasy.

You may feel you lack confidence in all areas of your life. While that may be true, you will do best to deal with one area at a time. Decide which area you want to work on first. In Chapter 9 on motivation and goal setting, you learned to set reasonable objectives. Rather than bite off too large a chunk of work to begin with, narrow your focus to one specific circumstance in which you feel self-doubt.

For illustration, let us suppose that you are constantly seeking the approval of your parents, your spouse, or some other loved one.

1. You may first want to use self-hypnosis to do some inner examination, some self-exploration. Try to determine why you seek a definition of yourself from other people in your life. Why should their view of you become your view?

2. Using the techniques of self-exploration, you can learn to let go of emotions that are unexpressed within you. Get in touch with these feelings, release them, and then put them behind you. Leave yourself free to concentrate on making the necessary *changes* in yourself.

3. While in a self-directed trance, you can recreate situations with people in which you felt you lacked self-confidence. Recognize your actions and better understand the reason for them.

4. Imagine an old situation with someone whose approval you sought, but now imagine new actions stemming from your perceptions of self-confident behavior.

5. Finally, rehearse again situations where you had self-doubt and give yourself posthypnotic suggestion cues that will reinforce your self-confident changes. After one success, your confidence in self-hypnosis will grow and all your future goals will be easier to reach.

A woman's liberation

A case that illustrates these processes well is that of Liz, a 28-year-old woman and daughter of a Navy officer. Because of her father's career, her family traveled extensively while she was growing up. She also had a weight problem—22 pounds too much.

Using self-hypnosis for self-exploration, Liz examined her own life. She felt that she was unable to go to college—a wish she had held for many years. She had a well-paying job, but it was not emotionally rewarding.

While in self-hypnosis and exploring her past, Liz realized that most of her life she had looked to her father to gauge whether she was doing well or doing the right thing. She also depended on her boyfriend to tell her whether she looked and acted okay. In short, she constantly depended on other people, particularly the men in her life, to tell her how she was doing.

Her father had told her she was better off with her present job and that college would be a waste of time. So she had given up the idea.

Her boyfriend wanted to marry her and have a family. She would then be helping him with his career. This was the story of her life: letting other people tell her what she should and should not do.

When she looked at her life and her desires, she saw far too many obstacles. Liz wanted to break out of this feeling of self-doubt and learn to take control of her own life.

Her first task was to establish some control over a small part of her life. A success, even a small one, is a building block in self-confidence.

She realized that her first, small success was in realizing what her problem was. She allowed herself to become angry at her father and feel frustration with her boyfriend, and to release some of her repressed, stored-up emotions.

She did this by writing each of them a long letter after a self-hypnosis session.

Liz saved these letters and at an appropriate time she gave each his letter. Her awareness and action resulted in an increase in her self-confidence. That was another success.

In those first few weeks of self-hypnosis practice, she was also giving herself suggestions for feeling more confident when talking with her father. She developed posthypnotic cues to use when she talked with him. For example, when her father began to tell her what to do or how to do something, she would softly rub the back of her neck. That was a signal for her to relax, remain calm, but be aware of the old pattern of control he was exhibiting, as if untying the string or her neck.

Another cue was clenching and then releasing her fist. That, along with a deep breath, signified the old control being released and her gaining new strength. She was taking charge of her own life. Her decisions and views about her life were more important than anyone else's, she told herself.

In another series of trance sessions, Liz imagined herself as a bird. At first, the bird couldn't fly; it only walked. It resembled a penguin.

Then she visualized a bird that could walk and fly just a little. The birds were a metaphor for her own transformation.

After a few weeks, she began to visualize a bird representing her future. This one was brightly colored, strong, and able to fly long distances. In her suggestions, she told herself that she could be as strong as that bird.

Liz suggested to herself that if some people saw the beautiful, colorful bird in flight, they might react in different ways. Some people might think it belonged in a cage. Others might think it should be in some other country. But their view didn't matter to the bird. It was exactly where it wanted to be.

Her life was like the bird's. She could be where she wanted, rather than where others wanted her to be. In successive self-hypnosis sessions, Liz gave herself suggestions of strength and power that were symbolized in her imaginary bird. As it could grow more colorful and strong, so could she.

Within eight months, Liz had enrolled in college and was doing well. Her relationship with her father was more distant, but much better.

Her relationship with her boyfriend was also much better than before. He liked the changes that had taken place in her, though occasionally he would relate to her as he had previously. When that happened, she would remind him that he was relating to a bird of a different color. Both of them could smile with that thought.

The 9-to-5 hive

The work place can be a very competitive environment. Often people may put you down so they can put themselves up. Some people use other people, manipulate them for their own gain. Perhaps they pay you double-edged compliments such as: *"That's nice, but can't you do better than that?"*

Sometimes people say things not meaning to undermine your self-confidence, but that is the result if you let it happen. They may be poor communicators with other people.

It's difficult to avoid some situations and some people like that. But you can do something about *your* reactions to them and how much time you spend listening to them.

While in a trance, separate other people's views of you from your own. Picture yourself in your work situation. Imagine that the six, 12 or 20 people there all buzzing about you at once like bees in a hive. All are saying something different. In fact, none of their points of view are the same. As they continue talking, you might even hear their comments differently and see their expressions change. The more you examine what they are saying, the less sense they are making. Why are any of their perspectives or opinions about you or your decisions more important than your own?

Others' comments about you might not be more accurate than your own view of yourself. Just as only you can change yourself, only you need judge what you want to change or accept.

Put a new frame around the critical comments of others. Rather than being "voices of truth," they can be like different channels on the radio or TV. You can choose to listen or not, or even change the station. If you were watching your own movie or TV program, as though your life and the people around you were a movie, you might even get a smile about some of those comments.

WORST CASE/BEST CASE STRATEGY

Another way to gain some perspective on a particular problem is to use "worst case/best case" imagery. Visualize how things might be if the very worst situation were to occur. Try to imagine what that condition would be like.

Then imagine what the "best case" would be. Imagine that as clearly and as detailed as you can.

Reality will usually lie somewhere between the two.

Here is a situation where the "worst case/best case" method of exploration helped a young woman finally achieve the best solution and feel great about it.

Gloria was responsible for setting up an exhibition booth for her company. The objective was to make the display accessible and to allow the customers to move through it in an uncongested manner.

She already had several different floor plans drawn up, but she wasn't confident that they were the best she could devise. Gloria decided to use her self-hypnosis skills to find more options.

While in a self-directed trance, Gloria imagined the "worst case" situation. In one scene, people were jammed into corners, unable to move. People tripped on the electrical wires on the carpet. Drinks were spilled onto equipment, which short-circuited and belched smoke. Customers began to get turned off and wandered down the aisle, away from her exhibit. In all, it was a disaster.

After that somewhat humorous yet terrible visualization, Gloria then imagined the opposite. With all the bad possibilities out and in the strong light of her imagination, she opened herself up to the "best case." In this scenario, she imagined how none of those horrible situations could occur.

Though she sometimes exceeded the realm of possibility in the new plan she visualized, she also came up with some new, more creative ideas that were workable. She used this form of practice several different times. And each time, when she finished her trance, she wrote down notes about her worst and best situations.

Her final floor plan was based on one of her original designs, with improvements and modifications gathered from her self-hypnosis. The design worked so well that she was asked to design an exhibit for another of the company's divisions.

REHEARSING DIFFICULT SITUATIONS — PUBLIC SPEAKING

You may find that your confidence is adequate in most situations, but that certain things unnerve you. One of the most common of these is giving a speech. Self-hypnosis rehearsal can be very useful in taking the anxiety and tension out of public speaking or any similar presentation situation.

How this is done is illustrated by the example of Steve, an administrator who had to give a speech once a month to a group of respected people in his town. He felt very controlled by the worry and pressure of what people would think if he messed up his speech.

You can apply the same method of imagery rehearsal and posthypnotic cues he used to any specific situation in which you feel a lack of self-confidence.

Steve was competent at his work and his preparation for his talk was always complete. It was the delivery in front of an audience that brought on his self-doubt. He looked to self-hypnosis for help. He began by learning how to develop a trance and become relaxed.

After feeling comfortable with self-hypnosis techniques, Steve examined what it was that caused him to feel uneasy about speech-making. Clearly to him, it was the possible embarrassment of botching the talk, forgetting what he wanted to say, or making some other "fatal" error.

While in a trance, his first step in defusing his lack of self-confidence was to use the worst case/best case strategy and *imagine* himself doing the worst possible job of delivering his speech. He pictured himself tripping over the podium, spitting as he spoke, forgetting his entire message, the public address system failing—every conceivable thing that could go wrong.

Most of these embarrassments were unlikely to ever happen; nonetheless, by imagining them he got all the negative possibilities out of his system. At times, he felt amused by, laughed, and enjoyed these parts of his self-hypnosis.

The process took several trance sessions. He used his imagery in this manner until he could think of no more negative events that could even remotely happen. This desensitized him to those negative possibilities. He also interpreted all of the possible negative situations more confidently. Then he was ready to work on positive images.

Steve next visualized himself giving an excellent speech. He saw the audience applauding. He used imagery to feel the sensations of the confidence he would feel after giving a very successful speech. He imagined these positive scenes in great detail.

He developed a set of posthypnotic cues, while in self-hypnosis, which would help him remain calm and focused while making his presentation. For instance, in most cases there was a microphone at the podium. He would have the opportunity to adjust it for a moment before he began. That moment of adjustment became a cue for him to feel the positive adjustments in himself, also.

One of his suggestions was: "*I know that I can adjust the microphone so that the audience can hear me better . As I adjust it to be a comfortable distance from me, I can also be adjusting myself to be comfortable and better able to communicate with the audience, clearly, confidently and more at ease.*"

Another cue was clenching his fist. He could do this just before he began speaking. His action was hidden from the audience and he could repeat it at any time during his speech.

His suggestion was: "*I may find that as I clench my fist and take a deep, satisfying breath, I squeeze all the tension and anxiety I feel into that hand. The tighter I clench it, the more I can gather the fear and self-doubt. As I exhale and open my fist, I can release that tension and self-doubt and feel much more comfortable and self-confident.*"

By using such cues, Steve overcame his self-doubts about speech-making.

OTHER METHODS OF PROBLEM SOLVING

Some of the most difficult problems we might need to deal with are those that involve our family and friends. In these situations, our emotions can run high, and often our feelings confuse our sound judgment. It is hard to be objective and to see situations clearly when we have strong underlying sentiments of loyalty, guilt, responsibility, anger, caring, disappointment, or other emotions.

If you are dealing with a problem or trying to make a decision that is clouded by emotional considerations, self-hypnosis can provide an arena of objectivity. Often this will open the way for new possibilities to be seen.

In your trance, you can consult with your inner self or what some people have called the "third eye." You can imagine conversations with those involved or with people whose opinions you trust and value. This may give you an idea of their point of view, without the emotional charge of a real discussion. In many instances, you may have already had several real discussions.

You might explore your own self-interest, devoid of hindering emotions such as guilt or sadness. Your goal is to find more alternatives, first. Then you can use your trance-state to evaluate the choices without the emotional baggage on the scales.

With self-hypnosis you will be better able to decide on a course of action or a solution that balances your interests with those of others involved.

The five-step decision

One dilemma facing many people today, that requires such balance of interests in family decisions, is what to do with aging parents. That was the challenge that Doris and her husband encountered.

Her widowed mother was reaching the point where her health made it unwise to live alone. Doris's husband had helped investigate the alternatives and was willing to have his mother-in-law live with them. They also had three teenage children who wanted the grandmother to live with them. However, the children were all at the age where they would be leaving home soon. Doris and her husband were looking forward to being alone together again.

The final decision seemed to rest on Doris's shoulders. After a great deal of conscious analysis of nursing homes, the domestic changes that would be required in her family, her responsibilities, her personal stress, and her mother's needs and happiness—Doris still couldn't make a decision.

She finally decided to use self-hypnosis to help her find a course of action. Over a series of six or seven different trance sessions, she went through a process that included:

1. An internal communication with herself to examine where her own family was in its growth and change. The children were soon to be gone. It would be the first time in 20 years that she and her husband might be alone together. She mentally listed all the benefits, joys, and anticipations she felt—*without feeling any accompanying guilt.* This was the first time she had allowed herself to do that.

2. She held an imagined conversation with her mother. The mother expressed her own needs to be close to her old friends, family, church, and familiar surroundings. She had lived near her mother for many years. Doris was able to appreciate the needs of her mother without feeling frustration and resentment.

3. Then Doris imagined the future and what it would be like with her mother in the house. She imagined the day-to-day routine. In another trance, she imagined what it would be like with her mother in a nursing home, not too far away. She visualized visiting her there and helping care for her.

4. In a unique fashion, Doris examined her own self-interests, using the symbolism of two pools of water. One was her mother's pool and the other her own. Years before, the two of them had gone swimming together for exercise, so this metaphor was drawn from that experience. In each pool Doris imagined inner tubes to represent the individual self-interests of each woman, without judging the merits of those interests. In the end, she counted more in her own pool. Yet she knew she was striving for balance.
5. In another conversation with herself, Doris examined all the possibilities again. She saw that she didn't want to make a permanent, irrevocable decision. When she realized that, she saw that a temporary solution, a trial period without a long-term commitment, was possible. This was a new concept, another option.

She finally decided on a one-year trial period of having her mother live with her. At the end of that time, she, her husband, and her mother would reconsider the entire situation. The mother agreed that this would be fine with her.

Though it seemed a logical alternative in retrospect, the notion of a trial period had never occurred to anyone before. Everyone had been polarized by their emotions into seeing an either/or situation.

As the year passed, the older woman's health began to fail even more. By the time the year was up, it was clear to everyone that the best care she could receive would be the 24-hour medical attention of a quality nursing home.

Though the decision was no less sad to make then, Doris and her husband felt the decision was in everyone's best interest. As it turned out, the children—two of whom had moved out of the house—visited their grandmother far more often, they said, than they would have had she gone directly to a nursing home the year before.

Frequently, we find that best solutions to our life's challenges are not easy. More often than not, there are no right or wrong ways. Rather there are many solutions, and each has a separate set of pluses and minuses. Only by following one particular path do we get to see what those add up to.

RELATIONSHIP DECISIONS

You may have a great deal of confidence in your work and in many other areas of your life, but suppose you lack confidence when you are relating to the opposite sex. The methods in the beginning of this chapter will also help you to rely on your own definition of your self-image rather than on that of someone you're romantically involved with.

Self-hypnosis can also be used to provide you more relaxation and a set of posthypnotic cues for remaining calm and self-confident when dating and in other relationship situations. This is a technique for putting you more at ease.

You may notice that when you are alone with your date or someone you are romantically interested in, you feel self-conscious. Perhaps you are afraid you will say something wrong or sound foolish. For this reason, you speak very little. Then you feel uneasy because you seem to be withdrawn and distant.

Does this sound at all familiar? How can you break the cycle of anxiety, fear, and self-doubt? First you must learn to relax in other situations.

Use your self-hypnosis experiences to develop cues to enable you to feel more calm and less tense in any situation. Give yourself suggestions that you can be relaxed and natural in any surroundings you choose. It is not necessary for you to be or act like someone you are not. You can be at ease, relaxed, and yourself.

Develop customized posthypnotic cues to relax, ones that can be used anywhere. Use cues such as clenching and releasing your fist, deep breathing, rubbing the back of your neck. Perhaps suggest closing your eyes for a moment and visualizing a color or image that you associate with relaxation.

While in a trance-state, you can rehearse an upcoming date or social situation that you may find yourself in. Rehearse the negative possibilities and then rehearse the desired positive outcome. Give yourself suggestions to reinforce the positive results.

For example, Jack had met what he felt was a wonderful woman. He was in love and, at the same time, afraid he would lose her. He wanted to tell her how he felt, but that was not easy for him to do. He had always found it difficult to share his feelings with women he was involved with.

Jack knew what he wanted to do, tell her how he felt. He knew that would get a lot off his mind. He used self-hypnosis to mentally rehearse how he would take this big step. He rehearsed it many different ways and with many different responses from his girl friend.

He still felt some anxiety the next week when he talked to her, but he was able to tell her about his feelings and was happily surprised when she responded with a "Me, too!" This sharing of himself became the foundation for a new way of being in a relationship for Jack.

Using self-hypnosis to gain confidence and make a positive change freed him to trust himself in other situations. One success often leads to another. If he could face himself and her in that way, he could face many other situations too.

In all your practice in building self-confidence, remember to set reasonable goals for yourself. You may find that when you go out after using self-hypnosis and developing some cues, you will feel a bit more at ease. You may notice that you are a little more talkative. You may laugh a little more easily. Or you may recognize other signs that your suggestions are taking effect.

There usually will be no sudden transformation. The changes are mostly gradual and cumulative. Build on your small successes. After you have some small positive result—perhaps your date or companion mentions that you seem to be in a good mood—use that in your next trance session.

Develop suggestions to strengthen your good feelings about any positive comments and review any negative ones to see if they have validity. If so, you may wish to use it as constructive input; if not, disregard the negative comments.

Reinforce any positive feeling, even if it's just a slightly more confident sensation you notice from within. Give yourself suggestions that if you can cause one small change like that, then you can build and expand on it. Remember the words of the Chinese philosopher who said, "A journey of a thousand miles begins with one step." And certainly, your journey of change is the best of all.

REFERENCES

Freedman, A.M., Kaplan, H.I. & Sadock, B.J. *Modern Synopsis of Comprehensive Textbook of Psychiatry.* Baltimore: Williams & Wilkins Company, 1972.

Hartland, J. *Medical and Dental Hypnosis.* Baltimore: Williams & Wilkins Company, 1971.

Maltz, M. *Psycho-Cybernetics for Creative Living.* New York: Pocket Books, 1974.

Newman, M. & Berkowitz, B. *How to Be Your Own Best Friend.* New York: Ballantine Books, 1971.

Pelletier, A.M. Three uses of guided imagery in hypnosis. *American Journal of Clinical Hypnosis,* Vol. 22, (July) 1979.

Robbins, A. *Unlimited Power.* New York: Simon & Schuster, 1986.

Stanton, H.E. Ego enhancement: A five step approach, *American Journal of Clinical Hypnosis,* Vol. 31 (March), 1989.

Wollman, L. Self-confidence achieved by hypnotic techniques. *Journal of the American Society of Psychosomatic Dentistry & Medicine,* Vol. 25, 1978.

21
Thin Meditations

If you have had a problem with weight control, you have likely tried many diets, pills, and conditionings before reading this book. There is no one method, formula, or series of suggestions that will be effective for everyone.

The reason you are overeating may be any one of a dozen or more possibilities. Perhaps you learned your eating habits from your parents. Maybe emotional factors cause you to overeat. There may be some specific compulsion or personality characteristic behind your eating problem.

In some rare cases there can be a metabolic problem. If you are severely overweight, you are advised to see a physician to determine that there is no organic problem. If no underlying physiological cause is found, you are left with the responsibility of your weight control. That can be the most difficult part of any weight loss program; changing your eating behavior and attitudes about food.

DO OTHER DIETS AND WEIGHT LOSS PROGRAMS WORK?

Actually, some do work. The failing often comes not from the effectiveness of the diet—but from the inability to keep the weight off.

Reliable observations and common sense show that overweight occurs when you take in more calories than you burn up. Emotions always play a part in self-control or self-denial. When this imbalance is reversed, you lose weight. Simple. Therefore, it would seem that a diet which accomplishes this reversal will insure a drop in weight.

But the high rate of relapse suggests that permanent weight loss can happen only with nutritional awareness, long-term physical fitness and exercise, altering emotional ties with eating, and changing poor eating habits into healthy ones.

Self-hypnosis can help you achieve these goals. However, make no mistake, *you make the changes in yourself.* We have titled this chapter *Thin Meditations* because self-hypnosis has meditative qualities and many of the exercises are like meditations with posthypnotic suggestions.

SELF-HYPNOSIS TO CHANGE YOUR EATING HABITS

Overeating is a personal and individual condition. You don't overeat for exactly the same reasons someone else does. Your life is unique and your experiences are different from those of your friends and neighbors. As you read this chapter, some techniques will seem more relevant to you than others.

All of these methods work, but you must select the ones which will work best for you. The most effective program is to use several different techniques together, at the same time.

There are several means of dealing with the symptoms of overweight:

1. *Symptom substitution:* Using posthypnotic suggestions and cues, you can "trade down" from one eating habit to other eating behaviors such as chewing gum or eating specific dietetic foods or vegetables and fruits.
2. *Symptom transformation:* You can change the compulsion to eat, through posthypnotic suggestion, into actions such as physical exercise, work, interest in community projects, child rearing, or window shopping. This is similar to symptom substitution, but it transforms the problem symptom into a less objectionable one without addressing the nature of the symptom itself.
3. *Symptom amelioration:* You can directly reduce the overeating. With posthypnotic suggestions, you deliberately eat less. The posthypnotic suggestions you give to yourself are aimed at teaching you that you are in control. You can just as easily eat less as eat more.
4. *Symptom utilization:* This encourages you to accept and redefine your eating habits. Your insistence that you "cannot stop overeating" is accepted rather than denied or attacked. You instruct yourself that you will continue to overeat a specific amount. That amount can then become less and less.
5. *Thin meditations:* These blend the above strategies while developing a special focus of awareness on thoughts, feelings, and unconscious processes surrounding food, eating, and nurturing. With thin meditations, you move yourself into a greater sense of self acceptance and you naturally select healthier eating choices.

Within these general categories—which can be used in combination—there are several specific self-hypnotic techniques that can also be used to reinforce your work toward improving your health and appearance and reducing your desire for food.

You may believe it is important to search through your past to uncover the reason you are a compulsive eater. If you feel strongly about that, then you can use Chapter 16 in this book on self-exploration. We will discuss the matter more in this chapter also.

Remove the tension

Relaxation is an integral part of weight loss and changing eating patterns. In looking at your own eating patterns, you may notice that you eat more when you are nervous, tense, or under pressure. Using self-hypnosis to deal with those feelings of tension and stress will help you to lessen your desire for food. Chapter 12 on stress management explains how you can directly influence stress also.

TASTING AND EATING MEDITATION

The following is a thin meditation you can read to yourself during self-hypnosis trance. It will help you relax and focus on what you are eating or tasting.

Before eating, I will close my eyes . . . say hello to my body . . . making sure my body is ready to eat.

I will breathe into relaxation . . . I can give my self a loving feeling through breathing and become more aware of what I am doing right now. I remind myself that I accept and love my inner self . . . as I am right now.

Right now, in the present moment, I am becoming more and more aware . . . I eat with joy . . . I drop all other purposes and let the act of eating envelope my whole being.

When I am eating, I let my whole consciousness be that of taste and smell . . . I can take my time . . . I can chew, then trust my taste buds. Smelling, and savoring the texture . . . I set all else aside for the right-now experience of eating.

When I do two things at once, I miss both experiences . . . I now can let food be meditative . . . I can be respectful of my ritual of eating and take my time to become more aware of food as nourishment.

What you are achieving by using self-hypnosis is a change in your eating habits that will keep you healthy and allow you to eat enough to reach and maintain your desired weight. If you wish to follow a nutritionally sound food diet along with your self-hypnosis work, that is fine.

This first exercise is to help you develop an increasing level of awareness of your eating. Practice your own form of eating and tasting meditation. Mentally play the meditation in your mind once a day for three weeks; additionally, each day, pause and think about the meditation for a minute.

USING SELF-HYPNOSIS FOR WEIGHT LOSS

Losing weight is not a spectator sport. You must become involved.

Most people focus on the physical body when they think of losing weight. Many experts agree that what we call the body is actually made up of three bodies or *selves*: physical, emotional, and mental.

All change processes, including weight loss, must integrate an awareness of each of these three selves to avoid a struggle between them which will sabotage permanent weight loss. In other words, if you ignore parts of your physical, emotional, or mental self when trying to lose weight, you are indeed "fighting with your self."

Here is an example. Mary, at age 41, was satisfied in her career, but dissatisfied with her recent marriage, her second. She had been thin and attractive earlier in her life, but a stressful marriage, a divorce and child custody battles, and refocusing on her career were big events in her life. She had grown bigger over the years.

From a comfortable 125 pounds, Mary had grown to 168 and seemed to be "more sad than happy lately," as she observed about herself. There were many emotional weights that hung on Mary along with physical and mental weight. She was still angry at her ex-husband for what she felt were injustices; she was tired and sometimes overwhelmed trying to raise her daughter and keep a career; there was much that she felt had been lost to her. Mary was pushing herself now in her work and realizing how empty she felt even after she had eaten.

Mary's self-hypnosis work combined trance sessions and journal writing three times a week to put onto paper all the emotions she was exploring in her trances. She would often compose letters (seldom sent) to people in her life to whom she still had something to say. For example, Mary's childhood upbringing had taught her that divorce was wrong. She wrote letters to her father, mother, priest, and even to herself, discussing the many feelings and perceptions she had about divorce. After writing a letter, she waited a week and then she read the letter again to decide whether or not to send it.

The trance work helped Mary to keep some distance from much of the pain of her memories and thoughts. She could watch events of the near or far past as if they were occurring on a movie screen. With time and practice, she let go of old feelings. Now understood and accepted, those feelings could be put in their place and let be.

In her journal, Mary wrote expressions that helped her release anger, resolve grief, and relieve inner conflicts. Like all of us, Mary, has different aspects of herself. These different parts or aspects of our selves can have different goals or priorities that may conflict. One part can say: "You should lose weight." Another cries out: "But I'm so hungry!" A third sympathetically says: "Maybe some indulgence is okay, you've worked so hard." Then another part of you says: "If you don't eat the whole thing, you're wasting food."

As long as there is this internal fighting or conflict, losing weight will always be a struggle. One part wants to be thin while other parts undermine the efforts.

You may have some idea of how this notion of different aspects of our personality or self can exist. Here is an exercise to help you develop more awareness of your different parts, particularly those affecting eating, food, and nourishment.

THE COMMITTEE MEETING

Your actions are driven by committee. Hold a committee meeting in your imagery. Imagine setting up a few chairs, gathering some pillows or cushions, in whatever way you choose. Imagine a committee made up of various parts of yourself assembling to discuss food or anything having to do with your goal.

Maybe there are some parts of you that you know should be at the committee, perhaps anger, fear, sadness, motivation, guilt, your inner child, your inner parent, or your ideal self. There may be three or four parts of you to meet this time or maybe there are six or 10. At different times, different parts of your self may wish to be heard. Take some time and allow this experience to happen, let each part of you have a voice, be accepted, without judging or arguing, allow all members of your committee to say a few words or as much as they want about something of which you would like greater awareness.

You might give hope a committee seat, or doubt, or indulgence, or the thin you and the fat you could have chairs and voice their perspectives. Committee members need to express all of their feelings out loud during self-hypnosis or you can write them down.

Next, set up a special chair for the "Watcher," that is the head of the committee, the observer part of you that listens and observes. The Watcher can see all these things you are doing, thinking, and feeling and ask, *"What part of me is this coming from? Whose voice is it?"* The committee trance can help you identify whose voice from within is influencing you—mother, father, priest, teacher, friend, an old part of you, or whoever.

The Watcher can help you decide to trust your self and help to understand what member of your committee may be speaking through actions. If unwanted actions have a voice at the committee, they will be less inclined to speak indirectly through sabotage, mixed feelings, or conflict.

This is a powerful exercise that you can do over and over again, each time learning something more or something different as you accept all parts of your self and your committee. This is a courageous exercise of self-understanding and expression. Give yourself credit each time you conclude a committee exercise and thank all parts of your self for speaking and being present.

SUGGESTION MATERIAL

Here are some specific suggestions. Put them in your own words. These can be included with any other suggestions or imagery you might choose to employ. As you will see, each one can be expanded and made personal to your situation. You have the responsibility for having put on your extra weight; take the responsibility and work toward freeing yourself from it.

1. *My appetite will be smaller than before and easily satisfied.*
2. *From the smaller portions I serve myself, I will get all the pleasure and satisfaction necessary for my physical and mental well-being.*
3. *I can take as long as I wish to eat.*
4. *I may find that more nutritious, lower calorie foods are what I really prefer eating.*
5. *I may find that there are better, healthier, more satisfying activities than eating between meals.*
6. *I can close my eyes at any time and visualize how I will look when I am at the weight I desire to be.*
7. *I can become more relaxed, more poised, more self-assured and confident as I get closer to the size and weight I desire to be.*
8. *The desire to eat can be replaced by a feeling of pride in my new ability to eat more healthfully and lose weight.*
9. *As I lose weight, I may find it easier than I thought to maintain my new image. My new eating habits are easy to keep because they are my habits, ones that I have created for myself.*

MORE WAYS TO CHANGE YOUR EATING PATTERNS

You can develop posthypnotic suggestions to transform your desire to eat into some other activity. This is symptom transformation.

Give yourself suggestions such as: "*I may find that certain times of the day I develop a craving for food. When this happens between my normal meal times, I may be able to take a brisk walk, or do some calisthenics, or perhaps some gardening. I may find that taking a walk or a drive can be just as satisfying as eating food. In fact, I may find that doing some exercise is so much healthier for me that I feel better after exercising.*"

Perhaps you can enroll in evening classes or begin reading books. Perhaps do some volunteer work or take up a hobby—sports, crafts, or other non-food related activities.

As always, use your own words to convey the meaning of your suggestions. Make the suggestions positive. Also, add some posthypnotic cues. For instance: "*I may notice that when my stomach begins to moan or my body in some other way tells me to eat, I know that I can use that signal, that desire, to motivate me to take a brisk walk. I will feel so much better, so much more energy from that walk, that I will enjoy the exercise and fresh air much more than eating.*"

Have several posthypnotic cues which you can suggest while in your trance. It is always best to have pre-planned those cues before you begin your self-hypnosis.

You can also develop cues from other actions you normally might take. Opening the refrigerator door can be a cue to open yourself up to other forms of consumption. "*When I open the refrigerator door to find some food to eat between meals, instead I may find that I can open up to a book that I will enjoy. Closing the door to the refrigerator is just as easy as closing my desire for food. I can close the door and leave behind the food, just as I can leave behind my hunger for extra food. I may ask myself, what am I really hungry or thirsty for? Companionship? Am I bored and thirsty for excitement?"*

When you develop such posthypnotic suggestions and cues, make them specific to eating at any time except mealtime. Avoid creating a conflict in your posthypnotic cues. Your suggestions will work best if you keep them in a positive form.

Another problem is eating correctly at your prescribed mealtimes. You may find that you do just fine avoiding between meal snacks, but at dinner you stuff yourself. Such extreme eating nullifies all the benefits of cutting out snacks. It is somewhat like washing your car with great care and then driving through a mud puddle.

Set intermediate goals

If your weight loss goals are substantial, you will need to put your goals into perspective. If you need to lose 80 to 100 pounds, or more, don't expect to lose it all in one or two months. Be patient.

You may not see any difference in your appearance after losing 10 or 12 pounds. But you certainly will *feel* the difference. You will feel more energy, you will feel better knowing you are being successful. After a few more weeks, you will start to look different.

In your self-hypnosis, just as you can feel the changes that are brought about by the trance-state, you can also feel the differences brought about by the small weight losses. Notice those changes—be aware of the feeling of less bulk. Think small. Feel small changes, make your weekly goals small, think of small portions of food and imagine yourself becoming smaller and thinner.

In your own program of weight loss, remember these points:

1. Check first with your physician to establish your level of health and the rate of *safe* weight loss. In most cases set a goal of no more than three pounds of weight loss per week.
2. It is best to have a weekly goal and daily checks. This will give you a target you can achieve in a reasonable period and will allow you to feel good about intermediate successes.
3. Give yourself a reward every few weeks of success. The reward should be nonfood—perhaps an outfit that you can reduce into, or a short trip to a peaceful, relaxing spot—the mountains, a beach, a park, or anywhere that you can take a healthy, refreshing walk. You may want to buy yourself a book or compact disc. Reward yourself with a long-distance call to an old friend.

BODY IMAGING

Body imaging has been found to be a very effective technique in self-hypnosis. While in a trance-state, picture yourself getting thinner and lighter. Imagine how you would like to appear. Visualize your arms getting thinner. See each part of your body as it can be when you are at your target weight.

Perhaps see yourself fitting into clothing that was previously too small for you. Your suggestions could include feeling thinner. Imagine people giving you compliments about how good you look in your new body.

Your imagining could involve a walk around a pond or in front of a store window—somewhere you can see your reflection. Visualize yourself in that reflection as you will appear in six or seven months or whatever time it will take you to achieve your desired weight loss. Create as clear an image as you can.

See yourself in some new clothes, looking slim, looking healthy. Imagine the colors. See your arms, legs, and waist as thin as you wish them to be. Know what you need to do in the next few months or so to make that picture of yourself become a reality.

Whenever you need motivation to continue your exercise, close your eyes, take a deep breath, and remember the reflections of yourself as you will be. Recreate that image in your mind as a cue to overcome the temptation to eat.

Make the imaging fun; be creative. Perhaps you'll want to imagine your reflection doing something like shopping for a new outfit. You might imagine yourself playing tennis or swimming.

Develop suggestions that let you feel good about losing weight and that reinforce your motivation. A set of suggestions might be something like these:

"As I sit here in self-hypnosis and can visualize myself as I am now, my body just as it is right now, I can see that there are some well-drawn goals that I have for how thin I want to look. These are goals of the slim appearance I will have six months from now. They are always with me in the back of my mind. But what I want to concentrate on now is today. I want to take each day as it comes, eating well, exercising, and gaining more control over my whole self."

WHAT IF YOU HAVE DOUBTS ABOUT SUCCEEDING?

You may have had many failures at trying to control your weight in the past. You may believe that it is impossible for you to lose weight. Maybe you've lost a few pounds, but then put the weight back on again. That is a very common problem.

Go to the committee exercise and give doubt a voice. Listen to "doubts" list of past experiences and hear the concerns that your doubting part has to say.

Listen and observe. Allow the doubt to be fully expressed, without argument or rebuttal.

Write something in your journal about doubts in the past, doubts about security, doubts about love, about being accepted, and listen to and observe everything you can about your doubts. Then accept that doubt can remain in the committee. Your Watcher part can always give attention to doubt even while acting in a new direction.

SATISFYING YOUR NEED FOR FOOD WITH LESS

By giving yourself suggestions and cues, while in trance, you can satisfy your desire for food with smaller portions and reduce your calorie intake. If you have a favorite diet program or low-calorie menu, go ahead and use it. Self-hypnosis suggestions can be a way for you to feel content with a smaller amount of food.

You can give yourself posthypnotic suggestions such as: *"I may find that I can chew my food more slowly. As I do this I know several good things are happening. I am helping my digestive system by chewing my food more completely. I am gaining more satisfaction from the food I eat because I can more fully appreciate the tastes and textures and aromas of my food by eating more slowly. Also, I know that as I eat more slowly, I will become full and satisfied perhaps before I finish all my food. I can stop eating then."*

AS YOU CONTROL YOURSELF—YOU CONTROL YOUR WEIGHT

While in your trance, feel more in control—more in control of your physical self. Notice the physical changes you can make with self-hypnosis: changes in skin sensations, heart rate, and feelings of lightness. Feel more in control of your emotional self, too.

Suggest to yourself that you can feel closer to a solution to a problem you may have been wrestling with. You may have had the extra weight for a long time. If it takes some time to get rid of it, that is all right. Be patient with yourself.

There is every reason to feel good about the work you are doing with self-hypnosis. You can let go of any feelings of frustration and disappointment along with the extra weight.

Don't expect miracles with self-hypnosis. Expect results that can last a lifetime. Your lifetime. And that can be a longer, healthier, happier life with the changes you can make.

Kroger and Fezler (1976) recommend concluding a trance session for weight control with some suggestions for motivating yourself. "Remember that you cannot will yourself to lose weight. The harder you try, the less chance you will have to accomplish your aims. So relax—don't press."

To paraphrase a piece of Chinese wisdom, relax and focus on the present, for even a journey of a 100 pounds begins with one step, one pound.

REFERENCES

Alman, B.M. (Ed. Ryan), *Thin Meditations*. In press, 1992.

Erickson, M.H. *Patterns of the Hypnotic Technique of Milton H. Erickson, M.D.—Vol. 2.* Cupertino, California: Meta Publications, 1977.

Erickson, M.H. The utilization of patient behavior in the hypnotherapy of obesity: three case reports. *American Journal of Clinical Hypnosis*, Vol. 10, (Oct), 1967.

Hartland, J. *Medical and Dental Hypnosis.* Baltimore: Williams & Wilkins Company, 1971.

Joaquin H. A. Brief group treatment of obesity through ancillary self-hypnosis. *American Journal of Clinical Hypnosis*, Vol. 19, (Apr), 1977.

Kroger, W.S. Comprehensive management of obesity. *American Journal of Clinical Hypnosis*, Vol. 12, (Jan), 1970.

Kroger, W.S. *Clinical and Experimental Hypnosis.* Philadelphia: J.B. Lippincott Company, 1977.

Kroger, W.S., & Fezler, W.D. *Hypnosis and Behavior Modification: Imagery Conditioning.* Philadelphia: J.B. Lippincott Company, 1976.

Mott, T. & Roberts, J. Obesity and hypnosis: a review of the literature. *American Journal of Clinical Hypnosis*, Vol. 22, (Jul), 1979.

Rajneesh, Bhagwan Shree, *Beyond Psychology*. West Germany: Rebel Publishing House, 1986.

Ryan, B., & Roughan, P. Women and weight: A treatment programme for both normal and overweight women preoccupied by eating and related issues. *Australian Journal of Family Therapy*, Vol. 5(4), (Oct), 1984.

Sanders, S. Self-hypnosis and problem solving in the treatment of obesity. *Psychotherapy in Private Practice*, Vol. 4(3), 1986.

Wadden, T.A. & Flaxman, J. Hypnosis and weight loss: A preliminary study. *International Journal of Clinical & Experimental Hypnosis*, Vol. 19, 1981.

22
Solve Your Sleeping Problems

Nearly everyone can have a problem getting to sleep at some time or another. This can be caused by quite understandable conditions: anticipation over an upcoming event—a trip, a speech to give, a visit from a relative; new or unsettling surroundings; noisy neighbors or an uncomfortable motel bed; physical discomfort, such as a toothache or a strained back.

Some people may seem to sleep eight hours, yet awaken fatigued, having tossed and turned all night. The quality of their sleep is poor. Still others may go right to sleep and awaken in the early hours unable to go back to sleep the rest of the night. The varieties of sleep problems are as numerous as their causes. According to the American Sleep Disorders Association, nearly 30 million Americans suffer from insomnia at some time in their lives.

If you suffer from a sleep disturbance that affects your daily functioning, it is advisable to have your physician examine for underlying physical problems. For example, adverse reactions to caffeine or alcohol can disrupt sleep.

Scientists are increasingly finding evidence that lack of adequate sleep can have serious health consequences. In fact, there is mounting evidence that sleep deprivation has become one of the most pervasive health problems facing Americans.

SLEEPING AND WAKING CONSCIOUSNESS

Most of us have grown up believing that sleep is unique and separate from our waking consciousness. This is nearly opposite the truth. In sleep, we have turned inward from the outside world.

But our sleeping self is not a different person. It is merely another side of ourselves. Asleep, we are the same personalities who loved, feared, rejoiced, became angry, laughed, and cried during the day.

Being aware of this oneness in our sleeping and waking selves helps us better understand why sleep can elude us. The effects of our daily lives spill over into our time of rest. So an irritating job, depression, domestic turmoil, or any waking problem or anxiety can translate itself into various sorts of sleep problems.

As Richard Garver (1990), a San Antonio clinician, observes, "your conscious mind has a memory for virtually all you do, including sleep patterns and behaviors. It records times of restful, high quality sleep and times of disturbed or poor sleep."

You can access memories of good, restful sleep during trance sessions and suggest to yourself: *"Positive sleep memories can be recalled right now, in trance, and experienced again tonight . . . and there is plenty of time to worry or think about problems, projects, concerns, or opportunities during my day time."*

What about using drugs or sleep medications?

Sleeping pills, prescription and nonprescription, can help you get through a temporary sleep difficulty—one or two restless nights or a transitory physical discomfort. But medications can intensify many sleep problems. They may also mask the underlying cause.

Also, some sedatives do not allow the quality of sleep you need to feel truly rested and renewed. They inhibit what is called REM sleep. Short for "rapid eye movement," REM describes a phenomenon associated with a dreaming period of our sleep.

Modern sleep research can monitor the wavy scratchings of brain rhythms as people slumber. Studies have shown that being deprived of REM sleep caused individuals to become hostile, irritable, and anxious. In some cases, distortions in personality were noted.

People prevented from getting this quality of sleep showed a "craving" for it. Extended use of medications and drugs that may induce unconsciousness but prevent this dream sleep do more harm than good in the long run and can become habit-forming.

ACUTE INSOMNIA

Acute insomnia is usually related to a specific event or situation such as those cited above. Often there is something going on in one's life that causes anxiousness that carries over from daytime to sleep time.

Self-hypnosis to relax and let go of such distracting thoughts can help most sleep sufferers.

Treating the symptoms

People with sleep problems often are thinkers. Many of the problems people have in getting to sleep stem from worry, tension, anxiety, fears, and emotional turmoil. If one common element were to be found that causes these factors to disrupt sleep, it would be over-thinking.

Many people have the tendency to try to solve their problems by thinking about them. Unfortunately, most problems are not resolved by over-thinking them.

Some challenges or obstacles, such as one's job or profession, require thinking in order to be solved. These may cause temporary sleep problems. But people in such a situation would still like to leave their excessive worry or concern resting at their desk when they crawl into bed.

Self-hypnosis can help break the habit of thinking too much at bedtime, whatever the reason. While in a self-hypnotic trance, recall your previous few nights of restlessness. Examine what has been going on in your life recently that would cause you to be anxious.

It is best to practice your self-hypnosis early in the day at first, long before sleep. Rather than look for expected results that same evening, expect them in a few days. Look for gradual comfort and change in your sleeping patterns, instead of "magic cures."

You might give yourself suggestions such as: "*I can build a good night's sleep just as I can plan anything in advance. Just as it takes a lot of energy to construct a complex building, I can direct my energy into building a mental vacation spot.*"

In elaborate detail, mentally design a mountain resort or a beach cottage. Describe it to yourself. Visualize the colors of the walls, the texture of the carpeting, the aromas of the flowers.

In this way you focus your thinking energy into an activity associated with relaxation and rest.

Give yourself suggestions that encourage control of your sleep time just as you can control your waking time. "*I know that through the day I can control my actions. I can eat when I am hungry, stretch when I am cramped, move about when I wish. I have the same control over my body when I am asleep. My nighttime consciousness is governed by the same process that I use in my daytime consciousness. I may sleep and feel rested just as easily as I may drive my car or eat a meal.*"

In addition to reinforcing your control over your sleeping self, program how you want the night to pass. How these suggestions are developed will depend on what your difficulty is. For example, if your problem is that you wake up one or more times through the night instead of sleeping straight through, here are some suggestions to use while practicing self-hypnosis:

There are many things in my daily, waking life that I can finish completely without interruption. I can drive from home to work without stopping the car engine. I can write a letter without interruption. Many times I focus my attention through an entire a movie. In fact, each and every day, I may go from morning till night without falling asleep or taking a nap.

"*In the same way that I can complete these other functions daily, without interruption, I may find that I am soon able to sleep completely and without interruption from evening until morning. It may not happen immediately. It may take several days, it may take several weeks, or it may happen even sooner than I might expect. Just as I can accomplish many waking routines uninterrupted, I may also sleep uninterrupted."*

Notice several things about the above suggestions.

1. They begin by reviewing many instances in which you have demonstrated control in your life. They suggest in a positive way that it is *possible*, not a certainty, but that it is possible to carry that same control over into your sleep.
2. It is always important to make suggestions open, permissive to being accepted at whatever pace your unconscious mind can work with. You would, of course, interject your own examples of processes, tasks, and life functions that *you* complete without interruption. Personalize the suggestions and fill them with as much detail as possible. You can make up some of your own—experiment.

In each instance, visualize the suggestions as you give them to yourself. Imagine the suggestions for sound, continual sleep also. Visualize yourself going to sleep in the evening and perhaps see the hands on your clock marking off the hours as you sleep soundly. Visualize yourself awakening at your prescribed time in the morning, having slept soundly and feeling refreshed. Rehearse the *feelings* of sleeping well.

Keeping a journal

A good way to use the insights and background material from your imagery is to write your feelings and thoughts in a journal, as well as the times and days of your self-hypnosis sessions.

You may want to write down your feelings while you are actually in a trance. Or you may want to wait until after the self-hypnosis. Find which way works best for you. You may even benefit from writing your dreams and reviewing them for guidance.

It may be that you express yourself best in images or drawings. That is fine, too. Write down insights or possibilities for solutions that might be presented in your imagery. Then you can review the material later and see if there are any threads of a solution to your real life worries and anxieties.

The information from your imagery can be used to construct positive solutions for your problems. For example, in your writing in your journal you may recognize that many days—say four out of seven—are bad days, you might know that there have been weeks before when you had six out of seven *good* days.

Recognize what it was about those good days and try to reproduce those conditions with your suggestions. Reinforce the positive experiences to displace the bad or negative ones.

POSTHYPNOTIC CUES FOR SLEEP

A part of treating the symptoms of sleep loss is to find a series of actions with which you can couple cues for sleep. In your morning self-hypnosis give yourself suggestions for actions that can lead to sleep later that night.

An example might be: *"I may notice that when I brush my teeth in the evening, just before bed, as I clean my teeth I can also clean my mind of worry, tension, and anxiety."* You might express this concept in your own words.

Further self-hypnosis suggestions to incorporate an action may involve removing your robe: *"As I take off my robe and hang it on the hook, I may also imagine that on my robe are pinned all of my problems, troubles, and worries from the day. I can see them now, like index cards or signs upon which are written all the worries that might keep me from sleeping. They are too small to read, but I feel that as I lift off my robe the weight of these worries and anxieties is lifted off me also. The robe and these worries are in the closet, and I can put them on tomorrow if I wish. But tonight I can sleep without them."*

Notice the progression and elements of these posthypnotic suggestions. Recognize the elements and write out your own self-worded suggestions to achieve the same goals.

1. The suggestions incorporate actions that you normally would take in preparing for sleep—taking off your robe, brushing your teeth, fluffing the pillows, closing the lights.
2. The suggestions use those actions similar to preparing for sleep in other ways. Brushing your teeth, for instance, is like clearing your mind and removing worries from your thoughts.
3. The suggestions imply ways that the worries and anxieties are small and you do not need to think about them at bedtime. You can spend time during the day taking care of those worries and thoughts. Or, you can set aside 10 or 12 minutes in the evening, while in self-hypnosis, and review all those distracting thoughts and then set them aside as you set aside your robe.
4. The suggestions are flexible and permissive. They provide the opportunity to set aside the distracting thoughts, but do not force them out of your mind. Be creative and find ways to lift any worries or concerns using your imagery—colorful balloons lifting your cares and concerns up and away, for instance.
5. Because the suggestions are less definite, you are posing no contradictory statements to your unconscious mind. There is nothing in the language which the unconscious mind must resist. You are proposing a persuasive set of possibilities—not commands.

Naturally, you would rather sleep than stay awake, so your unconscious will be more likely to follow your line of suggestions in this nonthreatening form.

In the beginning, practice self-hypnosis several times a day—perhaps three or four. The wording can change in different sessions, but the theme and cues can remain the same. During the first few self-hypnosis sessions, you may want to tape record the suggestions for yourself. Or you can read over your suggestions before practicing.

AN ACTIVE SELF-HYPNOSIS SLEEP TECHNIQUE

At some point in your day plan a five- or 10-minute walk. During the walk, give your physical self a chance to stretch, move, and let go of tension, thoughts, or concerns. Allow your thoughts to be considered, even absurd thoughts that may be creative and unrelated to other matters in your life.

Often accepting and allowing these ideas to be heard enhances your relaxed state of mind. You may even want to write, or otherwise record, some of your thoughts during your walk, to really get them out of your head. You know they won't be lost and you can review those notes later.

Also, during your walk you can allow your emotions to be felt. Accept whatever feelings you have to be aired and experienced. There are no "wrong" feelings. A walk is a good time to experience anger, sadness, frustration, hurt, disappointment and other emotions that can interfere with sleep if not acknowledged and experienced at some time.

After several weeks of taking physical walks, you may wish to take imaginary walks in your self-hypnosis to do almost the same thing. However, it is still helpful to physically walk to get a physical exertion and release with physical activity.

By accepting whatever feelings you have (perhaps even journal writing may be helpful here, too), you make your walk an active self-hypnosis period to take care of your WHOLE self so at bedtime you can have a WHOLE night's sleep.

Soak your anxieties before sleeping on them

You may know what has been on your mind and keeping you from sleeping well. It may be difficulties at work, an argument with your spouse or a family member, or financial worries.

When you know what causes your sleep problem, you can work on the problem while in self-hypnosis. But in order to work on the situation without creating more anxiety and tension, change the situation or setting of the problem.

One very effective way is to change the setting and the people involved to animals, insects, or even fish. That may sound ridiculous, but by doing so, you remove the reality from the situation. This allows you to think about it without generating even more tension than you already have.

This can be a valuable technique for several reasons. First and most immediately, now you can deal with an anxiety-producing situation or dilemma and not add more stress and tension in the process. Also, your sense of humor can be naturally relaxing.

Second, by separating the situation from a reality setting, you open your thinking up to more creative solutions. Your thoughts will not be restricted by the limits of conventional reality. You may find an insight to your problem.

Third, simply exploring the source of your sleep disruption may not actually solve the conflict or problem, but it will give your unconscious mind an opportunity to examine it. Spending several minutes in self-hypnosis and reviewing your problem in a nonthreatening way can help unravel some of the tension and anxiety you may be feeling.

Suppose your problem is a personality conflict at work—a common source of tension. By representing the situation, in your self-hypnosis, as fish in a tank or animals on a ranch, you can review the details and explore new possibilities. By placing the characters and setting in an imaginary form, you remove the threatening, anxiety-producing emotions that are present in the real setting.

This technique is better explained with an example. Let us suppose that you chose to represent a conflict at work as a large tank of fish. An overbearing, aggressive employer might be a barracuda. A troublesome coworker could be visualized as a carp or catfish. Your close friend is represented as an angelfish. And you might see yourself as a sunfish, a marlin, or a goldfish.

These fish can now act out roles representing their participation in your conflict or problem. You can explore various ways of dealing with that situation in a playful manner.

Perhaps you can tell off the barracuda. Yell, get angry, or swear—you can do anything you want in your imagery. Maybe imagine what the other fish might say back to you. In creative, imaginative ways, you can work out many of the possibilities for resolving your dilemmas.

Mental imagery is a way for you to create new ways of viewing situations. There is no threat of doing the wrong thing or saying something you'll regret. Through this imagery, you can vent your anxiety and tension enough to allow you to sleep better.

You may find a solution to your problem with this aquatic imagery, perhaps not. The important thing is that you allow your unconscious mind to express itself in these subtle ways. It is often the lack of an outlet for expression that causes your conscious mind to over-think your worries and problems and rob you of a good night's sleep.

You can use this sort of imagery with any kind of problem or interpersonal conflict—family or marital difficulties, friendships, insecurities, financial worries, or even physical problems and illness.

AN ERICKSON SLEEP TREATMENT

Some of us who worked with Milton Erickson observed a technique that he sometimes used with his patients, and that may work for you. It involved using posthypnotic suggestions that if you are unable to sleep, you get up and do something you really dislike.

When some patients had trouble sleeping, Erickson would prescribe that they get up from bed and clean the refrigerator, wash their car (yes, even if it were midnight), mop and wax the kitchen floor, sort out desk drawers, or perform some other task. Erickson helped such clients to recognize how much energy they used staying awake.

If you use a posthypnotic suggestion of this sort, it should also include the stipulation that when you are sufficiently tired from your task, you can stop and return to bed to sleep. That, of course, is the goal.

To try this technique for yourself, implant the suggestion that if you have trouble sleeping you will arise and perform a specific task. Give the suggestion to yourself in a morning trance session. It may take several days of practice to firmly implant the intended action.

Your suggestions should take the following form:

1. First, suggest that you *may* find that you rest comfortably, easily, and quickly. The word "sleep" may be too specific and direct for you. If you are sensitized or put off by the word "sleep," then use words like "deeply relaxed" or "completely restful." Avoid testing yourself with a loaded word.
2. Develop suggestions that should you be unable to fall asleep, you will get up and perform whatever task you have chosen. Don't be too easy on yourself; select a chore you've put aside for a while. Pick a piece of work that you'd rather not do at all.
3. In your suggestions, provide that when you grow so tired of working on your chore that you would rather go to sleep, you may stop work and return to bed to rest comfortably and deeply.
4. Make several suggestions for the same goal. Keep them open and flexible. Use words like "I may find," and "Perhaps I'll notice that . . ." A typical suggestion might sound like this: *"If I find that I'm unable to fall asleep, I may be able to get up and begin cleaning the stove. When I notice that I am too tired and fatigued to continue that task, I may find that I am able to return to bed and fall quickly asleep. I may even dream something pleasant or imaginative."*

The intent of all this is not to be constantly arising from bed to perform an unpleasant task. It is to go to sleep. After you do arise several times to work in the night, your unconscious mind will find it preferable to go directly to sleep.

MUSIC, TAPES, AND OTHER CUES

Some of you may have a favorite piece of music that you find soothing and sleep-inducing. You can use that as a cue for sleep. Set up your tape or CD player to play and shut off after you are in bed.

If you believe that creating a tape recording with your sleep suggestions would help, by all means do that. Suggest to yourself that the music or the tape will be a cue for you to drift into a natural, restful sleep.

Even reading a book or watching TV before sleeping can be used as a cue.

Visualize yourself, while in a trance, going through the actions of your cues and suggestions. In your imagery, feel yourself getting tired, yawning, feeling sleepy. Visualize yourself lying down, closing your eyes, falling asleep. Imagine how good and peaceful your sleep can be.

It is often normal for people's body temperature to cool slightly when they are deeply asleep. You might imagine that your temperature will slightly lower when you lower your eyelids at night. That can be another cue.

Your breathing, heart rate, blood pressure, and other body functions vary during sleep, just as during waking. But generally you begin with slow, regular breathing, along with a lowered heart rate and blood pressure. Through the control you have developed with your basic self-hypnosis techniques, you can slow your body down in preparation for sleep.

To aid all the other cues you have given yourself while in self-hypnosis, use progressive relaxation as you first lie down to sleep.

SOME FINAL NOTES ABOUT SLEEP

The world does not shut down and become quiet for us when we desire to sleep. People have been known to sleep in spite of the most horrendous noises—compressors, construction, freeway rumble, cat fights, war sounds, and blaring music.

Rather than seeing such noises as reasons for not being able to sleep, use the sounds as distractions and a focal point for your imagination.

Also, there is quite a variation in the amount of sleep each of us needs. Growing children sleep more because it is during sleep that the body does a great amount of physical growth.

The fact that you may be unable to remain asleep for a full seven or eight hours does not necessarily mean you are missing out. This is particularly true as we get older. Elderly people require less sleep since their bodies no longer require this "growth sleep" period.

In our culture, we have been conditioned to believe that there is something magical about eight hours of sleep. Advertisements, commercials, and other media have perpetuated the notion that seven or eight hours of shut-eye is normal.

Each of us is unique. What may be enough sleep for your neighbor or spouse may be too much for you. The bestselling author, Danielle Steele, reports she sleeps less than five hours per night.

Among the variables influencing how much sleep we need are external pressures such as job or professional dictates, personal temperament, heredity, and age. You cannot establish what is normal for you by comparing yourself with somebody else. Keep a journal for a few weeks to record your good days and bad days and how well and how long you slept before each.

Consider your past pattern of sleep behavior and see if your sleeping has changed over the years. If you are sleeping five hours instead of eight, that may be fine if you are 65 or 70 years old. Perhaps you don't need the extra time.

Studies have shown that even people who believe they "didn't sleep a wink" actually got more sleep than they realized. Our perceptions of how much we have slept can be very unreliable.

But if you do have a sleep problem, self-hypnosis is a safe, natural way to find a long-term solution—and sweet dreams.

REFERENCES

Bourke, D.H. *The Sleep Management Plan.* New York: Harper Collins, 1990.

Garver, R.B. Suggestions with sleep disturbance. In *Handbook of Hypnotic Suggestions and Metaphors* (Ed. C.Hammond). New York: W.W. Norton and American Society of Clinical Hypnosis, 1990.

Grings, W.W. & Dawson, M.E. *Emotions and Bodily Responses.* New York: Academic Press, Inc. 1978.

Hartland, J. *Medical and Dental Hypnosis.* Baltimore: Williams & Wilkins, 1971.

Langren, D. *Speaking of: Sleeping Problems.* New York: Consolidated Book Publishers, 1978.

Nardi, T.J. Treating sleep paralysis with hypnosis. *International Journal of Clinical & Experimental Hypnosis,* Vol.29 (Oct), 1981.

Toufexis, A. Drowsy America. *Time Magazine,* Dec 17, 1990.

23

Parenting Better with Self-Hypnosis

Parenting today can be difficult, frustrating, and rewarding. Often, both parents work. Many families do not have the benefit of nearby grandparents, aunts and uncles, and similar resources to assist in child rearing. Parents today need all the help and assistance they can gather.

Hypnotic principles can make the job easier and improve any parent's effectiveness. In this chapter you will discover: how to use self-hypnosis for yourself to help you relax and reduce tension and anxiety associated with parenting; how self-hypnosis can help you review your child rearing decisions and reactions; and how to use suggestion strategies directly with your child or your children to gain cooperation and improve behaviors.

Children are open to hypnosis, often more so than adults. Children have very active fantasy lives which are helpful for openness to positive self-hypnosis suggestions. They often seem to be absorbed in their inner world while watching television, eating, playing, or even just sitting daydreaming. Children frequently go into trance-states for brief periods of time each day.

Much research suggests that peaks of openness to hypnotic suggestion occur with children from preschool ages to adolescence. By adolescence, the demands of socialization are to be more rational and realistic. This often results in young people being more skeptical and less open to their imaginative skills.

Learning self-hypnosis can open up new worlds of self-control and imagination for both parents and children. And we believe that children who learn self-hypnosis will more likely carry those imaginative skills into adolescence and adulthood.

Formal hypnosis with children for clinical problems, such as chronic bed-wetting, hyperactivity, or encopresis should be done by a trained and qualified professional.

Hyperactivity, for example, is a symptom which is associated with central nervous system irritability, including metabolic, post-infectious, and even toxic influences. Neuropsychiatrist and behavioral neurologist Sydney Walker (1977) recommends that a differential diagnosis be conducted to clarify underlying causes of hyperactive symptoms. While such symptoms can be an expression of psychological or emotional factors, it is important to properly diagnosis or rule out physiological causes prior to treating the behaviors. This is recommended not only for hyperactive symptoms, but also for chronic bed-wetting, encopresis, learning problems, violent and overly aggressive behaviors, and other severe problems.

Contact the American Society of Clinical Hypnosis in Des Plains, Illinois or the chapter of the American Psychological Association or the American Association of Marriage and Family Therapists in your state for a referral in your locale. Never substitute self-hypnosis for conditions that require professional or medical attention. However, self-hypnosis can be used as an *adjunct* for additional help with many problems.

Parents can use informal hypnosis or suggestion strategies, and routinely do so, to gain cooperation, improve children's study skills and habits, reduce anxiousness, and achieve similar goals. The intention of this chapter is to help parents, teachers, or other responsible individuals and professionals to develop more successful patterns and strategies to resolve problems or enhance the child's development.

Children can benefit from self-hypnosis skills in many ways. Some areas where self-hypnosis can be used are: to reduce test-taking or performance anxiety; improving study or concentration skills; improving sleep patterns; reducing the anxiety of doctor or dental visits; managing fears of the dark, of animals, or other phobias; and helping modify behavioral problems, such as poor eating and thumbsucking.

We always advocate respect for the child's individuality and uniqueness. We understand that children are naturally responsive to suggestions from adults they love, trust, and respect. And you may be surprised at how even small children will be able to develop their self-hypnosis skills once you teach them some basics.

Both of the authors have taught self-hypnosis to their children, who have incorporated their new skills in creative ways. A key element to success is to be patient with the child and with yourself.

SELF-HYPNOSIS FOR PARENTS

Before you attempt to teach or use hypnotic strategies with your child, first be familiar with using it for yourself. This part of the chapter will help you use self-hypnosis to improve your parenting skills. If you have not yet read Section I of this book, it is essential you do so now.

When a parent is stressed or tense, this feeling can be communicated to the child, often nonverbally. You probably have noticed how closely your child or children watch you. Often they are very observant of you even when you are not aware of them. If you become stressed from work, from relationship difficulties, from financial concerns, or from problems directly related to your child, it will be noticed and may lead to stress developing in the child. Your child may then act out that stress in a behavioral way that causes you more stress and a cycle of stress response can begin and be more difficult to break out of.

Chapter 12 on stress management can be a valuable resource to you in managing your own stress. When you are more relaxed, you will find that children will be more relaxed and peaceful with you. This positive attitude is communicated to the child and stronger feelings of hope and growth are shared.

In addition to relaxation, another practical application is to use self-hypnosis to review and rehearse your interactions with your child. For example, Sam, a 36-year-old father of two boys, ages six and eight, used self-hypnosis in the following way.

Sam's boys would literally pounce on him when he first arrived home from work each evening. They would pull on his arms and clamor for him to play with them; he could barely take off his coat and catch his breath. He found himself becoming tense and irritable as he neared his home and by the time he walked to the front door he was wound up tight.

First, Sam used self-hypnosis to review how he was with the boys. He imagined his ride home from work, like watching a movie, the "Sam Comes Home" movie. As he watched himself through the drive home, he noticed how at certain points he would become more and more tense, even at some points observing that he considered in his mind stopping somewhere else first.

Sam recognized that taking the off ramp to his home from the freeway was the beginning of his negative feelings, a stop light that was nearly always red when he got there was another. Previously he would have thought it was the delay of the red light that caused him stress, but as he watched his "movie" he realized that at the red light he would be thinking of how the boys would jump on him soon; this is what really was causing him anxiety and tension.

Specific parts of his drive home had become negative cues that reminded Sam of what he would soon encounter. With that observation, he saw that by the time he opened the front door each evening he was anticipating the onslaught of pleas, begging, and tugging for his attention. Here is how he changed that self-fulfilling negative anticipation.

Now that he had this awareness, he decided to use self-hypnosis in a second way—to change how he responded to the drive home and how the boys could greet him.

He rehearsed several different ways of negotiating with his boys. He imagined bribing them with some gift, candy, or privilege to not storm him when he arrived home. He imagined sitting down with them and discussing how he felt and how he would like to be when he got home. Then he imagined their responses. He imagined discussing the matter with his wife to enlist her help with the matter. He imagined going with the flow and playing with the children before he took time to change out of his work clothes. In short, Sam attempted to come up with as many options as he possibly could before selecting any action.

In each instance, Sam would imagine the possibilities and the likely outcomes of each option. He finally decided, based on his self-hypnosis rehearsals (which took him several trance sessions to accomplish), that the best and most easily accomplished option was to combine coming home and first playing with the boys with rewarding them for allowing him to stop play, change, and relax. The reward would be taking some time with them to do a self-hypnosis imagery experience all together. Of course, he didn't call it self-hypnosis, he told them they would all play a game called "Imagine That."

So the new routine for Sam was he would come home, play ball, play video games, or carry out some other activity the boys enjoyed with him. After 20 minutes, he announced, as he had told them at the onset, that it was time for him to change clothes and eat dinner, then, if they behaved well, he would play a special game with them called "Imagine That."

As you might predict, right from the beginning they were very curious about this new game. He used their natural curiosity and told them he would explain it all and play it with them if they behaved. After they experienced the game, they came to anticipate it and more easily let him have some time to himself and with Mom.

The game consisted of them sitting on the floor of the boys' room (this is where Sam wanted them to play when they had finished the game) while Sam asked them to select a character of their choice from cartoons, storybooks, or anywhere that they would be. He selected one for himself, Zorro, from his own childhood days. Then he created a problem or obstacle, such as saving the life of a person they would each choose, such as a princess, Mom, the country, a kingdom, the family dog, or whatever.

Then they would close their eyes, breathe in deep, hold their breath, exhale slowly three magical times, and imagine how their character would save the day. Well, of course, each would get his turn to tell his "Imagine That" story.

The deep breathing, as you have already learned, helped the boys relax and quiet down their bodies. The sharing of the stories became the fun part for the boys to each have time to talk and tell. And Sam discovered he enjoyed hearing their fantasy adventures more than he had anticipated. The whole activity rarely took more than 15 minutes. And when they finished and he would leave the room, they were usually calmed and ready for bedtime.

Once he had decided on this plan, Sam used his self-hypnosis to mentally rehearse a new set of posthypnotic cues for his drive home. He wanted to prepare himself for a positive arrival home and a pleasant evening of mixed activities with the children and with his wife, plus time for himself alone, which was important to him.

The off ramp from the highway became an image of a playground slide. The red light became a signal to pause and take several slow deep breaths to relax and release the tensions and stresses of his day. Opening the garage door with his remote control could remind him of a toy remote control car and helped get him in a playful mood.

As Sam opened his front door, he was in a different frame of mind, ready to play for 20 minutes or so. He found he could now actually enjoy the games they would play. Naturally, the "Imagine That" game was modified many times as the boys eventually became bored and wanted change. Sam remained open to their suggestions as much as practical and always made the deep breathing his contribution to a new version.

Because the children really wanted that special time with their father, Sam was surprised how much easier it was to structure their time together and negotiate time for himself as well.

Needless to say, each and every evening was not always easy and without problems. However, Sam found that he was more patient and less stressed. His own ease transferred to the boys and, generally, evenings around his home on weekdays took on a much improved tone.

You will discover creative solutions by using self-hypnosis to open yourself up to more options. When you are relaxed, you will find you can imagine more possibilities, just as Sam did, to solve your specific problems as a parent.

TAKING THE CHILD'S AGE INTO ACCOUNT

Clinicians Karen Olness and Gail Gardner (1988) have done excellent research in the use of hypnosis with children and have outlined some important age-related differences in using hypnosis with children. For example, between ages two and four, the child can be given suggestions in the form of storytelling, speaking through a familiar stuffed animal or a favorite play activity such as blowing bubbles.

At ages four to six, imagery abilities are more developed and children can be encouraged to imagine helpful suggestions through imagery of a garden, storytelling, imagining a television or video scenario, or imagining activities such as playing ball or swinging.

Children between ages seven to 11 will respond to music, watching cloud shapes, imagining magical carpet rides, or imagery of favorite places. And older children and adolescents can be guided with some of the same images as you might use for yourself.

An example of self-hypnosis training for self-esteem is illustrated in Kelly, a sixth-grader. She was afraid to start junior high and was dreading in March the prospect of starting a new school in September. Her family had just moved to the area and she was finishing sixth grade in a new school.

Kelly was not outgoing and had felt very bad about the teasing and avoidance that new students often receive.

The school counselor helped Kelly learn some "visualization and guided imagery" skills, with the specific focus on reducing her fear and anxiety in social situations.

Kelly learned to relax easily with her eyes closed and then to imagine a television screen with a movie, video game, or anything on one of the channels she chose. She learned how to focus on the "school channel." On this channel, she could replay any scene from school or create any scene she wished.

At different times, Kelly would review parts of her school day, such as the time she was in the hall and a friend walked by without saying "Hi" or even acknowledging her. Kelly was sure that her friend was upset or angry with her for some unknown reason. This feeling of being ignored hurt her and those feelings caused her to avoid that friend later in the day.

That evening, on her self-hypnosis video screen, Kelly developed a mental rehearsal of how she would ask her friend at school the next day why she hadn't acknowledged Kelly in the hall. In the past, Kelly was too fearful of how uncomfortable she would feel asking a question she really wanted an answer to. Using self-hypnosis to rehearse the different ways she could observe herself asking the question and responding, she felt more at ease asking the next day.

When she asked her friend why she had not said "Hi," Kelly discovered that it was because her friend had been listening to music on her headphones and had not heard Kelly nor noticed her. Her friend wondered what the big deal was. Kelly was relieved.

Most importantly, this represented a change in Kelly. In the past she would have brooded over the perceived rebuff and acted further on it. Now she could review and rehearse the events and take action that was more successful for her. This led her to feel more capable and self-confident.

Self-esteem improves when a person feels he or she can make a difference in outcomes. One component of self-esteem, as Michael Yapko (1988) has pointed out in his work, is the ability to recognize when and how we are capable of having a positive effect on our environment. What Kelly did with her self-hypnosis was overcome a fear of asking certain people difficult questions, then she recognized how she could do something that she didn't feel she could do before. An improvement in her self-esteem resulted.

TEACHING RELAXATION

Teaching your child self-hypnosis for relaxation, breathing, and guided imagery has specific benefits. When you share the experience of self-hypnosis and model it for your child, a cooperative attitude can develop between you.

Here is an example. Sarah, eight years old, suffered from allergies and headaches. The symptoms started after her father died and this was considered a link. However, the problems continued even after counseling, though some improvement was observed. She was referred to learn self-hypnosis.

Sarah and her mother spent two hours a week practicing self-hypnosis together. They would breathe together, have their own imagery quietly, and then, because Sarah liked to draw, they would each draw some part of what they had visualized. That special time together became very important to Sarah and the more deep breathing exercises she did, the more her allergy symptoms improved.

The relaxed time spent in drawing and talking allowed Sarah to express in her own way how she felt about losing her Dad. In one poignant painting, she was on top of a mountain with her Dad in a cloud, so she could talk with him. Her mother encouraged her and they were able to be together and express their feelings and thoughts more comfortably.

INFORMAL HYPNOSIS FOR BEHAVIOR MODIFICATION

Parents are already in a powerful authority role and their suggestions will be effective in some measure without any hypnotic elements. However, there are several areas where a parent's observations of their children, coupled with awareness of suggestion strategies, can help make positive behaviors result.

For instance, bedtime for many parents is a time of struggle and a battle of wills. Children about two to six or seven years old are particularly prone to testing the limits of bedtime. One strategy is to read a story to the child and periodically substitute the words "sleep," "tired," "heavy," or similar words. The timing of such substitutions is most effective when you notice the child seems entranced by the picture or words.

It is not always possible to go against the agenda a small child has, so this strategy may take time to work or it may work only on some occasions. Don't be discouraged; if you are not successful try another approach, perhaps like the following:

Offer to play the "Humming Game" with your child. Demonstrate what you mean by humming and then ask her to hum along. Try to hum high pitches then low pitches. Model a breathing pattern of slow inhaled breaths, then hold for three seconds and hum as you exhale. Make the game as creative and entertaining as possible and fit it into the child's interest. For example, she could image a humming bird, a musical note, or even the hum of a radio when no channel was tuned.

In creating a way to have your child take slow deep breaths and experience relaxation, you are instilling in him or her a posthypnotic cue. Then as your youngster grows older, you can build on those basic skills.

Many children like having their backs or stomachs rubbed by Mom or Dad while they are reading stories, watching television, or doing some other passive activity. If this opportunity arises, you might try asking your child to take a deep breath and hold it for a moment while you massage a back muscle that feels tight. As the child begins to breathe in, massage with slightly more pressure and then release the pressure as he or she exhales. Again, you are suggesting deep breathing and relaxation to the child, coupled with a pleasurable experience from a loving parent.

While these strategies are effective with children, they will not work all the time nor with all children. Be patient and be creative with the techniques to adapt them to your particular situation.

A successful intervention of self-hypnosis with a four-year-old is described here to demonstrate some specific techniques.

Four-year-old Taylor was very quiet and seemed more shy than most children his age. The year before, he was talking and learning to speak fairly well, but now he had reverted to speaking little, thought he seemed to listen well.

Taylor's parents had taken him to the pediatrician who found no organic reasons for his behavior and recommended him to a psychologist who utilized hypnosis.

The self-hypnosis began with giving Taylor permission to talk to himself anytime he wanted (knowing that will take place quite a lot anyway, both consciously and unconsciously).

Next, he was taught how to watch the "Taylor Movie" with his eyes closed (parents can model closed-eyes imagery for best results). Then he was encouraged to "draw" what he saw . . . any color would do, any design was fine. Some children respond to drawing, others not as much.

Taylor was encouraged to guide the movie into what he wanted for himself. If he imagined or heard music in his movie, he was encouraged to hum some of it to himself. Soon his parents noticed that when Taylor was by himself he would seem to be humming a tune barely audibly. That was new behavior.

Gradually, Taylor began talking more each week until he was up to his appropriate level within three months. The root of the problem was discovered later when he revealed that he had developed a fear of saying something wrong and displeasing his parents.

The self-hypnosis experience helped teach *all* of them about how to relax and accept themselves. This also illustrates how a symptom can have a voice of its own and how understanding and compassion work.

TEACHING SELF-HYPNOSIS TO YOUNG PEOPLE

Children can understand self-hypnosis as pretending, daydreaming, or play trance. Therefore, they can be told quite honestly that they already know how to do guided storytelling or whatever you will choose to name this skill. The authors have found that their children accepted the term self-hypnosis easily.

A six-year-old boy, Adam, was taught self-hypnosis by his father, who had learned it as part of a training program at his work. Adam had been wetting the bed again in the past few weeks, since the start of the new school year. Their pediatrician found no physiological problem and felt the stress of a new class might be the cause.

Together, Adam and his father practiced relaxation breathing and then imagining different scenes.

Adam soon learned to control his breathing, while relaxing and imagining trucks. Trucks that could stop fast with very strong brakes. Adam's trucks also had big engines to really climb hills when they needed to. This imagery was encouraged by his father.

It really didn't matter what Adam imagined. Praising the child for any imaging abilities will reinforce that skill. The truck imagery was encouraged over about a week, until trucks had the power to fly or stop or go through barriers.

Soon, Adam learned that he could also go to bed (brakes for the day), and later get up and go to the bathroom (full power) even at night. In three weeks, he was much more calm and relaxed and was no longer wetting at night.

Parents benefit from training and coaching. Thomas Gordon (1975), in his book, *Parent Effectiveness Training*, suggests creating a learning agreement in which parents and children benefit from listening and sharing. We believe self-hypnosis can be just such a sharing and is a new learning experience that will become helpful in resolving conflicts.

One of the best techniques with young children is to involve them in a fairy tale that resembles their challenge. Have them picture the fairy tale with their eyes open or closed. As you add or have them add more details, close your own eyes. Children model after their parents and if you begin to tell parts of the fairy tale with your eyes closed, they will soon imitate you.

Within the story, suggest the solution that you believe will help your child learn something about the problem or challenge facing him or her. Ask the child questions and just listen to the answers without judging or commenting.

The first goal is to gain the cooperation of the child in learning this exciting new game (skill). If cooperation is present and you can excite the child to participate, then a solution will often begin to be seen in behavior soon.

You want the very best for your children. Teaching them new tools is giving them a lifelong gift. Helping your child grow up with relaxed confidence and self-esteem is one of the most important goals of parenting; it can also be one of the most rewarding.

Self-esteem is the protective shield against self-abuse in its many forms. Children who grow up to have good self-esteem have the best chances of being happy adults.

REFERENCES

Crasilneck, H.B. & Hall, J.A. *Clinical Hypnosis: Principles and Applications*. New York: Grune & Stratton, 1975.

Erickson, M.H. *Healing in Hypnosis*. (Eds. Rossi, Ryan & Sharp), Vol. 1. New York: Irvington Publishers, 1983.

Gardner, G.G. Parents: Obstacles or allies in child hypnotherapy? *American Journal of Clinical Hypnosis*, Vol. 17(1), 1974.

Gordon, T. *Parent Effectiveness Training*. New York: Plume Books, 1975.

Kuttner, L. Management of young children's acute pain and anxiety during invasive medical procedures. *Pediatrician*, Vol. 16(1–2), 1989.

Levine, E.S. Indirect suggestions through personalized fairy tales for treatment of childhood insomnia. *American Journal of Clinical Hypnosis*, Vol. 23(1), 1980.

Olness, K. & Gardner, G.G. *Hypnosis and Hypnotherapy with Children*, 2nd ed. Orlando: Grune and Stratton, 1988.

Smith, M.S., Womack, W.M. & Chen, A.C. Hypnotizability does not predict outcome of behavioral treatment in pediatric headache. *American Journal of Clinical Hypnosis*, Vol. 31(4), 1989.

Walker, III. S. *Help for the Hyperactive Child*. Boston: Houghton Mifflin Company, 1977.

Yapko, M.D. *When Living Hurts: Directives for Treating Depression*. New York: Brunner/Mazel, 1988.

24

New Strategies in Childbirthing

The birth experience is the miracle that all of us experience and few of us remember. For the mother, the physical resourcefulness to be flexible, to expand, and then to reduce any pain are benefits of a relaxed and confident birth. These are characteristics that self-hypnosis trance enjoys and which can flow into the birth experience.

In the last 100 years or so, childbirthing has taken a medical, at times even a surgical turn. Certainly, many experts believe that trauma at birth can profoundly affect the infant. Some psychologists specialize in using hypnosis to reach the birth experience of adults. This application of age regression can help uncover events that are still influencing behavior, attitudes, and feelings.

In the past, the role of the mother during birth was often reduced to that of a functioning object. Use of medications and anesthesia can cause a feeling of detachment from the birth process.

Fortunately, in recent years our culture has recognized the value of encouraging the mother-to-be to take an active role in labor and delivery beyond the reflex actions of her body. Lamaze and "natural childbirth" have become more popular. Hospitals are paying more attention to providing comfortable and "homey" atmospheres for labor, delivery, and postdelivery.

The reduction of fear and anxiety is one of the principal benefits of using self-hypnosis during childbirthing. However, the primary purpose is most often to reduce pain, and hypnosis has a long history of success with pain reduction.

There are several reasons for wanting chemical anesthesia to be reduced in normal, healthy labors and deliveries. They revolve around these two areas:

1. The undesirable aftereffects of the medication on both the mother and the baby.
2. Postdelivery depression that is associated with chemical anesthesia.

THE BENEFITS OF SELF-HYPNOSIS FOR CHILDBIRTH

Self-hypnosis with the expectant mother can have the following benefits:

1. A reduction in the amount of chemical anesthesia needed. Less anesthesia

reduces the undesirable postdelivery effects and minimizes the risks of anesthesia to both the mother and the child.

2. Self-hypnosis reduces the fear, tension, and pain before and during labor.
3. There is more control of often painful uterine contractions without the need of medication.
4. The recovery following delivery is accelerated.
5. The mother's resistance to fatigue increases and her exhaustion is minimized.
6. The mother experiences the delivery more and she can draw a greater feeling of accomplishment and fulfillment.

LAMAZE, "NATURAL CHILDBIRTH," AND SELF-HYPNOSIS

The Lamaze method of childbirth is derived from hypnotic techniques and then modified and popularized in the United States by Lamaze in the 1950s.

Both Lamaze and natural childbirth techniques use conditioned reflex training to block pain. Deep breathing and relaxation also play important roles in these two methods, as well as helping develop a self-hypnotic trance.

While Lamaze (1958) carefully avoids using any language that might indicate self-hypnosis, nevertheless, that is what expectant mothers are using. Their husbands or other partners are helping them develop a trance state through the controlled breathing exercises.

By whatever name you choose to call it, self-hypnosis can be used by nearly all expectant mothers for the benefits mentioned above. The short time it takes to learn the techniques earns comfort, confidence, and time saved in labor and delivery.

USING SELF-HYPNOSIS DURING YOUR PREGNANCY

Begin to work with self-hypnosis well before your expected delivery date. A good time to start is in the fifth or sixth month. Practice three or four times a week, at least. It takes only a light level of self-hypnosis to achieve real success with the techniques.

In separate sessions, work on relaxing, understanding your fears and worries, promoting a positive self-image, developing good habits of nutrition and exercise, and control of pain.

Bertha Rodger, M.D., (1990) focuses her patients on the inherent ability of each person to control aspects of the birthing process. She advises education of the whole birth process. Then, posthypnotic suggestions are used to reinforce relaxed breathing for control of temporary physical, emotional, or psychological stressors that can accompany pregnancy.

We agree with Rodger that using some of the natural events of childbirth to create posthypnotic cues is very effective. Such natural events can be the contractions, the presence of the partner, or even the specific activities of going to the hospital.

Other experts in this application of hypnosis for childbirthing, such as Erickson (1967), Kroger (1977), and Goldmann (1990), have done some excellent scripting of hypnosis for childbirthing. We have drawn on their fine work and others to create an effective, flexible, and relaxing script you can read, tape record, or even have your partner read and record. You might even take such a recording into the delivery room and listen to it there.

The following script for self-hypnosis contains many goal suggestions including those mentioned above. You may want to modify the script to add or include more suggestions of each separate goal.

If you're already involved in a good exercise and eating program, use self-hypnosis suggestions to reinforce those good habits. If you need to *develop* these habits, give yourself posthypnotic cues to help you get motivated to do the exercises and to eat well.

Be imaginative and creative both in how you use your self-hypnosis skills and in developing relevant images and visualizations to accompany your suggestions.

The script

"First of all, I'm going to relax. I will become as relaxed as possible and take time out to enjoy this experience. I will be relaxing in a way that gives me the most comfort . . . the most relaxation possible.

"I can move around and get myself into the position that is most comfortable for me. I can begin by taking a big . . . deep . . . satisfying breath. It is very natural . . . very easy. And I may notice, as I inhale . . . through my nose and mouth . . . that my body can naturally begin to relax. My breathing like the wind is natural and powerful, or like the soothing cycles of ocean waves.

"Labor is a natural process physically and emotionally. All contractions from the uterus are like all muscular contractions in the body. Every single contraction brings me closer to the moment of delivery.

"I can concentrate on my toes . . . or my head . . . or even my hands . . . and feel the tension there for a moment . . . I can feel it, and then release it. Perhaps my hands or my toes may begin to tingle when the tension is released. I may notice a numbness in my mouth . . . that's fine too.

"I can focus on any individual part of my body and that distracts me from other parts of my experience. Like with a radio dial or TV channel, I can tune into any one part of me at a time.

"I may feel the relaxation and comfort spreading throughout my entire body

. . . with each breath and each contraction . . . spreading to all the parts of my body. The comfort may begin on the outside . . . it will spread . . . it will soak in . . . absorb, and soon I will feel the relaxation deep inside me as well.

"My unconscious mind will help me relax with every contraction and every breath . . . my confidence gets stronger with each breath and each contraction. I am developing that control with each word of encouragement, or each touch of tenderness from those around me . . . including these very words of self encouragement.

"It's totally natural to allow myself to feel deeper . . . and deeper . . . and more relaxed. There's no reason to try to relax . . . there's no reason to try and go deeply asleep. The thoughts may come and go . . . I may be thinking about many different things . . . or perhaps just one.

"I may notice that my mind can go completely blank for a few moments. I can be sure that my conscious mind will be doing nothing of importance.

"As I take this time out for myself . . . a very special opportunity, which some people never take for themselves . . . I can allow myself to feel even more relaxed. Very naturally . . . without even concerning myself, my blood pressure has regulated and if helpful, adjusted . . . perfectly naturally. The blood is flowing through my body and to the baby . . . very even and very naturally . . . like rivers flowing into a lake. As I relax, it may be interesting to find that the baby relaxes too.

"And I know and understand that it's important for me to be relaxed during the time I'm getting ready for labor. It's important for me to take time out . . . to listen to myself . . . to practice these techniques . . . all by myself or with somebody . . . I want to feel more relaxed . . . more comfortable, more capable, with my potentials naturally flowing, from millions of years of programming and evolution.

"I know that during the actual experience of labor and delivery . . . that I will be able to feel a state of deep relaxation . . . very naturally. By taking a deep . . . satisfying breath, I can regain this same feeling of relaxation and comfort. I know my accomplishments will be respected by me years from now . . . even months, weeks, days, hours.

"My frame of mind will be very positive . . . and naturally my excitement will be present, and I can feel relief from most of my discomfort . . . that's right, perfectly naturally, very comfortably.

"The more I relax and breathe through each contraction, the more tingling and numbness I can feel . . . all over. My control like my breathing has an entrance and exit . . . and I know that entrances and exits are passing and temporary . . . just as any discomfort can be passing and temporary. I may be surprised at how much I can change my physical sensations and perceptions . . . of this breathing experience . . . from the beginning, through the middle . . . and all the way down through and past the moment of delivery.

"I may have a delightful surprise, finding that the experience I have, with my baby . . . is a living meditation . . . a communion . . . a rapport. I can find a quieting of my mind and tune in on the inner signals. The contents of my mind and of my baby's mind, will be freer of anxiety . . . more relaxed.

"I can pass on the physical changes of relaxation to my baby. I can appreciate the natural experience right now . . . and know how healthy this experience is for my baby, as well as for me.

"As I give birth to my baby, I can have the same degree of comfort and relaxation then, as I do now . . . by taking several deep, satisfying breaths, I can become relaxed . . . relaxed as I am right now. And naturally there may be some numbness . . . my body may feel some numbness in certain areas.

"This numbness can be felt, with or without any anesthetic. I am using a natural pain relief which has been used in hundreds of thousands of different deliveries. And the numbness I can feel in this deep state of relaxation . . . a numbness I might be feeling right now, is spreading to areas of my body.

"It may begin in my cheek . . . perhaps my right side or perhaps my left . . . it's not important where. A part of me can become numb, just as my gums and cheek would become tingling and numb after my dentist injected procaine. I may even be able to feel a part of me get numb, right now . . . just as if a part of me, such as my hand, had been injected with procaine.

"I can even move my hand toward my face . . . and the closer my hand gets to my face . . . the deeper and more relaxed I can become. When my hand reaches my face, I can take a deep breath and feel the numbness transfer from my cheek to my hand.

"Now, after I am certain that the area on my face is numb, I can remove my hand and my cheek will again feel normal and feel sensations. My hand will still feel the numbness and tingling. I can now place my hand on my abdomen . . . at my own pace . . . very naturally . . . and transfer the numbness to my stomach or to any other part of my body.

"I can do this anytime I wish, now or in the future. All I need to do is take several deep, satisfying breaths and touch my hand to my cheek and I'll regain this numbing, tingling feeling that I can transfer anywhere I wish on my body.

"I will find that as I practice this technique more and more . . . I will find that all I need to do is imagine in my mind, the part of my body that I wish to become numb. When I visualize the part of my body that I wish to become numb and painless . . . that part will begin to tingle slightly and will feel painless. The more I practice this . . . the easier it will become.

"The more I practice self-hypnosis, the easier it will become to reenter it the next time I practice. It is such a wonderfully relaxing feeling . . . to be so comfortable, so relaxed. This new experience is a different feeling . . . and it is a way for me to take care of myself and my baby.

"This is a relaxation ability that I have . . . built into my own system . . . into my mind and body . . . that can help in ways that I never knew possible. I may find that I can fall asleep very easily if I wish.

"By counting backward from 50 to 0, the closer I get to 0 . . . the deeper I can go towards complete relaxation. And if I wish to return to a wakeful, alert *level, I can merely count from 0 to 10 and the closer I get to 10 the more alert and awake I become.*

"And whenever I wish to reenter this state of deep, comfortable relaxation . . . all I need to do is take several deep, satisfying breaths and imagine how relaxed I can be.

"It will take only a few moments for me to become completely refreshed, alert, and awake . . . feeling good, as if I have had a nice long nap . . . very naturally. Inhaling through my nose and coming awake . . . feeling wonderful."

SUGGESTION STRATEGY FOR CRAMPS

Milton Erickson (1967) used hypnosis with pregnant women to help them have more comfortable childbirths and he used the following concepts, which you can incorporate in your trancework if you feel that cramps are a problem for you.

1. You have developed several expectations, including having this baby in the most comfortable way you can.
2. Imagine gripping your partner's hand. That means that if you must; get a cramp in your arm from that grip, be sure to let yourself have that cramp because, only you know what sort of discomfort, or distress, you may want to have while you labor.
3. What you know is you want to have a happy and agreeable labor and look upon the delivery of your child as a completely pleasing experience. Therefore, you might want a cramp in your right or left arm, or even an itch or tingling in or on your leg, so you can feel the labor contractions in three stages.
4. If you can feel the first stage of contraction, that will give you more time to study and be aware of the contraction. But you could feel the second stage or third stage, also, if you want to. You may even wonder what sex the baby will be.

SOME IMAGES WOMEN HAVE USED

You may want to visualize yourself giving birth. Visualizing the experience will allow you to rehearse childbirthing in a positive, relaxing way. Through self-hypnosis rehearsal, you can develop some posthypnotic cues to reinstate the feeling of comfort and relaxation at the times you will need it during the birth process.

Below are some comments and experiences from other women who have used self-hypnosis for their childbirth.

Judy: "I imagined my delivery as rose petals opening and unfolding to reveal a lovely new bud. With each deep breath I saw myself as that rose blossoming."

Liz: "I used each contraction as a posthypnotic cue to begin the next series of deep breathing. The breaths were a cue to help me relax. I imagined each breath as an ocean wave, each one mounting and building to the next contraction. But each one, each breath and wave, also brought more relaxation."

Gayle: "The more intense the contractions became, the more I rubbed my stomach. I pictured each breath I took as a rush of new life going in my nose and down to the baby. As I breathed deeper, I felt that that was also bringing more relaxation and calm to me and to my child. I had gone over this picture many times while I was in a trance in the weeks before my labor."

Wendy: "I used self-hypnosis for the birth of my two children. I made a self-hypnosis tape and listened to it daily the weeks before the deliveries so I was able to relax my body parts individually and in groups. While in a trance, I imagined a warm, sunny walk at a beautiful sandy beach with seagulls and a soft wind blowing my hair.

"I became aware of my breathing and I visualized that with each rise and fall of the contractions my cervix was opening more and more like a flower opening. It helped me create a positive, controlled, and aware understanding of a wonderful experience."

You can feel free to be as creative as you want in developing your own images and posthypnotic cues, such as rubbing your abdomen or gripping your partners hand, that can help you achieve more comfort and calm. If you do experience some discomfort during labor, focus on your breathing and breathe your way through that discomfort.

Your active participation with self-hypnosis in childbirthing will provide you with a great amount of satisfaction.

REFERENCES

August, R. *Hypnosis in Obstetrics*. New York: McGraw-Hill, 1961.

Chertok, L.S. *Psychosomatic Methods in Painless Childbirth*. New York: Pergamon Press, 1959.

Chertok, L.S. *Motherhood and Personality: Psychosomatic Aspects of Childbirth*. New York: Harper & Row, 1973.

Erickson, M.H. *Advanced Techniques of Hypnosis and Therapy* (Ed. J. Haley). New York: Grune and Stratton, 1967.

Fromm, E. & Shor, R. *Hypnosis: Developments in Research and New Perspectives*. New York: Aldine Publishing Co., 1979.

Goldmann, L. Childbirth Suggestions. In *Handbook of Hypnotic Suggestions and Metaphors*. (Ed. C. Hammond). New York: W.W. Norton & Company and American Society of Clinical Hypnosis, 1990.

Hammond, D.C. (Ed.). *Handbook of Hypnotic Suggestions and Metaphors*. New York: W.W. Norton & Company and American Society of Clinical Hypnosis, 1990.

Hilgard, E. & Hilgard, J. *Hypnosis in the Relief of Pain*. Los Altos, California: William Kaufmann, 1975.

Kroger, W.S. *Clinical and Experimental Hypnosis*. Philadelphia: J.B. Lippincott Co., 1977.

Lamaze, F. *Painless Childbirth*. London: Burke, 1958.

Malyska, W. & Christenson, J. Autohypnosis and the prenatal class. *American Journal of Clinical Hypnosis*, Vol. 9, 1967.

Martin, A.A. The effects of hypnosis and supportive counseling on the labor processes and birth outcomes of pregnant adolescents. *Dissertation Abstracts International*, Vol. 49(8-A), 1989.

Pratt, G.J., Wood, D.P., & Alman, B.M. *A Clinical Hypnosis Primer: Expanded & Updated*. New York: John Wiley & Sons, 1988.

Read, G.D. *Childbirth Without Fear*. New York: Harper, 1953.

Rodger, B.P. Outline of hypnotic suggestions in obstetriscs. In *Handbook of Hypnotic Suggestions and Metaphors*. (Ed. C. Hammond). New York: W.W. Norton & Company and American Society of Clinical Hypnosis, 1990.

Speigel, H. Current perspective on hypnosis in obstetrics. *New York State Journal of Medicine*, Vol. 63, 1963.

Zeig, J. Erickson's use of anecdotes. In *A Teaching Seminar with Milton H. Erickson, M.D.* (Ed. J. Zeig). New York: Brunner/Mazel, Inc., 1980.

25

Maximize Your Sports Performance

Self-hypnosis can be a useful tool for improving your weekend tennis or golf, playing better at volleyball or racquetball, even for more accurate bowling or pool. It is now understood that hypnosis, when correctly utilized in sports, can be of great value as mental training and performance sharpening.

Certainly, many professional athletes have benefited and will benefit from hypnosis to increase their performance, also. Boxer Ken Norton used hypnosis training before his famous victory over Mohammed Ali. That was the fight in which he broke Ali's jaw.

Many major league baseball players have used hypnosis to pull out of batting slumps or to sharpen their pitching skills. The Chicago Cubs' first baseman, Bill Buckner, began using self-hypnosis in August 1982. He went from a .278 batting average that year to a .405 for August. That included six home runs and 35 runs-batted-in for the month. He was the National League's Player of the Month for August.

Hypnotic techniques didn't turn a mediocre player into a superstar—Buckner had already been a National League batting champion in 1980. But self-hypnosis can help an athlete perform nearer to his or her best.

It can also provide for more focus and concentration so that you can learn faster and be more aware of your own areas of strength and weakness. You can also use that concentration to prevent your opponent from affecting your own play.

Jim Palmer, former Baltimore Oriole—turned ABC sportscaster—disclosed that one season he used hypnosis to calm the anxieties between pitching starts. He used it to help screen out the distracting thoughts about what the manager was thinking, what the fans were thinking, his last bad start, and other negative distractions.

Most professional athletes who use hypnotic techniques to help them perform are reluctant to discuss the matter openly because it may appear to indicate weakness or imply getting a boost from artificial means, or raise some other concern about publicity. However, mental training is a standard part of training of Olympic teams and of amateur athletes around the world.

You can also use the naturally occurring self-hypnosis state to give yourself positive suggestions for direct improvement in your sport. If you have experienced this trance-state while running or exercising you, are already familiar with one aspect of self-hypnosis.

Many people report that they are in a trance-state after they have been running or absorbed in activity for 15 minutes or more. This absorption is an altered state of awareness. It is marked by a higher production of endorphins, natural body chemicals that are associated with calm and relaxation.

MOTIVATING YOURSELF TO PLAY BETTER

Anyone who practices or plays a sport wants to play better. You don't need to search your past or look inside yourself to understand why you want to play better. Competing against your opponent or against your own levels of performance is a natural and healthy feeling.

Whatever your sport, self-hypnosis can help you perform your best. One quality sets sports and athletics apart from many other personal goals—high motivation to improve.

Learning the particular skills of your sport is important. Physical training can often seem like the easy part. How many times have you told yourself that you know *how* to do it, if only you would *do* the right thing when you are supposed to. If only you could *concentrate*, then maybe you would get it right.

Jack Nicklaus (1974) has stated many times that he believes that golf is 90 percent mental preparation and only 10 percent skill. He prepares for matches by visualizing problem putts and mentally rehearsing how he will execute each drive.

"I never hit a shot, even in practice," Nicklaus says, "without having a very sharp picture of it in my head. First I 'see' the ball where I want it to finish, nice and white and setting up high on the bright green grass. Then the scene quickly changes and I 'see' the ball going there. I watch its path, shape, and even its behavior on landing. Then there's a sort of fade-out and the next scene is of the swing that will turn that previous image into reality."

You can learn these same techniques with the added benefit of self-hypnosis. This chapter will show you how to reinforce that mental picturing and to create posthypnotic suggestions and cues for use before and during play. The cues will bolster your ability to concentrate while you stay relaxed.

TENSION VERSUS MENTAL ALERTNESS

In practically every sport—from tennis to horseshoes—mental concentration and alertness are important. But many people believe that to be mentally sharp they need to be tense and keyed up. And, true, it can be argued that some situations do demand extreme physical tension. Playing defensive tackle on a football team and lifting weights may be examples.

But in most individual and team sports, excessive *mental* tension is damaging to concentration and alertness. You will be able to play much better and execute your skills more effectively if you are in a relaxed and highly aware state of mind.

In his book, *Use Your Head in Tennis*, Bob Harman (1974) emphasizes above all else the need to relax . . . relax. He suggests that if you keep relaxation in mind while you're gettng ready to play, you'll be more relaxed when the match starts. That is the *first* thing self-hypnosis will do for you. It will get you relaxed and keep you less tense during play.

CALM POWER

You can develop what we call a state of calm power with self-hypnosis. This is a level of mental arousal with calmness that is associated with optimal performance.

While in self-hypnosis, you can suggest to yourself: *"As I take four or six deep and calming breaths, I can be focused and ready to act and react. Breathing in is an activating event. I take in oxygen to stimulate my brain and body to be at its best. Exhaling slowly calms my mind and body to focus my inner power."*

Self-hypnosis is often most effective when you are relaxed and focused on internal strengths. Letting go of outside distractions can help develop an inner rhythm that you take with you everywhere.

Mike, a 30-year-old professional tennis player, was known to have the potential to be one of the best on the circuit. However, he lost most of the big matches. He was a great second-place player, but seldom first.

Mike wanted to win, but also didn't want to beat anyone for the championship, especially himself. Instead of playing HIS game, he was responding to the other person. In his self-hypnosis, he reviewed his playing and discovered that he was beating himself in those critical matches. He was so anxious and overcharged that he was beating himself, reacting rather than acting purposefully.

In his self-hypnosis, Mike focused next on suggestions such as: *"I start the match with my healthy, winning self and have been finishing with my anxious, scared self. I will now play from my calm, powerful self . . . and with each swing of the racquet I bring the racquet back to my centered position and will bring my mind and my focus back to that centered position. Relaxed and confident . . . I can calm my mind to focus on purpose, while my body remains powerfully alert. My mind can act and my body can react."*

In this way Mike shifted from overpowering himself to calm power over his opponents. His success in big matches began to develop consistency and his standing in the circuit improved significantly over the next two years.

MENTAL REHEARSAL IN SELF-HYPNOSIS

You may be able to get just as much benefit from mentally rehearsing your sport as from actually playing. That may sound too good to be true, but studies have shown that basketball players who used mental rehearsal to practice free throws did better than players who only worked out on the court.

Researchers, such as Edmond Jacobson (1932), have found that when you mentally rehearse a skill, such as shooting basketball free throws, putting, serving a tennis ball, or shooting billiards, the muscles you would normally be using show a tiny amount of stimulation. The amount of nerve activity during this imagery is so slight that you would not be aware of it, but sensitive electronic equipment can detect the stimulation. Thinking is real practice.

Scientists theorize that while you are in a trance and you rehearse a particular skill, your muscles are stimulated just as they would be if you were physically practicing. In this way the muscles "remember" the practice in the same way that your brain remembers patterns of action and timing. The phenomenon is called "muscle memory" and the brain pathways are called engrams.

When you actually perform the movement, you benefit from the mental rehearsal in much the same way you would from having practiced on the court, field, or whatever. The difference is that in your mental rehearsal you need never make a mistake. All your shots or serves can be excellent and you reinforce playing, winning, and feeling well.

William Kroger (1977) relates this case study of self-hypnosis for sports improvement:

> A leading pro golfer was having trouble with his putting. Whenever he reached the green, the spectators caused him to become so nervous that his exceptionally long drives were being nullified by shaky putting.
>
> He was taught self-hypnosis and imagery techniques and gave himself the suggestions that he could become completely oblivious to the crowd around him. Also, he suggested to himself that he would be able to "see" a dotted line from his ball to the cup. Additionally, the cup would appear to him to be two or three times its normal size.
>
> He would imagine strokes as being successful before they were made and he suggested to himself that he would not be shaken if he made a bad shot. Though this golfer already could hit a long ball, he suggested increased power and accuracy for himself.
>
> In a short time, with this conditioning and self-hypnosis practice, his putting and driving both improved. A short while later, he tied the course record in the National Open and barely missed winning. Several months afterwards, he won a coveted championship and attributed a good measure of his success to the self-hypnosis.

You can use this same method of mental rehearsal to improve your own sports or athletic performance. After developing a comfortable trance-state, become as relaxed as you can. Give yourself suggestions that you can return to this relaxed state of mind anytime you wish. Taking several deep, satisfying breaths, you can *regain* this feeling of deep relaxation *anywhere, anytime.*

Once you are relaxed and in a trance-state, begin to see the court, field, or whatever playing environment your sport involves. Visualize and remember it as vividly as you can. Imagine yourself in the scene, perhaps as if you are watching yourself from the sidelines. Or see the action through your own eyes during play. Maybe you can best imagine as if from over your own shoulder. It is fine to change the point of view of your visualizations. You may even want to imagine watching yourself on a TV or movie screen.

Whatever way suits you best, use it. Picture in your mind the racquet, the ball, the net, the walls, the markings on the field or court—visualize all the physical elements that are in your sport activity.

Imagine yourself moving around in your mental setting. This may take some practice. Be patient with yourself. If it takes two or three self-hypnosis sessions before you are able to easily visualize your playing condition, that's fine. Some people are able to do this quickly, some take a bit more time. The time it takes to develop this imagery has no bearing on the success you can have with the techniques.

Give yourself posthypnotic cues that fit in with your particular sport. If your sport is tennis, you might suggest to yourself that whenever you step onto the tennis court, that will be a cue for you to relax. Give yourself these posthypnotic suggestions and imagine them regularly, *a week or two before you play.*

Visualize yourself stepping onto the court. Give yourself suggestions such as: "*I will associate the feeling of concentration and readiness with stepping onto the court. My stretching exercises before a match can be a complete stretch. My physical flexibility and my mental readiness can begin with those exercises.*"

As you are able to become aware of all *external* parts of your experience, you can also become aware of the *internal* changes that take place. In your imagery, you may notice that as you run and move about, your breathing becomes more rapid and your heart begins to beat faster. You can recognize in your imagery internal changes—you sweat more, you can become more alert as the blood flows faster, and your stamina builds as you imagine playing.

WINNING IMPROVEMENTS

In most sports, there are three areas that you will want to improve: (1) concentration; (2) timing; and (3) technique.

Concentration is important even before the game or event begins. You can start building your concentration as you're getting dressed to compete. You can start by suggesting increased concentration with nearly all your activities, in the days or weeks before your events.

Begin your process of developing your concentration by eliminating all the outside concerns and worries you might have. Discard your problems and thoughts about your financial, job-related, or personal situations.

You might give yourself the suggestion, while in self-hypnosis: "When I change into my my sports attire, I will leave behind old problems and I'll be fresh in my mind for the game I will be playing."

You could suggest this cue: "When I wipe my face with a towel, once out on the court or field, I can also wipe away distracting thoughts from my mind. I can toss the towel along with the distracting thoughts to the side of the court."

Whenever possible, give yourself some tangible symbol, like the towel or getting suited-up, to reinforce a suggestion.

Drs. George Pratt and Errol Korn (1986) have also emphasized concentration with hypnosis. An image they use with athletes is: "You know that the playing field is composed of lines and angles. You also know that the ball travels in a direction that is determined by the precise angle at which it is struck. You may find that you know, even without thinking about it, the precise angle at which the ball must be struck in order to travel to the desired place. By taking a deep breath a few moments or seconds before you strike the ball, you can develop a deep concentration within you. Imagine that occurring right now."

Another posthypnotic suggestion for developing concentration could be: "As I lace up my shoes and tighten the laces for a firm, comfortable fit on my feet, I know that I can also use that action as a cue to tighten up my concentration on the game to be played."

Give yourself several posthypnotic cues for each area of improvement: "When I first step out on the court, I can notice that there are lines marked off for the boundaries. I may be able to form boundaries in my concentration that mark those actions and events that are in bounds and pay attention only to them.

"I can also ignore those actions, sounds and events that are out of my mental bounds for this game. I can allow them to pass through me without interrupting my concentration. If I am distracted, I'll be able to see the distraction as momentary. As if I'm on automatic pilot, I can return to my game and focus."

Notice that your suggestions are in a positive form. Use positive words that suggest what you *will*, *can*, or *may* do, rather than negative words such as "no," and "not."

You can form suggestions and cues from nearly any action or element in your sport. The grip you have on your racquet, club, or paddle can symbolize how you have more grip on your concentration. A net, goal, or other marker can suggest that there are divisions on the field of play as there are divisions in your field of attention and concentration.

Be creative and find those actions or things in your own sport that can be used as cues for developing your focus on your game. Set these suggestions and cues into your unconscious mind by rehearsing your game with your imagery and "seeing" yourself respond to the cues in your visualized play.

Timing may be required in making contact with the ball and racquet, club, or coordinating your own movements. This eye-to-hand coordination is normally achieved through repetition. You can enhance this timing with self-hypnosis practice.

Imagine the critical moments of your sport. Suppose your activity is racquetball. As the ball is hit by your opponent, you must prepare yourself to return the shot. Your ability to time your movements to coincide with the action of the ball will put you in the best place to return your opponent's shot.

Visualize the more difficult returns. See yourself in the back of the court defending against a shot hit in the lower left corner. See yourself responding as the ball leaves your opponents racquet and sense the direction of the shot. Practice your timing in as many possibilities as you can. Imagine yourself responding to all situations in precisely the correct way.

You'll want to spend some time imagining your *technique* with your self-hypnosis rehearsal. Imagine yourself executing each shot. Feel the ball or racquet in your hands and allow each play to evolve in slow motion.

Visualize your technique in all its components. The placement of your feet, your hands, your head and shoulders. See all your movements and all the techniques you know are correct. Imagine each of your movements being perfect and well executed.

See the ball travel, in slow motion, toward the target areas. Feel your own follow-through. Imagine how good you feel when you make a basket, score a point, or whatever your sport requires.

You might imagine seeing a thin wire going from your racquet to the spot you want the ball to hit. Visualize the ball traveling along that wire. Or, as in an earlier example, see a dotted line going exactly where you want the ball to go. Maybe imagine the scoring area being twice as big as normal.

Rehearse these successful maneuvers. Pay attention to both the external images of success and your internal feelings of success. *Feel* the glow of making your perfect shot. Your feelings are just as important in improving your performance as is visualizing the ball traveling where you intended.

Jeff McCullough (1984), USPTA professional tennis instructor, instructs his students to mentally imagine the correct path the racquet takes for each specific shot, ground stroke, forehand volley, lob, etc. Students are asked to spend some time between physical practices doing such mental practicing. He find that students who spend time using this mental rehearsal learn more quickly and retain their skills longer than students who rehearse only on the court.

MENTAL TRAINING PROGRAM

The work you will do in each area of concentration, timing, and technique can be broken into these parts:

1. *Self-hypnosis rehearsal* of the desired action or specific reaction, such as making a shot or a defensive move or controlling the racquet, bat, or club.
2. *Posthypnotic suggestions and cues* to create a specific positive response and winning feeling before and during play. Develop cues to relax, to concentrate, to eliminate distractions, and to increase your stamina.
3. *Review of your work* on the above two items, a day or so after the game or sport. You can use this review time, while in self-hypnosis, to strengthen your posthypnotic cues and to find new ways to positively develop your own goals of relaxed concentration, timing, and control techniques.

Combine all the elements

In your rehearsal imagery, combine the elements of concentration, timing, and technique. As you prepare to serve the ball in tennis, for instance, feel relaxed and focused. Know that you can shut out all unnecessary distractions and concentrate on completing a perfect serve.

As you toss the ball up, visualize how you will hit it with your racquet at just the right angle and at just the right moment to send it to your target in your opponent's court. Feel the entire serve in one fluid movement, perhaps in slow motion.

Then imagine seeing the ball traveling over the net and landing exactly where you intended.

You will see it when you imagine it

When you do this self-hypnosis imagery and rehearsal, make your images as vivid and as clear as you can. Visualizations that are more detailed and clear are more effective.

Don't worry if your efforts seem to take some time to work. The results you get from self-hypnosis may come quickly or may take more time to develop. *Keep working* on the mental rehearsals for a couple of weeks before you try to evaluate how effective they are.

The benefits are *cumulative and build on one another.* Just as your muscles can become accustomed to performing a task and build their strength, your unconscious mind can build up ability with mental practice.

Avoid the trap of overthinking your movements

When Michael Jordan gets a quick pass and shoots a basket, he doesn't think each move through, consciously. If he did, the ball would get slapped out of his hands in a second. It is a pattern that he has practiced many times. It is "muscle memory," a pattern of muscle behavior that is recorded in the brain. His shot to the basket is a habit of the same sort that walking is to most people.

A common trap that many people fall into is overthinking their actions and reactions. By examining your physical responses during a game, you can become a victim of *paralysis through analysis.*

While you are playing a game and trying to do your best, that is not a time to try new strategies or techniques. Let your unconscious mind respond and direct your muscles. Do your analysis and review of your moves while you are in self-hypnosis afterwards. Postpone close scrutiny of your game for another time, perhaps when you are deliberately playing to practice a new technique you've learned. If you're in a game with an opponent, that's the time to do your best and use those skills and abilities that you have been practicing.

You can use your conscious mind to scan for the movements of the ball or for moves of your opponent. Keep your conscious mind focused and away from distracting thoughts.

This will allow your unconscious mind to work for you while you are playing. As you mentally rehearse your actions and reactions in a trance-state, you will create the muscle memory that directs your moves, unconsciously, during play. Your self-hypnosis can become a personal coach you always have with you.

Mental training such as described here can provide a competitive edge and will help you to achieve nearer to your personal best. Keep in mind that, like any other form of training, mental training also functions best when you practice it regularly and are attentive to the fundamentals of good nutrition and adequate sleep.

REFERENCES

Benson, H. *The Mind/Body Effect.* New York: Simon & Schuster, 1979.

Hammond, D.C. *Handbook of Hypnotic Suggestions and Metaphors.* New York: W.W. Norton & Company and the American Society of Clinical Hypnosis, 1990.

Harman, B. *Use Your Head in Tennis.* Kennikat Press, 1974.

Jacobson, E. Electrophysiology of mental activities. *American Journal of Psychology,* Vol. 44, 1932.

Kaplan, J. He's in a zone of his own. *Sports Illustrated,* Sep 13, 1982.

Kolanay, B. *The effects of visual motor behavior rehearsal on athletic performance.* Unpublished Masters Thesis. Hunter College, City University of New York, 1977.

Kostrubala, T. *The Joy of Running.* Philadelphia: J.B. Lippincott Company, 1976.

Kroger, W.S. *Clinical and Experimental Hypnosis.* Philadelphia: J.B. Lippincott, 1977.

Leonard, G. *The Ultimate Athlete.* New York: Avon Books, 1975.

McCullough, J. *Two-Handed Tennis.* New York: M. Evans and Company, 1984.

Nicklaus, J. *Golf My Way.* New York: Simon and Schuster, 1974.

Pratt, G.J. & Korn, E.R. Using hypnosis to enhance athletic performance. In *Hypnosis:*

Questions & Answers, (Eds. Zilbergeld, Edelstein, Araoz). New York: W.W. Norton & Company, 1986.

Prokop, D. The inside story of hypnosis. *Runner's World*, (Sep), 1981.

Robinson, R. Look deeply into my eyes and you'll hit .300 again. *TV Guide*, (Aug 13), 1985.

Unestahl, L.E. *The Mental Aspects of Gymnastics*. Orebro, Sweden: Veje Publishers, 1983.

26
Successful Thinking About Money and Your Career

You may be wondering how self-hypnosis can be used to help you make money and be more successful in your career. The answer is it can help by enlisting your unconscious mind to help you work toward your goals.

PROGRAMMING YOURSELF FOR SUCCESS

Your unconscious mind can be a valuable aid to you in your career development. Self-hypnosis can help you program yourself for success by helping you:

1. *Clear away negatives.* Progress often begins as you recognize and understand your present attitudes and beliefs about money and success. Self-hypnosis can help you identify and acknowledge any unproductive ideas and negative thinking about money or success. With self-hypnosis you can then replace negative with positive thinking. (The Committee Meeting exercise from Chapter 21 can help).
2. *Set clear goals.* You can accomplish much more, sooner, if you have a clear idea of what success is for you and what you want in your career.
3. *Create imagery of your goals.* By using imagery and visualization, you can feel and build success in your unconscious mind. That will allow your mind to work toward getting you the "dream home" or other material things you wish. Imagery sets in motion what you need for the next step— *action.*
4. *Take action toward your goals.* Success doesn't happen just with imagination. You must act. You must engage in some sort of activity that will lead you in the direction of your goals.
5. *Be patient.* Self-hypnosis can help you develop the patience and perseverance to continue working toward your career goals, even if they seem far off in the future.

You will obtain the most progress when you can accept yourself as you are right now. No matter what age you are, regardless of what disadvantages you may feel you have, in spite of how remote your goals may seem, *first* acknowledge and accept yourself, as you are presently. This means that if you have negative thinking about money or success, it is better for you to recognize that first, then move on.

Should you have poor work habits, don't try to fool yourself. Accept your shortcomings and vow to make changes from this point on. Denying your weaknesses will work against you. Pretending you have no faults may fool your conscious mind a bit, but not your unconscious mind.

Make a list of your bad habits, weaknesses, and shortcomings. Write down any traits that work against you or hamper your success. This is the point from which you can proceed. Your unconscious mind can clearly work on those areas you acknowledge and really *want* to change.

Eliminate negative thinking about money or success

Do you think that devious, tricky, corrupt people make the most money? Do you think money is the root of all evil? Are you resentful of people who are rich? Do you believe that in order for you to succeed, someone else must fail?

If any of these statements cause you to nod your head, even just a bit, you likely have some negative thoughts about money or success.

If you are unsure of your attitudes about these questions, try doing some self-exploration while in self-hypnosis. Focus, while in a trance-state, on being open to an insight into your unconscious thoughts about these questions. See Chapter 16 for help in developing methods for self-exploration.

Negative ideas in your unconscious mind often stem from things your parents may have said when you were young. Or you may have developed these unhealthy attitudes from some other source. Where you got them is less important than how to get rid of them. Don't dwell on the origins of what Zig Ziglar (1975) calls "garbage dump thinking" about money and success. Spend your energy on converting "stinkin thinkin" into positive thinking.

While in self-hypnosis, you may give yourself suggestions such as: "*I recognize that my attitudes about money and success may have prevented me from achieving those things. It can be difficult to achieve a goal that I believe to be unworthy. But I can now see that it is possible for me to be successful without depriving someone else of success. The world is bountiful and full of opportunities for anyone willing to work for money and success. I can choose to work toward having money and success.*"

You can further rid yourself of negative thinking with suggestions like: "*Being successful and having money will allow me to accomplish more good and contribute more back to society. I can feel anticipation toward success without feeling guilty. The more successful I am, the more I can help others to achieve success, if that is my wish. I am working on change right now and that improvement can continue every time I make a decision.*"

Set clear, achievable, and specific goals for yourself

There is no favorable wind for a ship without a destination, to paraphrase an old proverb. For you to make use of your energy and work, you need to have a clear picture of what your goals are.

Spend some time writing out exactly a detailed description of the success you seek. Just to want lots of money, a big house, and a boat is vague. Be as specific as you can.

An example of a well-defined goal might be: "To become district manager of my company in three years. To have a home such as the one I cut out of a magazine—four bedrooms, a patio, a swimming pool, and a large kitchen. To have a new dark blue Corvette. I will work to have these things all within five years."

Another approach could be: "Each step I take, each decision I make, each choice or option I discover, will bring me closer to my goal. I will achieve my pleasures easier and easier, especially as I detach and let go of my fears and old destructive beliefs. I am building a more daring attitude. I am feeling more and more in the mood for prosperity . . . emotionally, physically, and mentally. A whole improvement, a new belief in myself, designed by me and full of respect is developing right now."

A set of goals such as these could be more specific and have a time frame built around them. They are achievable and something to look forward to with positive anticipation.

You must set your own goals. If you want material things, find pictures of them in magazines and cut them out. While in your self-hypnosis, visualize them. Put yourself in mental movies of your "dream home" or behind the wheel of your "dream car."

You might even want to hang the pictures of your material goals where you will see them every day. Use whatever methods you can to implant the details of your goal in your unconscious mind.

Wayne Dyer (1989) teaches people to go beyond their limitations. He helps people focus on their conditioning (upbringing) as the roots of their negative thinking about money, self, and career. His books and tapes are very useful and can provide you with ideas and concepts for your self-hypnosis suggestions.

Self-hypnosis is an excellent tool for changing old patterns and beliefs that may prevent you from achieving your best or performing up to your potential. The best way to develop new ideas and be creative is to relax while developing success imagery.

THE IMPORTANCE OF IMAGERY IN REACHING YOUR GOALS

Here is the reason why imaging is so valuable as part of your career process.

Within the structure of the human brain is the reticular formation. This is the part of our mind that acts as a gatekeeper to awareness. If our mind had to handle equally all the incoming stimuli from our environment, we would be much less able to focus our attention and concentration when necessary.

The reticular system screens input from the environment while scanning for information that is important for survival or relevant to us.

An example will help illustrate this phenomenon. Perhaps you recall purchasing a car. As you drove about your city, you may have noticed how many cars of your make, model, and color went by. You didn't notice those cars the same way before because it was not as relevant to you.

This reticular activation process can be harnessed and guided with self-hypnosis goal-setting. The process is a goal-directed inner mechanism we all possess and can learn to use more effectively.

While you are in self-hypnosis, use imagery and visualization to mentally picture your goals. Imagine yourself in the role of company owner or as a "super" salesperson. Visualize yourself in action. Imagine yourself doing that job or performing that role.

We make decisions daily, weekly, monthly—hundreds, even thousands, of small choices in life. When we hold a clear, well-defined, achievable goal in our mind, all our choices, all our options and decisions can benefit from the selective knowledge base, even though it may be unconscious.

Suppose you want to be a successful artist or performer. Imagine yourself painting a fine work of art. "See" yourself onstage in a Broadway play or on a movie set. No matter what your idea of success is, visualize yourself as having already reached it. Your unconscious mind will help you incorporate knowledge, experience, and awareness to make decisions that will move you closer to your goals.

It is not a perfect system. Mistakes are made in the service of learning. Focus and persistence do pay off.

You can visualize whatever it is that you want. Put the image into your unconscious mind by using self-hypnosis. Allow your unconscious to help you make decisions that will achieve your goals.

Napoleon Hill (1960), author of *Think and Grow Rich*, recommends using what he calls the "subconscious mind." He describes the subconscious as the "connecting link between the finite mind of man and infinite intelligence." He suggests that you develop the Seven Major Emotions:

- Desire
- Faith

- Love
- Sex
- Enthusiasm
- Romance
- Hope

He recommends developing "money consciousness" by filling your mind with positive emotions. We endorse that approach. With self-hypnosis, you relax and absorb and fill your suggestions with the positive emotions you want.

In *"Hyper-Performance: Releasing Your Business Potential"*, Korn, Pratt and Lambrou (1987) help people take their work stress and transform it into positive mental energy. They recommend reducing negative emotions and hostility and converting that energy to positive workaholism.

Hyper-performance's positive workaholism channels the passion, enthusiasm, and energy of motivation towards specific, well defined, and achievable goals, while becoming aware of and reducing harmful, negative emotions. It is the negative emotions, such as anger, hostility, fear, and a perception of little control over one's situation, that lead to the health problems associated with excessive work and what have been called "Type A" behavior.

They advocate the use of active relaxation, imagery of the end result you desire, and mental rehearsal of the processes you will take to achieve your goals.

ESTABLISH INTERMEDIATE GOALS

If your primary objective is very large or far off in the future, then set intermediate or "stepping stone" goals. Suppose you have just finished college and your long-range goal is to have your own computer software company. That is fine.

In the meantime, you can set goals that will lead you toward your larger target. Perhaps you can identify a particular job and a company at which you wish to work to gain experience. You might set some specific financial goals that will give you the resources to purchase or set up your own company.

Within your intermediate goals, you may have many short-term targets that will give you more immediate gratification and reward. Mentally imagine and work toward saving for a vacation or toward buying a better car. As you achieve these smaller objectives, you will be reinforcing your ability to reach larger goals. Reinforce both intermediate and long-range goals with suggestions of success while in your self-hypnotic trance.

ACTION SPEAKS LOUDER THAN WANTS

It is not enough to just put clear specific goals into your unconscious mind. The catalyst to make them happen is your action. You can want something very badly, but that alone will not make it materialize. You must *act*.

The path of work and perseverance is made easier when you can see what is at the end. A clear goal will provide you with more motivation to keep up your efforts.

You can give yourself posthypnotic suggestions that the more you work toward your goals, the closer they will become. You can also provide posthypnotic cues to help you take action, such as: *"I know that whenever I close a sale or complete a project, I will feel a little closer to my ultimate goals. I know that as I get up each morning and prepare for work, I am preparing myself for one step nearer to my goal (describe your specific goal)."*

As you proceed in your work and achieve some of your short-term goals, you will change your cues. Experiment with the cues to find the ones that are the most effective for your situation.

BE PATIENT WITH YOURSELF

As you work toward what you seek from life, you may feel that you're not making progress. There will always be lows in your progress, as there will be high moments. Keep encouraging yourself. Learn from the mistakes and focus on your successes.

In your self-hypnosis, recognize that your goals will take time to reach. Be patient. Keep working.

In his book *The Greatest Salesman in the World*, Og Mandino (1968) devotes an entire chapter to persistence. He observes:

"The prizes of life are at the end of each journey, not at the beginning; and it is not given to me to know how many steps are necessary in order to reach my goal. Failure I may still encounter at the thousandth step, yet success hides behind the next bend in the road. Never will I know how close it lies unless I turn the corner. I will persist until I succeed."

You may have setbacks or failures in pursuing your path to career success. But perceive these as opportunities to learn. Use your self-hypnosis to examine them and learn from your mistakes.

There is a fine statement in Richard Bach's (1977) *Illusions*: "There is no such thing as a problem without a gift for you in its hands. You seek problems because you need their gifts."

The thoughts you put in your unconscious mind are the ones you must live with. Just as you can perceive a glass as half full or half empty, you can see obstacles and setbacks as failures or as gifts of experience. Choose the more positive view.

Your self-hypnosis can give you relaxation and relief from stress to help you continue in the face of adversity. You can also give yourself posthypnotic cues to deal with situations of tension and problems that might sap your motivation. Chapter 12 on stress and relaxation can help you.

Here is an example of how a business owner used some of the principles of self-hypnosis in his company.

Dan had attended a class in self-hypnosis for stress management at a local community college. He owns a computer software firm with eight employees.

After using the skills he had learned for several weeks, he began to see the positive effects his training provided in his business and personal life. He hired a stress management consultant to come to his place of business for a four-hour training session.

He was surprised how enthusiastic his employees were at the prospect of learning the new skills. With audiotaped examples of self-hypnosis, he provided his staff with conference room time each day to practice with the tapes or on their own.

It became a team-building experience of sharing ideas, learning something new together, with the example and encouragement of their leader, the staff developed a new camaraderie. The relaxation qualities in the office and personally were noticed not just by the employees and their families, but comments were made by customers and vendors.

Dan's business grew to 27 employees and showed a proportional increase in sales over the three years following. He periodically brings in the self-hypnosis training when new employees are hired, which also serves as a refresher for the other employees.

As you work toward your career and financial goals, you will employ many different professional or occupational tools. You can think of self-hypnosis as another of those tools.

Also, you may have read various books on the topic of motivation and success. There are many fine volumes on the bookshelves that can give you further insights into successful thinking and positive attitude development.

Use your self-hypnotic practice to reinforce the concepts you have learned from this book and others. Develop posthypnotic cues to put into practice successful ideas and positive behavior changes that will enhance your career.

REFERENCES

Bach, R. *Illusions*. New York: Delacorte Press, 1977.

Brothers, J. *How to Get Whatever You Want Out of Life*. New York: Simon and Schuster, 1978.

Carnegie, D. *How To Win Friends and Influence People.* New York: Simon and Schuster, rev. ed. 1981.

Dyer, W. *You'll See It When You Believe It.* New York: W. Morrow, 1989.

Hill, N. *Think and Grow Rich.* New York: Fawcett Crest, 1960.

Korn, E.R., Pratt, G.J. & Lambrou, P.T. *Hyper-Performance: The A.I.M. Strategy for Releasing Your Business Potential.* New York: J. Wiley & Sons, Inc., 1987.

Maltz, M. *Psycho-Cybernetic Principles for Creative Living.* New York: Pocket Books, 1974.

Mandino, O. *The Greatest Salesman in the World.* New York: Frederick Fell, Inc., 1968.

Sharp, B. B. & Cox, C. *Choose Success: How to Set and Achieve All Your Goals.* New York: W. Clement Stone, 1970.

Ziglar, Z. *See You At The Top.* Gretna, Louisiana: Pelican Publishing Company, 1975.

27
Self-Hypnosis for Generations

Self-hypnosis is a deep and absorbing state. We are more open to new ideas in this natural self-induced experience. Self-hypnosis has historical roots that are perhaps millions of years old. It is likely that the ability to be hypnotized has been programmed into our central nervous system genetics.

One can imagine ancient fire chants under a starlit night sky, with all the community members focused and determined to receive answers about life. Within these powerful rituals and beliefs are the roots of modern day self-hypnosis. We believe that all hypnosis is actually developed and maintained by the self that is experiencing the trance. Almost all people desire more skill at reaching states of awareness in which self-change is most easily created.

In the far distant future, people will be even more open to enhancing physical, mental, emotional, and creative abilities. Self-hypnosis will assist in unfolding those desired changes. The use of "focused unconscious time" or "untime" will be used to access hypnotic states and to seed suggestions toward personal development.

Learning self-hypnosis will be part of almost every school curriculum for concentration, motivation, and self-esteem building. Tapping into one's own unconscious potential will be accepted and encouraged because the results have proven the process.

As a way of describing how hypnosis has evolved and how we believe it might develop in the future, we thought that we would describe some of the milestones of the past and then go forward into the future. In part, the future headlines we have created are based upon current research directions and extrapolation. It will be interesting to see what future generations will discover about the mind's capabilities.

Here is a brief view of the past, present, and possible future signposts of how your capacity for self-direction through hypnotic processes has appeared and may appear in the future:

1959—Viktor Frankl, who survived a Nazi concentration camp, describes his discovery that "It is a peculiarity of man that he can only live by looking to the future." His book, *Man's Search for Meaning*, describes how man is self-determining.

1976—After surviving a nearly fatal condition, Norman Cousins writes

Anatomy of an Illness, offering a picturesque example of recovery and the mobilization of healing resources from within. He illustrates how overcoming fear, panic, and helplessness helps the brain write elaborate prescriptions for our bodies.

1978—As a result of research with terminally ill cancer patients, Carl Simonton publishes *Getting Well Again*, describing how his team had trained 159 patients who had been branded as "incurable." Although these patients had all been expected to die within a year, most survived for at least 20 months, while more than one-fourth recovered partially or completely. Simonton attributed these results to his revolutionary "self-awareness and imagery techniques."

1982—Dr. Jean Houston in her book, *The Possible Human* describes exercises for the human ability to enhance physical, mental, and creative abilities. She encourages each individual to be playful about experiencing one's own rhythm of awakening the mind and body.

1986—Author Ernest Rossi publishes *The Psychobiology of Mind-Body Healing*, describing physiological evidence that what we think and believe has a profound effect on disease. He outlines the electro-biochemical connection between neural systems in the brain and the immune system. The mechanisms of the Simontons' work of the prior decade are better understood.

1987—*Discover* magazine's February issue describes the work of psychoneuroimmunology researchers Gerard Renoux, Candace Pert, Ed Blalock, Nick Hall, Hugo Besedovsky and others. Guided imagery and visualization are described as methods of initiating communication to the immune system.

1995—Three Fortune 500 companies report self-hypnosis training for managers has reduced the incidence of cardiovascular disease in senior management. These companies will institute self-hypnosis or "mental fitness" periods during the day for all employees to reduce stress-related illness and to improve productivity.

1996—Reports are published on the use of self-hypnosis within couples and families—to create more intimacy—to develop better communication—to add new dimensions to their mutual understanding.

1997—Journal article reports that clinicians have used hypnosis for age-regression to allow patients to reenter specific ages for days at a time, in controlled settings, to learn developmental processes that have impeded emotional growth and more adaptive behavior. They report that the openness to learning while in trance is accelerating progress. What took years previously can now be accomplished in months.

1999—Major league baseball team announces plan to include mental imagery and self-hypnosis exercises in spring training camps. All players, not only the pitchers, will attend daily exercises on relaxation, concentration, and mental rehearsal for skill-building. The players who have been using self-hypnosis are excited at the prospect of experiencing the new group trance exercises aimed at improving performance.

2001—Health insurance coverage, for the first time, supports training in self-hypnosis as an adjunct to medical treatments for inducing the immune system to function at its maximum potential against disease.

2004—Geriatric researchers report that training in lucid dreaming and self-hypnosis taught to elderly patients results in less need for medication, more energy, and longer life spans.

2006—State school system mandates self-hypnosis within curriculum of all elementary school and secondary schools to assist students in academic achievement, self-esteem building, and wellness.

2015—Scientists discover how self-hypnosis has been able to access components of the immune system as a "sixth" sense. Using trance for inner communication with consciousness, the immune system can detect airborne chemical signals given off by the emotional processes of others. Individuals who have trained with self-hypnosis can bring to awareness and interpret these signals. What were called "hunches" or intuition now have been traced to this sixth sense cultivated and more easily accessed through self-hypnotic trance states.

YOUR FUTURE GENERATION

Advances and new discoveries in how we can use our mental abilities for health maintenance and life improvement are unfolding rapidly. The more we discover about ourselves, the more we are awed by the power and strength we possess as individuals. The forecasts of today will likely be the news reports of the future, perhaps as we have portrayed above.

Our body is like a miniature world, more complex and synchronized within than the most sophisticated computer could design. Our unrevealed and dormant potential for improving our physical and mental life is perhaps one of the greatest resources on our planet.

The hypnotic phenomenon is certainly one avenue for exploring and improving the world within each of us. What we have learned about each person's natural hypnotic ability for self-discovery is as encouraging as space exploration or the unraveling of the mysteries of human genetics.

You have begun to access this phenomenon by reading and practicing the techniques in this book. In a real sense, you are at the leading edge of personal breakthroughs in dismantling the barriers between mind and body. You can learn to use your mind more efficiently for enhancement of physical health and prowess, emotional development, and personal achievement.

The future is yours to create and enjoy.

Glossary

Absorption—Experience of complete involvement in an activity. It is this state that preoccupies one's attention and focuses concentration on an object or activity.

Acute pain—Sudden onset of discomfort that usually lasts for a short time, but can be recurring.

Age regression—(See Time regression)

American Society of Clinical Hypnosis—A professional organization that specializes in the training and education of health-care professionals in the specialty of hypnotic strategies.

Analgesia—The absence of pain sensation or the relief of pain without the loss of consciousness.

Anesthesia—An agent that causes an insensitivity to pain. There are two types of anesthetics: general anesthetics, which produce sleep, and regional or local anesthetics, which cause a specific area of the body to be insensitive to pain.

Catharsis—The release of fears, conflicts, or emotions by bringing them to consciousness for expression, verbally, physically, and/or emotionally.

Chronic pain—A discomfort of long duration. Pain which lasts more than six months is usually referred to as chronic.

Conscious thoughts—The part of human perceptions that focuses on logical, rational, analytical, or concrete thoughts. These are the waking awareness thoughts associated with day-to-day actions and also with the past, present, and future.

Direct hypnosis—The technique of hypnotic suggestions that emphasizes language that is commanding or authoritative in nature.

Distraction strategy—The experience in hypnosis of focusing on sounds, feelings, objects, or thoughts in order to take you out of some other experience, as with distraction away from pain, or distraction to a focus.

Desensitization—Breaking the bond of association of a particular stimulus (action or thought) to a mental or physical reaction. For example, flying in an airplane may be unconsciously associated with fearing loss of control over one's immediate environment. One can break such a bond by gradually increasing proximity to the stimulus while practicing relaxation strategies.

Emotions—A state of mental excitement characterized by an altering of feelings and often by physical changes in the body which may or may not be outwardly apparent.

Endorphins—Naturally occurring body chemicals that have a morphine-like action, usually found in the brain and associated with pain relief and other body responses.

Engrams—Mental pathways in the mind which develop from stimulation and can influence thought processes and muscle functioning and are part of the basis for memory.

Eye fixation—One of the oldest known styles of creating a hypnotic trance that emphasizes staring at an object, usually leading to eye closure, physical and psychological comfort, and receptiveness to suggestions. A form of absorption.

Hypnosis—A phenomenon characterized by an individual's increased openness to acceptable suggestions while in a state of heightened and focused concentration.

Hypnotherapy—The utilization of hypnosis as a means of physical, emotional, or psychological relief of symptoms, causes, or other change.

Hypnotic susceptibility—The likelihood of hypnotic success using the technique or techniques of hypnosis being tested for. The reliability of such tests is affected by such factors as the nature or length of the preexisting relationship with the hypnotist, prior expectations and beliefs, motivations concerning hypnosis, and many individual differences.

Imagery—The natural ability to use one's memory and imagination to perceive or mentally create or recreate ideas, pictures, or feelings through any or all of the five senses.

Indirect hypnosis—The approach of hypnotic suggestions that employs permissive, flexible, and choice-oriented language. This method often incorporates words, symbols, and imagery that are familiar to the individual.

Metaphors—Suggestion language that uses one familiar subject or idea to create an association with a desired suggestion idea. For example: "*My pain can be washed away just like the soap suds when I take a shower.*"

Neuro-linguistic programming (NLP)—The study of the interrelationship between communication styles, learning, and responding in one's environment.

Phobia—An obsessive, persistent, unrealistic, intense, or limiting fear of an object or situation. A phobia often arises from an unconscious process of transferring an internal and unconscious conflict to an external object that may be symbolically related to the conflict. Other phobias arise from an exaggerated response to a real situation or object.

Placebo—An inactive substance given to satisfy a patient's desire for some therapeutic benefit. Also used as a comparison for testing various drugs and treatments.

Posthypnotic behavior—Actions carried out after the completion of hypnosis and in response to suggestions given while in trance.

Posthypnotic cues—Signals or symbols suggested while in trance that trigger a posthypnotic behavior some time after the trance.

Progressive relaxation—A technique of relaxing by focusing on specific muscle groups and relaxing them systematically. One variation is to tense the muscle group beyond its present tension level and then release the muscular tension, allowing greater relaxation of the muscle group. Often done in combination with controlled deep breathing.

Psychiatry—The branch of medicine dealing with the diagnosis and treatment of mental disorders.

Psychology—The study of the mind and mental processes, feelings, desires, and behavior.

Psychoneuroimmunology (PNI)—The study of how mental or psychological processes interact and affect the immune system functioning.

Rapid eye movement (REM)—The experience during sleep associated with dreaming and which indicates certain physical and psychological activity.

Self-hypnosis—The natural ability to use one's own inner processes of focused awareness and concentration to develop a state of increased responsiveness to suggestions for positive change.

Symbolism—The use of suggestion words or ideas describing one concept or idea to represent some other suggestion concept or idea. For example, descending a stairway can be a symbol for entering a deeper level of self-hypnosis trance. Symbolism is often contained in suggestion metaphors.

Time progression—A mental exploration to future experiences through hypnotic suggestions. The use of the unconscious potential to forecast and create is emphasized.

Time regression—A mental return to earlier levels of development or experiences through hypnotic suggestions. There are various degrees of time regression that can involve some or many areas of the unconscious mind. Time regression or age regression can be used as a therapy tool for understanding and exploring past events and emotional feelings about them.

Trance—A natural state of focus and absorption. This altered state of awareness can be used, as with self-hypnosis, to create desired changes through specific suggestions.

Unconscious thoughts—Those thought processes which are not in waking or conscious awareness. Those processes which are often associated with the part of the mind involving imagination, memory, dreaming, and creativity, and which are particularly more accessible through trance.

Visualization—The ability to perceive experiences, images, or emotions by mentally picturing them. A visual form of imagery.

Index